C000057188

Indian Banking in the Globalised World

Indian Banking in the Globalised World

R.K. Uppal

New Century Publications
New Delhi, India

NEW CENTURY PUBLICATIONS
4800/24, Bharat Ram Road,
Ansari Road, Daryaganj,
New Delhi -110 002 (India)

Tel.: 011 – 2324 7798, 4358 7398, 6539 6605
Fax: 011 – 4101 7798
E-mail: indiatax@vsnl.com
www.newcenturypublications.com

Editorial office:
34, Gujranwala Town, Part-2,
Delhi - 110 009

Tel.: 27247805, 27464774

Copyright © 2008 by R.K. Uppal

All rights reserved. No part of this book may be reproduced, stored in a retrieval system, or transmitted in any form or by any means, mechanical, photocopying, recording, or otherwise without the prior written permission of the publisher.

First Published – **June 2008**

ISBN: 978-81-7708-174-9

Published by New Century Publications and printed at Salasar Imaging Systems, New Delhi

PRINTED IN INDIA

The Book

Banking sector reforms in India are aimed at induction of best international practices and technological changes for competing globally. The Reserve Bank of India (RBI) has time and again emphasised transparency, diversification of ownership and strong corporate governance to mitigate the prospects of systemic risks in the banking sector. Banking sector reforms have supported the transition of the Indian economy to a higher growth path, while significantly improving the stability of the financial system. In comparison with the pre-reform period, the Indian banking system today is more stable and efficient. However, the gains of the past decade need to be consolidated, so that these could be translated to drive the institutions, markets and practices into a mature financial system that can meet the challenges of globalisation. The banking system would, therefore, not only need to be stable, but also supportive of still higher levels of planned investments by channelling financial resources more efficiently from surplus to deficit sectors.

Competitive pressures as well as prudential regulatory requirements have made banks risk-averse as reflected in their tendency to investment in relatively risk-free gilt instruments. The behaviour and strategies of banking business need changes in favour of risk-taking even while performing core activities. Also, there is a need to ensure long-term finance to support development and growth in the economy, even as restructuring takes place through mergers and universal banking.

The present book addresses issues like Basel – II Accord guidelines, second generation banking sector reforms, cost-benefit and productivity analysis of Indian banks, danger zone banks, privatisation and comparative efficiency of Indian banks and the recent reform measures.

Vital statistics regarding the Indian banking sector and the recent Annual Policy Statement, 2008-09 of the RBI has also been discussed.

Author's Profile

Dr. R.K. Uppal did his M.A. in economics from Punjabi University, Patiala in 1986. Thereafter, he obtained M.Phil. degree from MDU, Rohtak in 1987 and Ph.D. degree from Punjabi University, Patiala in 2003. Specialising in banking and finance, Dr. Uppal has 11 books to his credit and has published 40 research papers on the subject in reputed national and international journals.

He has also presented more than 35 research papers in national and international conferences in Hawaii, Indonesia, Finland, Costa Rica, Australia, London and the UK. Presently, he is head of the Department of Economics, DAV College, Malout, Punjab and Principal Investigator of a UGC-financed research project on Indian banking. He is also Director of an ICSSR sponsored major research project on Indian banking.

Preface

Banking developments in India after Independence in 1947 has been, by and large, a state-induced activity. The Reserve Bank of India was nationalised in 1949 followed by the nationalisation of Imperial Bank of India (now the State Bank of India) in 1955. In 1969, 14 major commercial banks were nationalised and the exercise was repeated when 6 more commercial banks were nationalised in 1980. Thus, prior to economic reforms initiated in early 1990s, banking business in India was a near-monopoly of the Government of India. The underlying philosophy of this approach was to encourage growth, via availability of adequate credit at reasonable/concessional rates of interest in areas where commercial considerations did not allow for disbursal of credit.

Prior to reforms, the banking sector suffered from lack of competition, low capital base, inefficiency and high intermediation costs. Ever since the bank nationalisation of 1969, the banking sector had been dominated by the public sector along with a high degree of financial repression characterised by administered interest rates and allocated credit.

The process of interest rate liberalisation began in September 1991 with the discontinuation of sector-specific and programme-specific prescriptions, except for a few areas like agriculture and small industries. Loans above Rs. 2 lakh were freed from various prescriptions, subject to the minimum lending rate prescribed by the RBI. The process of deregulation was carried forward with the withdrawal of the minimum lending rate in October 1994, thereby providing banks full freedom to determine lending rates for loans above Rs. 2 lakh. Thus, deregulation of interest rates was central to the new market-oriented monetary strategy in terms of rejuvenating the price discovery process

With interest rate deregulation and the consequent

flexibility in the market-determined rates, the associated risk factor for market participants has also increased. This necessitated the development of derivative products for hedging risks by participants. Accordingly, banks and financial institutions were allowed in July 1999 to adopt risk management tools such as forward rate agreements (FRAs) and interest rate swaps (IRS) for their balance sheet management and hedging of interest rate risks by using the implied rates from any market segment such as money, debt or foreign exchange segment, for their own benchmarking.

There has been a distinct downward movement in interest rates and significant improvement in the liquidity of financial intermediaries. The increase in foreign exchange assets and cuts in CRR have also added to the liquidity. However, these favourable developments have failed to result in an appreciable increase in credit flow to the commercial sector. The dismal performance of the stock market and absence of alternative avenues of investment have led to an increase in bank deposits despite falling deposit rates.

The focus of on-going reforms in the banking sector is on soft interest rate regime, increasing operational efficiency of banks, strengthening regulatory mechanisms and technological up-gradation.

Reforms in respect of the banking as well as non-banking financial institutions have focused on creating a deregulated environment and ensuring free play of market forces. With a view to providing greater choice to customers and promoting competition, the RBI has become more liberal in permitting the entry of new private banks and foreign banks.

Financial sector reforms introduced since the early 1990s have brought about a significant improvement in the financial system. The commercial banking sector, which constitutes the most important segment, has witnessed a remarkable improvement both in stability and efficiency parameters such as capital position, asset quality, spread and overall profitability. It is significant to note that the improvement has been noticed in respect of all bank groups.

The most significant achievement of financial sector reforms has been a marked improvement in the financial health of the commercial banking sector, which constitutes the most important segment of the Indian financial system. Asset quality of commercial banks, which before the initiation of reforms, was at a very precarious level, improved significantly even as norms were tightened over the years and the economy slowed down. The capital position of commercial banks also improved significantly and was somewhat higher than the prescribed level. Profitability of the commercial banking sector improved despite decline in spread, which itself is a measure of efficiency. Although commercial banks still face the problem of overhang of NPAs, high spread and low profitability in comparison with banks in other emerging market economies, reforms have been successful in enhancing the performance of commercial banks in terms of both stability and efficiency parameters.

In the banking sector, the particular focus has been on imparting operational flexibility and functional autonomy with a view to enhancing efficiency, productivity and profitability, imparting strength to the system and ensuring financial soundness. The restrictions on activities undertaken by the existing institutions were gradually relaxed and barriers to entry in the banking sector were removed. In case of non-banking financial intermediaries, reforms focussed on removing sector-specific deficiencies.

Banking sector reforms in India are aimed at induction of best practices and technological changes for competing globally. The Reserve Bank of India (RBI) has time and again emphasised transparency, diversification of ownership and strong corporate governance practices to mitigate the prospects of systemic risks in the banking sector.

RBI has continued to monitor the progress of implementation of the Basel II framework, which was to be operationalised by banks and other financial institutions by

March 2007. To enable banks operating in India to acquire Basel II, the RBI on January 25, 2006 issued detailed guidelines, for raising capital funds to meet market as well as credit risks. The Basel II accord 1998 had specified a three-tier capital structure for banks.

Tier 1 covered permanent shareholders' equity; perpetual non-cumulative preference shares; disclosed reserves; and innovative capital instruments.

Tier 2 included undisclosed reserves; revaluation reserves; general provisions/general loan-loss reserves; hybrid debt capital instruments (a range of instruments which combine characteristics of equity capital and debt); and subordinated term debt.

Tier 3 consisted of short-term subordinated debt for the sole purpose of meeting a proportion of capital requirements for market risks.

The RBI issued detailed guidelines for the merger/amalgamation in respect of the private sector banks on May 11, 2005. These guidelines were applicable to merger proposals between two banking entities or between a banking company and non-banking financial company (NBFC); the same governing principles would be applicable, as appropriate, to public sector banks (PSBs) also. The merger of an NBFC with a banking entity would be subject to satisfaction of the Board of the banking entity on certain safeguards.

In July 2005, the RBI issued detailed draft guidelines on the sale/purchase of non-performing assets where securitisation companies and reconstruction companies are not involved. The draft guidelines covered (a) procedure for purchase/sale of nonperforming financial assets by banks, including valuation and pricing aspects and (b) prudential norms relating to asset classification, provisioning, accounting of recoveries, capital adequacy and exposure norms and disclosure requirements. The guidelines, *inter alia*, provided that a NPA in the books of a bank shall be eligible for sale to other banks, only if it has remained as NPA for at least two years in the books of the selling bank and such selling should be only on cash basis; a NPA should be held by the purchasing bank in its books at least for a period of 15 months before it is sold to other banks; banks should ensure that subsequent to the sale of a NPA to other banks, they should not have any involvement with reference to the assets sold and do not assume operational, legal or any other type of risks relating to the financial assets sold.

To protect customers' rights, enhancing the quality of customer service and strengthening grievance redressal mechanism in banks, RBI initiated several measures on an ongoing basis. To facilitate customer service in banks under a single window, RBI set-up a separate Customer Service Department (CSD) in July 2006. Its main functions, among other things, include the following.

1. Disseminating instructions/information relating to customer service and grievance redressal by banks.
2. Administering the Banking Ombudsman (BO) scheme.
3. Acting as a nodal department for the Banking Codes and Standards Board of India (BCSBI); ensuring redressal of complaints received directly by the RBI on customer service in banks.
4. Liaising between banks, Indian Banks Association (IBA), BO offices and the regulatory departments within RBI on matters relating to customer service and grievance redressal.

In his 2008-09 budget speech, the Union Finance Minister maintained that Government's policy of a careful and calibrated opening of the financial sector had proved successful and it would continue to take measured steps in this direction. The final report of the Committee on Financial Inclusion was received by the Government and the Minister announced the acceptance of two its recommendations to begin with: (a) to advise commercial banks, including RRBs, to add at least 250 rural household accounts every year at each of their rural and semi-urban branches and (b) to allow individuals such as retired bank officers, ex-servicemen etc to be appointed as business facilitator or business correspondent or credit counsellor.

Banks would be encouraged to embrace the concept of Total Financial Inclusion. Government would ask all scheduled commercial banks to follow the example set by some public sector banks and meet the entire credit requirements of Self-help Groups (SHG) members, namely (a) income generation activities, (b) social needs like housing, education, marriage etc and (c) debt swapping.

In order to increase the resource base of NABARD, SIDBI and NHB, the Minister proposed to tap into the resources of scheduled commercial banks to the extent that they fall short of their obligation to lend to the priority sector. Accordingly, it was announced to create the following funds:

- A fund of Rs. 5,000 crore in NABARD to enhance its refinance operations to short-term cooperative credit institutions.
- Two funds of Rs. 2,000 crore each in SIDBI, one for risk capital financing and the other for enhancing refinance capability to the MSME sector.
- A fund of Rs. 1,200 crore in NHB to enhance its refinance operations in the rural housing sector.

Other announcements made by the Finance Minister were as under:

- Take measures to develop the bond, currency and derivatives markets that will include launching exchange-traded currency and interest rate futures and developing a transparent credit derivatives market with appropriate safeguards.
- Enhance the tradability of domestic convertible bonds by putting in place a mechanism that will enable investors to separate the embedded equity option from the convertible bond and trade it separately.

- Encourage the development of a market-based system for classifying financial instruments based on their complexity and implicit risks.

In response to reforms, the Indian banking sector has undergone radical transformation during the 1990s. Reforms have altered the organizational structure, ownership pattern and domain of operations of banking institutions and infused competition in the financial sector. The competition has forced the banks to reposition themselves in order to survive and grow.

Apart from increasing integration of various segments of financial markets, the distinctions between banks and other financial intermediaries are also getting increasingly blurred. Another important aspect of reforms in the financial sector has been the increased participation of financial institutions, especially banks, in the capital market. These factors have led to increased inter-linkages across financial institutions and markets. While increased inter-linkages are expected to lead to increased efficiency in the resource allocation process and the effectiveness of monetary policy, they also increase the risk of contagion from one segment to another with implications for overall financial stability. This would call for appropriate policy responses during times of crisis. Increased inter-linkages also raise the issue of appropriate supervisory framework.

Banking sector reforms have supported the transition of the Indian economy to a higher growth path, while significantly improving the stability of the financial system. In comparison of the pre-reform period, the Indian banking system today is more stable and efficient. However, the gains of the past decade have to be consolidated, so that these could be translated to drive the institutions, markets and practices into a mature financial system that can meet the challenges of sustaining India on a higher growth trajectory. The banking system would, therefore, not only need to be stable, but would also need to support still higher levels of planned investments by channelling financial resources more efficiently from deficit to surplus sectors. The banks would need to reassess their core banking business to view how best they could undertake maturity transformation to step up the lendable resources in support of real economic activity.

Competitive pressures as well as prudential regulatory requirements have made banks risk-averse and their investment in relatively risk-free gilt instruments. The behaviour and strategies of bank business would need to change from the present so that they can factor in their own risk assessment even while performing their core activities. There is a need to ensure long term finance to support development and growth in the economy, even as restructuring takes place through mergers and universal banking.

Malout   R.K. Uppal
June 2008

Contents

- Monitoring of Frauds
- Ownership and Governance of Banks
- Payment of Dividends
- Managerial Autonomy for Public Sector Banks
- Mergers and Amalgamation of Banks
- Exposure Norms
- New Capital Adequacy Framework (Basel II Norms)
- Investment Norms
- Securitisation of Standard Assets
- Management of NPAs by Banks
- Anti-Money Laundering Guidelines
- Credit Information Bureau of India Ltd. (CIBIL)
- Off-site Monitoring and Surveillance
- Supervision of Financial Conglomerates
- Customer Service

1

Indian Banking and Basel II Accord

Introduction

In implementing Basel II, the Reserve Bank of India (RBI) is in favour of gradual convergence with the new standards and best practices. The aim is to reach the best standards in a phased manner, taking a consultative approach rather than a directive one i.e. a consultative and participative approach has been adopted for both designing and implementing Basel II. The RBI has set up a steering committee to suggest migration methodology to Basel II. Based on recommendations of steering committee, in February 2005, the RBI proposed "draft guidelines" for implementing new capital adequacy. Prior to 1988, central banks in different countries allowed varying definitions of capital in order to make their country's commercial bank and other financial institutions appear solid than they actually were. In order to provide a level playing field for various participants and also to ensure uniformity, the concept of regulatory capital was standardised in Basel I.

Along with definition of regulatory capital a basic formula for capital divided by assets was constructed and an arbitrary ratio of 8 per cent was chosen as minimum capital adequacy. However, there were drawbacks in the Basel I as it did not did not discriminate between different levels of risk. As a result a loan to an established corporate was deemed as risky as a loan to a new business. Furthermore, it assigned lower weightage to loans to banks and as a result banks were often keen to lend to other banks.

The Basel II accord proposes getting rid of the old risk weighted categories that treated all corporate borrowers the same replacing them with limited number of categories into which borrowers would be assigned based on assigned credit system.

Greater use of internal credit system has been allowed in standardized and advanced schemes, against the use of external rating. The new proposals avoid sole reliance on the capital adequacy benchmarks and explicitly recognize the importance of supervisory review and market discipline in maintaining sound financial systems.

At present banks in India are following the capital adequacy norms introduced by RBI of India in April 1992. These norms are based on Basel 1 Accord.

Under the current system, the balance sheet items are assigned prescribed ratio (at present 9 per cent) on the aggregate of the risk weighted assets and other assets on ongoing basis.

In June 2004, Basel II accord (International Convergence of Capital Measurement and Capital Standards: Revised Framework) has been brought and RBI had issued detailed draft guidelines to Indian banks for implementation of the same vide their circular dated 15.02.2005. A summary of the guidelines is discussed hereunder. The Basel II norms in respect of market risk have already been implemented as on 31.03.2006.

Basel II aims to build on solid foundation of prudent capital regulation, supervision and market discipline and to further risk and financial stability. Implementation of new framework will require substantial commitment on the part of field functionaries.

RBI expects banks to adopt the standardized approach for credit risk and basic indicator approach for operational risk. After adequate skills are developed both by banks and also by the supervisors, some of the banks may be allowed to migrate to the internal rating based (IRB) approach.

On current indicators implementing of Basel II will require more capital for banks in India due to the fact that operational risk is not covered or captured under Basel I, and the capital charge for market risk was not prescribed till recently. The cushion available in the system, which at present has a capital to risk asset ratio (CRAR) of over 12 per cent provides for some comforts but the banks are exploring various avenues for meeting capital requirements under Basel II.

Table 1.1: An Overview of the Basel II Accord

Basel II		
Pillar 1 Minimum Capital Requirement	Pillar 2 Supervisory Review	Pillar 3 Market Discipline

1. Capital for credit risk
• Standardized approach
• International Rating based approached
  - Foundation
  - Advanced
2. Capital for market risk
• Standardized method
  - maturity method
  - duration method
3. Capital for operational risk
• Basic indicator approach
• Standardized approach
• Advanced measurement approach
	1. Evaluation risk assessment
	2. Ensure soundness and integrity of banks internal process to assess the adequacy of capital
	3. Ensure maintenance of minimum capital
	4. prescribed differential capital where necessary i.e. where internal processes are slack
		1. Enhance disclosure
		2. Core disclosure and supplementary disclosure
		3. Semi annually submission

The RBI on its part has issued policy guidelines enabling issuance of several instruments by the banks viz. innovating perpetual debt instruments (IPDI), perpetual non cumulative preference shares and hybrid debt instruments so as to enhance their capital raising options.

Three-Track Approach in India

In India, we have 85 commercial banks which account for about 78 per cent (total assets) of the financial sector, over 3000 corporate banks which account for 9 per cent and 196 RRB's which accounts for 3 per cent. Taking in account the size, complexity of operations, relevance to the financial sector, need to ensure greater financial inclusion, the capital adequacy norms applicable to these entities have been maintained at different levels of stringency.

Given the differential risk appetite across banks and their business philosophies, it is likely that banks would themselves select their own approach, which in turn is likely to engender a stabilizing influence on the system as a whole.

On first track, the commercial banks are required to maintain capital for both credit and market risks as per Basel I framework. The co-operative banks on the second track are required to maintain capital for credit risk as per Basel I framework and through surrogates for market risk. The Regional Rural Banks on the third track have a minimum capital requirement which is however, not at par with Basel I framework. Consequently, we have a major segment of systematic importance on a full Basel I framework, a portion of minor segment partly on Basel I and smaller segment on a non Basel framework.

Consistent with these approaches, currently all commercial banks in India have been advised to start implementing Basel II with effect from 31 March, 2007.

Issues and Challenges in Implementing Basel II in India

While there is no second opinion regarding the purpose, necessity and usefulness of the proposed accord-the techniques and methods suggested in the consultative document would pose considerable implementation challenges for the banks specially in a developing country like India.

1. Capital Requirement: The Basel II implementation will increase the level of capital to be maintained by banks as per their risk profile. Capital requirement for credit risk may go down due to adoption of more risk sensitive models; however the same will be offset by additional charge for operational risk plus increased capital for market risk. This partly explains the current trend of consolidation in the banking industry.

2. Profitability: Competition among banks for highly rated corporate, needing lower amount of capital may exert pressure on already thinning interest rate speed. Further, huge implementation may also impact profitability for smaller banks.

3. Risk Management Architecture: The new standards are amalgam of international best practices and call for introduction of advanced risk management system. It would be a daunting task to create the required level of technological architecture plus human skills cross the institution.

4. Rating Requirement: For adopting the standardized approach, the banks require greater penetration of verdict rating agencies in India. Also, rating in India is restricted to issue plus non issuers-encouraging rating of issues would be a challenge.

5. Choice of Alternative Approaches: The new framework provides for alternative approaches for computation of capital requirement of various risks. Banks adopting IRB will be more sensitive, resulting in high risk assets flowing to banks or standardized approach as they would require lesser capital for these assets. Hence, the system as a whole may maintain lower capital than warranted plus become more vulnerable.

6. Absence of Historical Database: The implementation of various approaches requires creation of historical database which is a time consuming process plus may require initial support from supervisor.

7. Supervisory Framework: The supervisory cadre has to be properly trained for understanding of critical issues for risk profiling of supervised entities and validating plus guiding development of complex IRB models.

8. Corporate Governance Issues: The banks BOD has the responsibility for setting basic tolerance levels for various types of risks. It should ensure that management establishes a framework for assessing risks, develop a system to relate risks to the bank's capital levels and establish a method for monitoring compliance with internal policies.

9. Disclosure Regime: Pillar 3 purports to enforce market discipline through stricter disclosure requirements. However, this will only help the supervisory authorities, since the general public lacks the ability to comprehend and interpret the disclosed information. Also, too much disclosure may cause information overload and may even damage financial position of banks.

10. Disadvantage for Smaller Banks: The new framework calls for revamping the entire management information system and allocation of substantial resources. Therefore, it may be out of reach for many smaller banks.

Gist of Basel II

- Threats posed by risk prone assets held by the banks are to be counter balanced not only through holding prescribed minimum capital, but also by supplementing by effective supervisory review of capital adequacy plus accepted market discipline implying public disclosure. These constitute the three pillars of the Basel II accord.
- The underlying implication of the new accord is greater risk sensitive. It embodies the principles of
  - -flexibility,
  - -menu of approaches, and
  - -incentives for better risk management.
- Banks with advanced risk management tools would be permitted to use their own internal credit system for evaluating credit risk by process of internal based rating (IRB) approach. The use of this approach would be subject to the approval of the supervisory based on standards established by the committee.
- The new accord intends to cover all types of risks to which banks are exposed in addition to credit risk.

Three Pillar Approach

The capital framework proposed in the New Basel Accord consists of three pillars, each of which reinforces the other. The first pillar establishes the way to quantify the minimum capital requirements and is complemented with two qualitative pillars, concerned with organizing the regulator's supervision and establishing market discipline through public disclosure of the way that banks implement the Accord. Determination of minimum capital requirements remains the main part of the agreement, but the proposed methods are more risk sensitive and reflect more closely the current situation on financial markets.

Table 1.2: Basel II Accord

Pillar 1	Specifies new standards for minimum capital requirements along with the methodology for assigning risk weights on the basis of credit risk + market risk + operational risk.
Pillar 2	Enlarges the role of banking supervisors giving them power to review the bank's risk management system.
Pillar 3	Defines standards and requirements for higher disclosure by banks on capital adequacy, asset quality and other risk management processes.

First Pillar: Minimum Capital Requirement
The first pillar establishes a way to quantify the minimum capital requirements. While the new framework retains both existing capital definition and minimal capital ratio of 8 per cent, some major changes have been introduced in the measurement of risks. The main objective of Pillar I is to introduce greater risk sensitivity in the design of capital adequacy ratios and, therefore, more flexibility in the computation of banks' individual risk. This will lead to better pricing of risks.

Capital Adequacy Ratio signifies the amount of regulatory capital to be maintained by a bank on account for various risks inherent in the banking system.

The Capital Adequacy ratio is measured as:

$$\frac{\text{Total Regulatory Capital (unchanged)}}{\text{Credit Risk} + \text{Market Risk} + \text{Operational Risk}} = \text{Bank's Capital (minimum 8\%)}$$

Regulatory capital is defined as the minimum capital banks are required to hold by the regulator, i.e. *"The amount of capital a bank **must** have"*. It is the summation of Tier I and Tier II capital.

1. Credit Risk: The changes proposed in the measurement of credit risk are considered to have most far reaching implications. Basel II envisages two alternative ways of measuring credit risk.

- **The Standardised Approach:** The standardized approach is conceptually the same as the present Accord, but is more risk sensitive. The bank allocates a risk-weight to each of its assets and off-balance-sheet positions and produces a sum of risk-weighted asset values. Individual risk weights currently depend on the broad category of borrower (i.e. sovereigns, banks or corporates). Under the new Accord, the risk weights are to be defined by reference to a rating provided by an external credit assessment institution that meets strict standards.

- **The Internal Ratings Based Approach (IRB):** Under the IRB approach, distinct analytical frameworks will be provided for different types of loan exposures. The framework allows for both a foundation method in which a bank estimates the probability of default associated with each borrower, and the supervisors will supply the other inputs and an advanced IRB approach, in which a bank will be permitted to supply other necessary inputs as well. Under both the foundation and advanced IRB approaches, the range of risk weights will be far more diverse than those in the standardized approach, resulting in greater risk sensitivity.

The risk components include measures of:

(a) Probability of default (PD),
(b) Loss Given default (LGD),
(c) Exposure at default (EAD), and
(d) Effective Maturity (M).

Option 1 = Risk weights based on risk weight of the country

Option 2a = Risk weight based on assessment of individual bank

Option 2b = Risk weight based on assessment of individual banks with claim of original maturity of less than 6 months

Retail Portfolio = 75 per cent

Claims secured by residential property =35 per cent

NPA's = If specific provision is less than 20 per cent = 150 per cent.
If specific provision is more than 20 per cent = 100 per cent.

Table 1.3: Proposed Risk Weight Scale

Credit Assessment	AAA to AA-	A+ to A-	BBB to BBB-	BB+ to B-	Below B-	Unrated
Sovereign (Central banks)	0%	20%	50%	100%	150%	100%
Claims on the banks						
Option I	20%	50%	100%	100%	150%	100%
Option 2 a	20%	50%	50%	1005	150%	50%
Option 2b	205	20%	20%	505	150%	20%
Corporate	20 %	100%	+0	150%		100%

2. Operational Risk: Basel II Accord sets a capital requirement for operational risk. It defines operational risk as "the risk of direct or indirect loss resulting from inadequate or failed internal processes, people and systems or from external events". Banks will be able to choose between three ways of calculating the capital charge for operational risk – the Basic Indicator Approach, the Standardized Approach and the Advanced Measurement Approaches.

Second Pillar: Supervisory Review Process

The supervisory review process requires supervisors to ensure that each bank has sound internal processes in place to assess the adequacy of its capital based on a thorough evaluation of its risks. Supervisors would be responsible for evaluating how well banks are assessing their capital adequacy needs relative to their risks. This internal process would then be subject to supervisory review and intervention, where appropriate.

Third Pillar: Market Discipline

The third pillar of the new framework aims to bolster market discipline through enhanced disclosure by banks. Effective disclosure is essential to ensure that market participants can better understand banks' risk profiles and the adequacy of their capital positions. The new framework sets out disclosure requirements and recommendations in several areas, including the way a bank calculates its capital adequacy and its risk assessment methods. The core set of disclosure recommendations applies to all banks, with more detailed requirements for supervisory recognition of internal methodologies for credit risk, credit risk mitigation techniques and asset securitization.

Objectives of the Study

- To study the implementation of the guidelines of Basel II Accord in Indian banks and to have an explicit picture of the concepts of operational risks and facilitate its management.
- Whether the Basic indicator approach for calculation of charge is an effective tool to measure the operational risk.
- To see the Impact of capital allocation for credit risk and to value collaterals w.r.t Haircut strategies.
- Whether Basel II is likely to improve the risk management systems of banks as the banks aim for adequate capitalization to meet the underlying credit risk plus strengthen the overall financial system of the country.
- To identify the areas of operational risk and evaluate the same in each product, activity, process and system.

Methodology

A. Credit Allocation for Market Risks: Basic indicator approach states operational risk and the calculation of capital charge.

Operational risk = KBIA = $(\{(GI\ N\ *)\}/N$

KBIA=capital charge under Basic indicator approach

GI = gross income, where positive over the previous year

N =number of previous three years for which GI is positive

- All credit exposure were risk weighted 100 per cent
- Regulatory retail portfolio is defined and it carries a uniform risk weight of 75 per cent. CRAR is 755 on retail loans.
- Off balance sheet items are first calculated and then risk weights are applied.

B. Credit Mitigation Techniques: Collateralised Transactions: A collateralized transactions is one in which banks have a credit exposure and that exposure is hedged in whole or part by collateral posted by a counter party or by a third party on behalf of the counter party and banks have a specific lien on the collateral and the requirement of legal certainty as mentioned here in above are met.

- **Overall Framework and Minimum Conditions:** In addition to the general requirements for legal certainty, the legal mechanism by which collateral is pledged or transferred must ensure that the bank has a right to liquidate or take legal possession of it in a timely manner in the event of default, insolvency or bankruptcy. Reserve Bank has further advised that they must take all steps necessary to fill those requirements under the law applicable to the bank's interest in the collateral for obtaining and maintaining an enforceable security interest.

In order for collateral to provide protection, the credit quality of the counterparty and the value of the collateral must not have a material positive correlation.

Under this comprehensive approach, when taking collateral, banks will need to calculate their adjusted exposure to a counter party for capital adequacy purposes in order to take account of that collateral. The adjustments in the value of collateral is called haircut. The application of haircut will produce volatility adjusted amount for both exposure and collateral. The volatility adjusted amount for exposure is higher than the exposure and the volatility adjusted for the collateral is lower than the collateral.

- **Eligible Financial Collateral:** The following are the eligible financial collateral instruments:
1. Cash,

2. Gold,
3. Securities issue by central and state governments,
4. Indira Vikas Patra, Kisan Vikas Patra and NSCs,
5. Life insurance policies,
6. Debt securities rated by recognized credit rating agencies,
7. Debt securities rated by not recognized by credit rating agencies,
8. Undertaking of collective investments in transferable securities and mutual funds.

- **Haircuts:** RBI has advised two ways of calculating the haircuts.

1. standard supervisory haircuts using parameters set by committee, and
2. own estimate haircuts using internal estimate of market price volatility.

RBI has advised that the banks in India will use standard haircuts for the exposure as well as collateral.

C. Credit Mitigation Techniques: Guarantees: A range of guarantees are recognized under Basel II Accord. The detailed operational guidelines for guarantee eligible for being treated as a CRM are as under:

1. A guarantee must represent a direct claim on the protection provider and must be explicitly referenced to specific exposures or a pool of exposures.
2. A guarantee must be irrevocable.
3. The guarantee must be unconditional.
4. On the quality default/nonpayment of the counterparty, the bank may in timely manner pursue the guarantor for on monies outstanding under the documentations governing the transactions.
5. The guarantee is an explicitly documented obligation assumed by the guarantor.
6. The guarantee covers all types of the payments the underlying obligor is expected to make under the documentation governing the transaction.

Conclusion

A. Implementation of Basel II: Implementation of Basel II is likely to improve the risk management systems of banks as the banks aim for adequate capitalization to meet the underlying credit risk plus strengthen the overall financial system of the country.

It is apparent that advantage lies in favour of encouraging central banks/banking sector regulators to implement Basel II framework at their own pace plus in a manner appropriate to their economies, banking systems and supervisory mechanisms. In India, banks are likely to comply with the Basel II norms by March 2007. In the short term, Indian commercial banks may need to augment their regulatory capitalization levels in order to comply with Basel II. However, in the long term, they would derive benefits from improved operations and credit risk management practices. As the deadline of implementing Basel II approaches, the Indian banking is still preparing to solve the risk puzzle for a more transparent and risk free financial base.

1. The Standardised approach yields little in linking capital to risk while the IRB approach looks complex to implement and difficult to monitor. The banks adopting IRB approach would be more risk sensitive than the Banks on the Standardised approach, since even a small change in degree of risk might translate into a large impact on capital requirement for IRB Banks.

2. For the Banks adopting the Standardised Approach, the relative capital requirement would be less for the same exposure and would be inclined to assume the exposures to high risk clients, which were not financed by IRB Banks. As a result, high risk assets could flow towards bank on Standardised approach which needs to maintain lower capital on these assets. Hence, the system as a whole may maintain lower capital than warranted.

Keeping in view the above, we suggest a Centralised Rating based (CRB) approach where RBI dictates a rating scale and asks the Banks to rate borrowers according to the centralized scale.

RBI thus would be able to monitor and control their capital sufficiency in relation to risk much more effectively. The Banks would thus by CRB approach have their own Rating Scales in consultation with RBI and use them as a reference tool.

B. Challenges in Implementation of Basel II Norms Are:

1. **Costly Database Creation and Maintenance Process:** The most obvious impact of BASEL II is the need for improved risk management and measurement. It aims to give impetus to the use of internal rating system by international banks. More and more banks may have to use internal model developed in house and their impact is uncertain. Most of these models require minimum 5 years bank data which is a tedious and high cost process as most Indian banks do not have such a database.

2. **Additional Capital Requirement:** In order to comply with the capital adequacy norms we will see that the overall capital level of the banks will raise a glimpse of what was seen when the RBI raised risk weightages for mortgages and home loans in October 2004. Here there is a worrying aspect that some of the banks will not be able to put up the additional capital to comply with the new regulation and they may be isolated from the global banking system.

3. **Large Proportion of NPA's:** A large number of Indian banks have significant proportion of NPA's in their assets. Along with that, a large proportion of bank loans are of poor quality. There is a danger that a large number of banks will not be able to restructure and survive in the new environment. This may lead to forced mergers of many defunct banks with the existing ones and a loss of capital to the banking system as a whole.

4. **Relative Advantage to Large Banks:** The new norms seem to favor the large banks that have better risk management and measurement expertise. They also have better capital adequacy ratios and geographically diversified portfolios. The smaller banks are also likely to be hurt by the rise in weightage of inter-bank loans that will effectively price them

out of the market. Thus banks will have to restructure and adopt if they are to survive in the new environment.

5. **Increased Pro-Cyclicality:** The appropriate question is not then whether Basel II introduces pro-cyclicality but whether it increases or not. The increased importance to credit ratings under Basel II could actually imply that the minimum requirements could become pro-cyclical as banks are required to raise capital levels for loans in times of economic crises.

6. **Low Degree of Corporate Rating Penetration:** India has as few as three established rating agencies and the level of rating penetration is not very significant as, so far, ratings are restricted to issues and not issuers. While Basel II gives some scope to extend the rating of issues to issuers, this would only be an approximation and it would be necessary for the system to move to ratings of issuers. Encouraging ratings of issuers would be a challenge.

7. **Cross Border Issues for Foreign Banks:** In India, foreign banks are statutorily required to maintain local capital and the following issues are required to be resolved:

- Validation of the internal models approved by their head offices and home country supervisor adopted by the Indian branches of foreign banks.
- Date history maintained and used by the bank should be distinct for the Indian branches compared to the global data used by the head office.
- capital for operational risk should be maintained separately for the Indian branches in India.

Compliance with Basel II norms would give banks:

(a) Better position to fight with three primary risks which they face, namely – credit, market and operational.

(b) Put Indian banks on equal footing with that of international banks and help improve their credibility.

2

Indian Banks: Changing Paradigms

Introduction

Banking as a major part of the financial sector, is a life blood for the whole industry, necessary to survive. It plays a decisive role in accelerating the rate of economic growth in each economy. In the wake of contemporary changes in the world economy and other domestic crises like adverse balance of payment problem, increasing fiscal deficits etc. our country too embarked upon economic reforms. As banking sector reforms represents financial sector reforms, they are necessary for faster economic growth to meet the emerging challenges. To improve the adverse situation in banking, banking sector reforms were introduced in 1991 and 1998 by the Committee constituted under the chairmanship of Mr. M. Narasimham.

Rationale of Banking Sector Reforms

Banking sector reforms were introduced to remove the deficiencies in the banking sector. Following were the problems the Indian banking sector was facing prior to the reforms:

- highly regulated by the RBI.
- eroded productivity and efficiency of public sector banks.
- continuous losses suffered by public sector banks year after year.
- increasing NPAs.
- deteriorating portfolio quality.
- poor customer service.
- obsolete work technology.
- inability to face the competitive environment.

Hence, need of the hour was to introduce some policies to remove the above said deficiencies. So, in the light of above distortions, Narasimham Committee was appointed in 1991 and it submitted its report by November 1991, with detailed measures to improve the adverse situation of the banking industry. The main motive of the reforms was to improve the operational efficiency of the banks to further enhance their productivity and profitability.

First Phase of Banking Sector Reforms
The first phase basically contained:
1. Reduction in SLR and CRR,
2. Deregulation of interest rates,
3. Transparent guidelines or norms for entry and exit of private sector banks,
4. Public sector banks allowed for direct access to capital markets,
5. Branch licensing policy liberalized,
6. Setting up of Debt Recovery Tribunals,
7. Asset classification and provisioning,
8. Income recognition,
9. Asset Reconstruction Fund (ARF), and
10. At least 40 pc of the total advances for the priority sector.

The first phase of banking sector reforms, termed as 'Curative' measures, came up with the main objective to improve the operational efficiency of the banks. Although first phase of banking sector reforms witnessed revealed improvement in the performance of the banks, yet competition also increased with liberalization, privatization and globalization. With better use of technology, new entrants were able to spur competition, but public sector banks suffered as they were not using the technology to a large extent mainly due to opposition from trade unions and high initial costs of installation.

Second Phase of Banking Sector Reforms
In spite of the optimistic views about the growth of banking industry in terms of branch expansion, deposit mobilization etc, several distortions have still crept into the system which are enumerated as follows:
• increasing competition,

- increasing NPAs, and
- obsolete technology.

Hence, while observing above distortions, the Government of India appointed the Second Narasimham Committee under the chairmanship of Mr. M. Narasimham in 1998 to review the first phase of banking reforms and chart out a programme for further reforms necessary to strengthen India's financial system so as to make it internationally competitive. This situation arose mainly due to the global changes occurring in the world economy, which has made each industry very competitive. The Committee reviewed the performance of the banks in light of first phase of reforms and submitted its report with some repaired and some new recommendations. There were no new recommendations except the following:

- merger of strong units of banks, and
- adaptation of the 'narrow banking' concept to rehabilitate weak banks.

As the process of second banking sector reforms is going on since 1999, it has proved improvement in the performance of banks and on the other side, many changes have come occurred due to the entry of our banks into the global market.

Since a decade of banking sector reforms has been completed, it is essential to review the various issues of banking sector reforms, especially its post reforms' impact on NPAs, interest income, non-interest income, capital adequacy, priority sector advances and SLR & CRR. This study is mainly concerned with the efficacy of banking sector reforms, major weak areas need to be further considered and some possible reforms need to be added in third reforms.

The present chapter is divided into six sections. After a brief introduction of the banking sector reforms, section II reviews some related studies. Section III describes the objectives and database and research methodology. Section IV analyses the results whereas section V suggests some possible reforms which may be termed as third phase of reforms. Last part of the paper concludes the discussion.

Review of Literature

Ballabh, J (2001) analyzed challenges in the post-banking sector reforms. With globalization and changes in technology, financial markets world over have become closely integrated. For the survival of the banks they should adopt new policies/strategies according to the changing environment.

Kaveri, V.S. (2001) studied the non-performing assets (NPAs) of various banks and suggested strategies to reduce the extent of NPAs. In view of the steep rise in fresh NPA advances, credit should be strengthened. RBI should use some new policies/strategies to prevent NPAs.

Singh, R (2003) analyzed profitability management of banks under the deregulated environment with some financial parameters of the major four bank groups i.e. public sector banks, old private sector banks, new private sector banks and foreign banks and concluded that the profitability has declined in the deregulated environment. He emphasized to make the banking sector competitive in the deregulated environment with preference for non-interest income sources.

Vashisht, A.K. (2004) studied recent global developments, which has transformed the environment in which commercial banks operate. Globalization has expanded economic interdependence and interaction of countries greatly. Under the regime of globalized environment, the financial performance of the commercial banks has changed and the commercial banks will face new challenge and also new opportunities in the coming years.

Wahab, A (2001) has analyzed the performance of the commercial banks under reforms. He also highlighted the major issues that need to be considered for further improvement. He concluded that reforms have produced favourable effects on performance of commercial banks in general but still there are some distortions like low priority sector advances, low profitability etc. that needs to be reformed again.

From this review, we conclude that banking sector reforms has changed the financial environment with new challenges that are emerging along with immense opportunities.

Objectives and Research Methodology

The present chapter is basically concerned with the following objectives:

- To study the rationale of banking sector reforms;
- To study and analyze the efficacy of banking sector reforms; and
- To suggest third banking sector reforms in the globalized environment.

Present study is concerned with the performance of Indian banking industry under reforms to analyze the efficacy of banking sector reforms. The universe for the study is Indian banking industry. Five major bank groups, as defined by RBI, are taken for the study. These bank groups are:

G-I	SBI and its Associates
G-II	Nationalized Banks
G-III	Old Private Sector Banks
G-IV	New Private Sector Banks
G-V	Foreign Banks

The present study is concerned mainly with post-second banking sector reforms period i.e. from 1998-99 to 2003-04. Various ratios are examined to analyze the efficacy of the banking reforms. The statistical results are obtained by using SPSS Version 10.

- Gross NPAs as percentage of Gross Advances
- Net NPAs as percentage of Net Advances
- Interest Income as percentage of Total Income
- Non-Interest Income as percentage of Total Income
- Interest Paid as percentage of Total Expenditure
- Priority Sector Advances as percentage of Total Advances
- Capital Adequacy Ratio
- SLR & CRR.

Results and Discussion

Non-Performing Assets (NPAs): The improvement in the

financial health of the banking system is reflected in declining share of NPAs in the total advances of all the bank groups. From Table 2.1, it is examined that gross NPAs to gross advances ratio of all the bank groups is showing a decreasing trend during 1998-2004.

Table 2.1: Gross NPAs to Gross Advances (per cent)

Years	G-I	G-II	G-III	G-IV	G-V	Average	S.D.	C.V. (%)
1998-99	17.17	16.51	13.03	5.41	7.53	11.93	5.28	44.26
1999-00	15.32	14.77	11.22	4.03	7.32	10.53	4.85	46.06
2000-01	12.73	12.16	10.90	5.10	6.84	9.55	3.39	35.50
2001-02	11.23	11.01	11.00	8.90	5.38	9.50	2.49	26.21
2002-03	8.68	9.72	8.90	7.60	5.25	8.03	1.73	21.54
2003-04	6.98	8.21	7.60	5.00	4.62	6.48	1.59	24.54
Average	12.02	12.06	10.44	6.01	6.16			
S.D.	3.88	3.12	1.91	1.84	1.22			
C.V. (%)	32.28	25.87	18.30	30.62	19.81			

Note: G-I, SBI & its Associates, G-II, Nationalized Banks, G-III, Old Private Sector Banks, G-IV, New Private Sector Banks and G-V, Foreign Banks.
Source: Performance Highlights (*various issues*), 1998-2004, Indian Banking Association, Mumbai

It decreased at a tremendous rate despite tightening of norms relating to NPAs. On an average, it is the least in case of G-IV i.e. 6.01 pc followed by G-V with 6.16 pc, it is half the NPAs share compared to G-I & II while variations are maximum in G-I i.e. 32.28 pc. In 1998-99, an average percentage of gross NPAs to gross advances were 11.93 pc, which decreased to almost half to 6.48 pc in 2003-04.

Table 2.2 shows the trends in net NPAs to net advances reflecting a declining trend in all the bank groups in all the years under study except G-IV, which shows a fluctuating trend. In 1998-99, average ratio was 7.36 pc with 33.70 pc co-efficient of variations, and decreased almost three times to 2.71 pc in 2003-04. It is the least i.e. 3.43 pc in case of G-IV followed by G-V with 3.45 pc, but highest in the case of G-III i.e. 6.82 pc whereas variations in terms of C.V. is maximum in case of G-V i.e. 77.39 pc.

Table 2.2: Net NPAs to Net Advances (per cent)

Years	G-I	G-II	G-III	G-IV	G-V	Average	S.D.	C.V. (%)
1998-99	9.22	8.69	9.13	3.49	6.28	7.36	2.48	33.70
1999-00	7.76	8.08	8.10	2.06	7.43	6.69	2.60	38.86
2000-01	6.27	7.01	7.30	3.10	1.82	5.10	2.48	48.63
2001-02	5.45	6.01	7.10	4.90	1.89	5.07	1.96	38.66
2002-03	4.12	4.74	5.50	4.60	1.76	4.14	1.42	34.30
2003-04	2.71	3.13	3.80	2.40	1.49	2.71	0.86	31.73
Average	5.92	6.28	6.82	3.43	3.45			
S.D.	2.37	2.09	1.91	1.15	2.67			
C.V. (%)	40.03	33.28	28.01	33.53	77.39			

Source: Same as in Table 2.1.

Interest Income and Expenditure: Interest is a cost and income of the banks. Due to the deregulation, interest rates are decreasing continuously to meet the competition. It adversely affects the interest income earned from advances and investments. Banks have initiated to pitch into the fee-based activities market, income from these sources is going to increase which is further helping the banks to set off their losses due to reduction in interest margins.

Interest Income to Total Income: Table 2.3 reveals that all the bank groups show fluctuating trend in share of interest income in the total income in all the years under study but decreased in 2003-04 in all the cases which is mainly due to reduction in interest rates. In 1998-99, the average ratio was 85.84 pc which further decreased to 76.57 pc in 2003-04 with maximum variations during 2001-02 i.e. 6.06 pc C.V. On an average, from all the bank groups, G-II shows the highest interest income ratio i.e. 85.91 pc followed by G-I whereas G-V witnessed the highest decrease from 80.61 pc in 1998-99 to 69.09 pc in 2003-04 with the highest variation of 5.69 pc C.V.

Table 2.3: Interest Income as Percentage of Total Income (per cent)

Years	G-I	G-II	G-III	G-IV	G-V	Average	S.D.	C.V. (%)
1998-99	85.61	89.48	88.15	85.57	80.61	85.84	3.40	3.96
1999-00	85.81	88.38	88.57	81.91	79.16	84.77	4.13	4.87
2000-01	86.40	88.84	79.65	85.87	79.03	83.96	4.37	5.20
2001-02	86.56	85.48	79.65	79.40	74.54	81.13	4.92	6.06
2002-03	83.63	83.32	79.07	76.01	74.49	79.30	4.15	5.23
2003-04	78.93	79.97	78.99	75.94	69.09	76.57	4.40	5.75
Average	84.49	85.91	82.35	80.75	76.14			
S.D.	2.92	3.73	4.67	4.39	4.33			
C.V. (%)	3.46	4.34	5.67	5.44	5.69			

Source: Same as in Table 2.1

Non-Interest Income to Total Income: Reforms have led to diversification in the banking activities away from their core intermediation business to fee-based services such as credit card transactions, merchant banking etc. The rising share of non-interest income in the total income of all the bank groups is manifest in Table 2.4 which shows that the trend in this ratio is increasing in all the years except 2000-01 in all the bank groups.

An average proportion of non-interest income in the total income of all the bank groups increased from 14.12 pc in 1998-99 to 23.42 pc in 2003-04, but in case of G-V, it increased at a greater rate. On an average, the share of non-interest income in the total income is the highest in case of G-V i.e. 23.86 pc followed by G-IV but variations are still the highest in case of G-III i.e. 27.22 pc. Hence, share of interest income is decreasing accompanied with increasing share of non-interest income in the total income, which further contributes to their profitability positively.

Interest Expenditure to Total Expenditure: The more the deposits and borrowings, more is the interest expenditure. Now a days it has decreasing due to decreasing interest rates, which again contributes to reduction in total expenditure.

Table 2.4: Non-Interest Income as Percentage of Total Income (per cent)

Years	G-I	G-II	G-III	G-IV	G-V	Average	S.D.	C.V. (%)
1998-99	14.39	10.52	11.85	14.43	19.39	14.12	3.39	24.01
1999-00	14.19	11.62	14.95	18.09	20.84	15.94	3.58	22.46
2000-01	13.60	11.16	11.43	14.13	20.97	14.26	3.97	27.84
2001-02	13.44	14.52	20.35	20.60	25.46	18.87	4.92	26.07
2002-03	16.38	16.62	20.92	23.99	25.61	20.70	4.19	20.24
2003-04	21.07	20.03	21.01	24.06	30.91	23.42	4.45	19.00
Average	15.51	14.08	16.75	19.22	23.86			
S.D.	2.92	3.72	4.56	4.43	4.37			
C.V. (%)	18.83	26.42	27.22	23.05	18.32			

Source: Same as in Table 2.1.

From Table 2.5, it is examined that the share of interest expenditure in the total expenditure shows fluctuating trends in all the bank groups and years under study except G-III which shows a continuous decrease. However, it still decreased in 2003-04 in case of all the bank groups where G-V witnessed a decrease at greater rate than others. In 1998-99, average share of interest paid in total expenditure was 66.06 pc which decreased to 53.37 pc in 2003-04 with the highest variations in this year i.e. 14.93 pc. On an average, G-V shows the least percentage of interest paid to total expenditure i.e. 51.02 pc followed by G-I whereas, it is the highest in case of G-IV. Overall, this ratio decreased during 2003-04 for all the bank groups.

Overall, it is concluded that profitability of public sector banks is dependent more on interest income where as new private sector banks and foreign banks are able to step up their non-interest income effectively in comparison to public sector banks.

Priority Sector Advances
Priority sector advances to total advances ratio represents the

banks' credit pattern in the priority sector against the given target by RBI i.e. 40 pc of the total advances (32 pc in case of foreign banks). Table 2.6 shows that the share of priority sector advances to total advances firstly decreased till 2001-02 and then started to increase in other years under study. In 1998-99, its average share was 27.35 pc which increased to 29.22 pc in 2003-04.

Table 2.5: Interest Paid as Percentage of Total Expenditure (per cent)

Years	G-I	G-II	G-III	G-IV	G-V	Average	S.D.	C.V. (%)
1998-99	60.91	64.67	72.82	74.11	57.78	66.06	7.20	10.90
1999-00	63.50	65.14	69.74	68.77	53.72	64.17	6.38	9.94
2000-01	61.65	62.53	69.06	69.30	52.55	63.02	6.85	10.87
2001-02	64.28	62.98	65.33	63.43	52.78	61.76	5.10	8.26
2002-03	61.34	59.38	62.97	65.61	49.53	59.77	6.16	10.31
2003-04	54.88	53.98	59.26	58.98	39.76	53.37	7.97	14.93
Average	61.09	61.45	66.53	66.70	51.02			
S.D.	3.32	4.19	4.96	5.24	6.12			
C.V. (%)	5.43	6.82	7.46	7.86	12.00			

Source: Same as in Table 2.1

Table 2.6: Priority Sector Advances as Percentage of Total Advances (per cent)

Years	G-I	G-II	G-III	G-IV	G-V	Average	S.D.	C.V. (%)
1998-99	30.51	32.25	32.99	18.89	22.12	27.35	6.42	23.47
1999-00	29.15	31.65	33.58	16.32	21.60	26.46	7.27	27.48
2000-01	29.07	31.53	31.69	15.30	21.45	25.81	7.20	27.90
2001-02	28.92	31.46	31.02	15.97	21.48	25.77	6.79	26.35
2002-03	28.94	33.84	29.94	18.18	21.90	26.56	6.36	23.95
2003-04	30.81	36.25	31.56	24.15	23.23	29.22	5.43	18.58
Average	29.57	32.83	31.80	18.14	21.98			
S.D.	0.86	1.90	1.32	3.25	0.71			
C.V. (%)	2.91	5.79	4.15	17.92	3.23			

Source: Same as in Table 2.1

Co-efficient of variation is maximum in 2000-01 i.e. 27.90 pc. On an average, the share of priority sector advances in the total advances is the highest in case of G-II i.e. 32.83 pc followed by G-III, whereas G-IV shows the least share i.e. only 18.14 pc. It is examined that not even a single bank group have succeeded to meet the target of RBI but still had somewhat rising contribution to this sector. One major reason for lesser share of priority sector advances is the absence of sufficient credit takers in this sector.

Capital Adequacy

Capital adequacy ratio reflects the overall financial condition of the banks and also their ability to meet the need for additional capital. An adequate capital base is essential for banks to absorb credit risk but in the pre-reform years, a large number of banks were undercapitalized, as they were unable to add to their capital base by increasing reserves due to declining profits. Since 1991, it was much below the internationally accepted CRAR of 8 pc. But after the reforms were introduced, a target of 10 pc CRAR in 2003-04 was fixed. Table 2.7 shows that CRAR of all the bank groups is fluctuating, but still met the target. However, in the case of G-IV, it decreased from 12.01 pc in 1998-99 to 10 pc in 2003-04 whereas G-V shows the highest ratio even three times the target CRAR, and further it reduced from 36.77 pc in 1998-99 to 15 pc in 2003-04. Such a favourable development indicates the banking system's growing strength to absorb credit risk, which may arise on account of its advances going bad, resulting in losses.

Table 2.7: Capital Adequacy Ratio (per cent)

Years	G-I	G-II	G-III	G-IV	G-V
1998-99	11.98	9.95	12.60	12.01	36.77
1999-00	11.95	9.82	12.32	12.63	34.94
2000-01	12.43	10.39	11.73	11.47	32.38
2001-02	12.96	10.81	12.65	10.79	46.32
2002-03	13.50	12.20	12.96	11.50	15.20
2003-04	13.50	13.10	13.85	10.00	15.00

Source: Same as in Table 2.1.

SLR and CRR

It represents the required percentage of the banks' time and demand liabilities that need to be reserved/deposited with the RBI on daily basis. Before the banking sector reforms, it was much more and have blocked the banks capital resulting in a ban to invest these funds in other better opportunities that might increase their profitability. After that, it was reduced as recommended by the Narasimham Committee, which improved the banks' financial and liquidity position. During the banking sector reforms, CRR and SLR is continuously falling and due to this the banks have more funds for credit to various sectors and they have more funds for investment (Table 2.8).

Major Issues

The foregoing analysis shows that reforms have paved the way for building our banking system capable to meet the requirements of an open and competitive economy. But on the other side, some deficiencies have persisted despite these reforms, like:

- low level of priority sector advances,
- decreasing interest income,
- high share of NPAs, and
- growing influence of foreign banks witnessed by their tremendously increasing non-interest income, decreasing NPAs and good CAR.

Agenda for Third Phase of Reforms

Rethinking for financial sector reforms have to be accorded the highest priority, with restructuring of the public sector banks in particular, to strengthen the Indian financial system and make it sound to meet the challenges of globalization. The on going reforms process and the agenda for third phase of reforms will focus mainly on making the banking sector reforms viable and efficient so that it could contribute to enhance the competitiveness of the real economy and face the challenges of an increasingly integrated global financial architecture. The future agenda for third reforms would certainly have to address to the following core areas:

Table 2.8: Cash Reserve Ratio (CRR) and Statutory Liquidity Ratio (SLR) (per cent)

Years	CRR	SLR
1991-92	15	38.50
1992-93	15	37.75
1993-94	14	34.75
1994-95	15	33.75
1995-96	14	31.50
April 1996	13	31.50
July 1996	12	31.50
October 1996	11.5	31.50
January 1997	10	26.70
1997-98	8	25
1998-99	8	25
1999-2000	8	25
End Dec. 2001	5.5	25
2003	4.5	25
March 2004	4.5	25
April 2005	5.00	25
December 2006	5.25	-
November 2007	7.50	-
May 2008	8.00	25

Source: Report on Trend and Progress of Banking in India (*various issues*); Macroeconomic and Monetary Developments, 2007-08 – Reserve Bank of India

Management of NPAs: The level of NPAs in the Indian banking industry is of a greater concern and thus urgent cleaning up of bank's balance sheets has become a crucial issue. Although the ratio of net NPAs to net advances has reduced to some extent, yet it is high in absolute terms. So, NPAs would have to be reduced drastically and for the same purpose, following measures are suggested:

• reducing the existing NPAs and curbing their further build up

- do not consider projects with old technology for finance
- do not consider financing term loans for maturities over 5 years except in case of agriculture, infrastructure and SSI
- increasing the number of Debt Recovery Tribunals
- complete ban on generalized loan waivers
- provide financial help to form ARF to banks at individual level
- collect interest from clients on monthly basis instead of quarterly collection
- compulsory annual review of borrower accounts with sufficient disclosure in balance sheet. For this purpose, change the review format to analyze both quantitative and qualitative data
- train the staff to closely monitor creditworthiness of borrowers and the end use of bank loans to avoid major post-defaults
- at the time of credit appraisal, observe and consider the list produced by RBI of defaulters and suit-filed cases thoroughly
- regional managers should visit the branches periodically for monitoring preventive actions taken by the branches
- separate credit-monitoring and audit cells should be installed in the banks
- eliminate political interference in disbursing loans.

The above said set of reforms should be considered to arrest the trend of ever increasing level of NPAs.

Technology Upgradation

New entrants, with the use of new technology and full computerization of their branches, have been able to spur the global competition but our public sector and old private sector banks are still waiting for some other alternatives and are far behind the new entrants and hence, unable to meet the competitive challenges. The need of the hour is that public sector banks should adopt a cautious approach in adoption of technology i.e. e-banking which enhances their capacity in handle more and more customer demands without loosing time. Because, e-channels like

ATMs, I-banking, M-banking and Tele-banking etc. help to enhance the deposits, advances and other fee-based earning sources, it further contributes to their profits. All loopholes in the use of IT should be plugged so that once technology is in place, there is no further reason or excuse for slackness on the part of public sector banks. For this purpose following steps can be considered to reform:

- complete computerization of entire branch network through integrated software or with the centralized server
- provide branches with online nodes to receive customer requests and to provide them across the counter services
- appoint skilled manpower and train the existing ones to remove hesitation
- all branches should be interconnected with regional servers through reliable network media
- banks should be provided some tax benefits to motivate them to use more technology
- place proper security infrastructure for routing secure transactions through the public network
- as cost of installation of technology infrastructure is much higher, government should provide subsidy to the banks, particularly to the public sector banks
- banks should take more initiative for customer awareness regarding computerization, particularly e-delivery channels
- special arrangements should be made to motivate the rural branches to adopt technology. Rural branches should be fully exempted from taxes for such income and provide subsidy for installation cost.

The above said measures will help the public sector banks to compete with the new entrants and improve their performance.

Further Reduction in SLR and CRR

As we know that with the reduction in SLR & CRR, banks have been able to utilize their surplus funds in other profitable activities. If it is further reduced, the funds for all the banks will increased and they can invest these surplus funds in government securities, foreign stock markets, more advances, etc., which will result in:

- increase in interest income and income from dividends,
- increase in foreign reserves,
- improved liquidity position, and
- enhanced goodwill in foreign markets.

We hypothetically feel that SLR should be reduced to 20 pc and CRR to 4 pc.

Priority Sector Advances

The tendency of declining share of priority sector advances in the total advances, need to be checked if the banking system is to be geared up to meet the specific requirements of Indian economy. On the basis of above analysis, the following recommendations should be considered for third reforms:

- reduction of present 40 pc target limit to 35 pc, besides motivating banks to finance in this sector more than their target and reward those banks with some extra benefits like tax exemption to possible extent, increase in their credit limits etc.
- simplify the procedure for loan application form, agreements and other documents
- delegating power to branch managers
- order the banks to make their loan policy transparent and stop mutual adjustments of various aspects of priority sector advances
- initiate self-evaluation programmes to evaluate borrower accounts and security values by internal professionals and by external experts to prevent default in accounts
- eliminate political interference and provide loans only to confident parties and for productive purposes only
- promote more advances for agriculture and SSI by enhancing the credit limits for them.

These recommendations should be considered in third reforms to manage the priority sector advances in the right direction.

Rationalisation of Interest Rates

Interest income is declining continuously due to deregulation of interest rates, entry of NBFCs with easy financing options and intense competition. On the other side, non-interest income is increasing which is a good indicator of increasing profitability. To manage the interest rates, following suggestions can be considered:

- evolve a Reserve Bank Reference Rate of Interest, which will be the basis for determining the entire gamut of interest rates
- adopt cautious step by step approach rather a rapid deregulation of interest rates
- adopt more and more fee-based activities like merchant banking, advisory services etc. Public sector banks should be further motivated to initiate fee-based activities
- the government should reduce the rate of interest on housing loans and also on loans for infrastructure development activities.

Development of Rural Banking

Public sector banks have more rural branches than new entrants, a major reason for their slow development. The following steps should be considered while initiating third reforms to further develop our rural banking:

- new private sector banks and foreign banks should be motivated to open their rural branches by providing them with some extra benefits like tax exemption, increased credit limits etc.
- start more programmes to aware the people about the functioning of banking and their benefits
- appoint skilled and nice-natured staff in these branches so that they help the customers to solve their problems
- computerize all the rural branches and also motivate them to adopt IT. For this purpose, people in the rural sector should also be made aware about the functioning of e-channels and tell them the benefits of using IT
- merge two or more rural branches to strengthen them for

better and effective functioning
- create direct link with regional and zonal offices

New Credit Assessment Skills

So far the focus of attention in the Indian banking industry has largely been extending finance to agriculture and manufacturing sectors covering small, medium and large industries. However, banks should now capture service class also. Through IT, banks therefore, have to sharpen their credit assessment skills and lay more emphasis in providing finance to the wide range of activities in the services sector.

WTO and Indian Banking Industry

As WTO provisions come into force, countries including India have to provide greater market access to other countries by eliminating Quantitative Restrictions (QR), regarding tariff barriers and liberalizing the market for financial services. The impact of these developments on various sectors of the Indian economy would be critical.

The banks will have to keep themselves updated on sector specific developments taking place in the world, particularly in countries that are India's major trading partners and advise their corporate clients to help them to prepare for competition with multinational companies.

Miscellaneous Recommendations

In spite of the above said reforms, following are also core competitive areas which need to be considered for third reforms:
- reduction in the government stake in public sector banks' capital up to 33 pc which would be beneficial for the banks as witnessed in the case of by 12 public sector banks like SBI, PNB, Syndicate Bank, OBC, Punjab & Sindh Bank, Bank of Maharashtra etc.
- implement VRS with some new attractive and effective policies and recruit efficient, skilled and innovative professionals

- RBI should liberalize various policies for the merger of weak banks. Other banks should also merge to compete in the global market. Banks should also go for merging some of their activities under core competition rather to merge for the whole business. Particular branches of the banks should also be allowed to merge with each other
- all the banks should be motivated to set up specialized committees like Audit Committee, Risk Management Committee, Compensatory Committee etc., which will strengthen the corporate governance
- in the deregulated environment, banks should enter retail banking with some attractive policies. It will help in increasing their fee-based income
- enter universal banking with three tier structure of capital
- RBI should give more autonomy to the public sector banks to access the capital market

In the post-era of IT Act, global environment is continuously changing and creating new directions, dimensions and immense opportunities for the banking industry. Keeping in mind all the changes, RBI should appoint another committee to evaluate the on-going banking sector reforms and suggest third phase of the banking sector reforms in the light of above said recommendations.

Conclusion

The conclusion emerging from this study reflects that reforms have produced favourable effects on the performance of commercial banks in general witnessed by their achievement of minimum capital adequacy norms and increased non-interest income. However, on the other side, the poor performance in terms of priority sector advances, persistence of large NPAs and decreasing interest income are issues which call for careful attention in the subsequent dose of reforms. Hence, there is a need to consider the above listed measures for third banking sector reforms to improve the performance of the banks particularly of public sector banks. Need of the hour is to provide some effective measures to guard the banks against financial fragilities and vulnerability in an environment of growing financial integration, competition and global challenges. The challenge for the banks is to harmonize and co-ordinate with banks in other countries to reduce the scope for contagion and maintain financial stability.

3

Cost-Benefit Analysis of Commercial Banks

Introduction

Globalization through the ways of liberalization, privatization and deregulation in the financial sector has stimulated financial innovations. Globalization is affecting each activity of the banking sector. Breath taking developments in the technology of telecommunications and electronic data processing is adding fuel to the fire in these changes. Banking being one of the most dominating part of financial sector, IT is responsible for a paradigm shift in banks (Bhide, Prasad and Ghosh).

At a time, when the banking world over is undergoing a radical transformation due to the all pervasive influence of technology advancements, banking has become more competitive and hence, demands special care to tackle challenges of recent transformation. Transformation in banks through IT is taking place at a rapid speed to catch up with the best practices in the world (Uppal & Rimpi).

The major challenge for the banks is asset and liability management especially funds creation and the disbursement of these funds into profitable portfolio to earn enough. To meet these challenges the use of technology assumes a critical role. Indian banks are working in a high-tech environment (Rangarajan). Technology must be used to strengthen internal control, improve accuracy of records management and facilitate provision of new products and services. Now-a-days, 90 per cent of the banking business is done electronically with the advent of ATMs, Credit/Debit/Smart Cards, Internet-banking, Mobile-banking, Tele-banking etc. which has influenced deposits and fee-based income at a large scale and on the other hand demat services along with other available ways of electronic fund creation have also influenced the investments too and hence resulted in increased income. The big challenge for each bank is to choose the optimum portfolio of funds i.e. from where to create funds at least cost and where to invest these funds to earn enough with efficient risk management.

The key to any commercial bank's source is the selection of its sources and use of funds. If we review the balance sheets, the largest of all the liabilities, is the amount of deposits and among the assets, the largest share is of advances whereas other liabilities like borrowing funds and investments are also playing crucial role in the total funds of the banks. The decision to get the type of deposits which are less costly and from where to borrow money to pay the least and then to get maximum returns, where to invest these funds, so that the cost of creating funds can be recovered, are major challenges for all commercial banks at the moment. Here, it is necessary to mention various available sources and means of funds.

It is difficult to decide that amongst all the instruments of funds, which is more profitable and risk free and this is termed as funds management. From the review of commercial banks' balance sheet, it is observed that the portfolio of investment consists very largely of the securities of central and state government and treasury bills, which constitutes 90 per cent of the whole investment portfolio and remaining 10 per cent is utilized in other approved securities to fulfill the statutory obligation under section 24 of Banking Regulation Act. Management of loan portfolio is no doubt subject to price constraints. In case of deposits, saving deposits have greater share whereas among the borrowing fund's portfolio, borrowings from RBI has a dominating share. The problem is not over here, but started from the time of selection of source that would be cheap to create funds and to decide about more profitable investments. Hence, funds management is a major problem requiring effective means to take good care of its efficient management.

The present chapter deals with the cost-benefit analysis of these funds and evaluates their functioning and popularity with the Indian public. The present chapter attempts to provide optimum portfolio through cost-benefit analysis of these funds which will further help the banks to manage their funds efficiently with enough earnings and negligible risk.

Objectives

- To study and analyze the cost of funds to get the cheapest source of funds.
- To study and analyze the returns from funds invested to get the highest beneficial investment.
- To compare the cost of funds with the returns to get the most profitable investment.
- To suggest some strategies for the efficient management of funds.

Hypotheses

- There is no significant correlation between the cost of deposits and return on advances and investments separately.
- There is no significant correlation between the cost of borrowing funds and return on advances and investments separately.
- There is no significant correlation between the cost of total funds and return on advances and investments separately.

In the present chapter, Indian banking industry is taken as universe and further four major bank groups are taken for the inter-bank group comparison of cost-benefit analysis of their funds.

    G-I – SBI and Its Associates

    G-II– Nationalized Banks

    G-III – Foreign Banks

    G-IV – New and Old Private Sector Banks

Parameters for the Cost-Benefit Analysis

For the cost-benefit analysis, following ratios have been examined:

- Cost of Deposits (Interest on Deposits as Percentage of Total Deposits);
- Cost of Borrowing Funds (Interest on Borrowing Funds as Percentage of Total Borrowing Funds);

- Cost of Total Funds i.e. Deposits + Borrowing Funds (Interest on Total Funds as Percentage of Total Funds);
- Return on Advances (Interest on Advances as Percentage of Total Advances);
- Return on Investments (Interest on Investments as Percentage of Total Investments);
- Total Deposits as Percentage of Total Liabilities;
- Total Credit as Percentage of Total Deposit;
- Total Investments as Percentage of Total Deposits; and
- Credit + Investments as Percentage of Total Deposits.

Average and simple growth rates are used to achieve the desired objectives. Further correlation-coefficient is used to test the hypotheses. All calculations are based on SPSS 10.00 version.

Cost of Funds (Deposits/Borrowings/Total Funds)

Table 3.1 shows that all bank groups show a declining trend in their cost of deposits during 2000-05. On an average, it is the highest in G-I with 6.59 per cent and G-IV is in succession with 6.23 per cent but it is the least in G-III i.e. 5.02 per cent because this bank group shows the highest overall decline of 54 per cent in their cost of deposits whereas, G-IV shows 47 per cent decline in their cost of deposits. G-III shows the highest variations in terms of 30 per cent C V that proves their highly competitive environment.

Table 3.2 shows a declining trend in cost of borrowings of all bank groups during the study period with the highest decline of 82 per cent in G-II and G-V which is in succession with 72 per cent decline. On an average, cost of borrowing funds is the least in G-IV i.e. 2.23 per cent and the highest in case of G-III i.e. 5.66 per cent as this group registers a 72 per cent decline in the cost of borrowings.

G-III shows the highest fluctuations i.e. 84 per cent in terms of C V, their main strong point being better management of their business because more the competition more will be the qualitative business.

Table 3.1: Cost of Deposits (X_1)

(Per cent)

Years	G-I	G-II	G-III	G-IV
2000-01	7.58	7.17	6.74	7.80
2001-02	7.57	6.95	6.08	7.34
2002-03	7.02	6.21	5.31	6.62
2003-04	5.83	5.15	3.87	5.26
2004-05	4.96	4.56	3.11	4.13
Overall Growth	-34.56	-36.40	-53.86	-47.05
Average	6.59	6.01	5.02	6.23
S.D.	1.16	1.13	1.51	1.52
C.V.	17.60	18.80	30.08	24.40

Note: G-I – SBI and its Associates; G-II – Nationalized Banks; G-III – Foreign Banks; G-IV – Private Sector Banks
Source: Statistical Returns of Banking in India (2000-01 to 2004-05)

Table 3.2: Cost of Borrowings (X_2)

(Per cent)

Years	G-I	G-II	G-III	G-IV
2000-01	5.62	8.78	7.48	5.55
2001-02	4.26	7.13	7.30	1.52
2002-03	2.08	5.37	5.13	0.96
2003-04	1.43	4.40	4.56	1.58
2004-05	2.58	1.56	3.81	1.53
Overall growth	-54.09	-82.23	-49.06	-72.43
Average	3.19	5.45	5.66	2.23
S.D.	1.71	2.75	1.65	1.87
C.V.	53.61	50.46	29.15	83.86

Source: Same as in Table 3.1.

Table 3.3 exhibits that cost of total funds goes on decreasing in all the bank groups under study where the decline is the highest in G-III i.e. 53 per cent but its cost, on an average is the least i.e. 5.2 per cent. Overall, the decline is the least in G-I i.e. 35 per cent having an average cost which is the highest i.e. 6.48 per cent. It shows that the cost of total funds is more in public sector banks with a decline at lower rates as compared to that of foreign banks and private sector banks.

Table 3.3: Cost of Funds (Deposits + Borrowings) (X_3)

(Per cent)

Years	G-I	G-II	G-III	G-IV
2000-01	7.50	7.19	6.96	7.67
2001-02	7.47	6.95	6.47	6.31
2002-03	6.88	6.20	5.26	5.45
2003-04	5.69	5.14	4.04	4.72
2004-05	4.86	4.42	3.29	3.80
Overall Growth	-35.20	-38.53	-52.73	-50.46
Average	6.48	5.98	5.20	5.59
S.D.	1.16	1.18	1.56	1.48
C.V.	17.90	19.73	30.00	26.48

Source: Same as in Table 3.1.

Overall, we may conclude that foreign banks are gainers with the least cost of deposits and total funds but in case of cost of borrowings, private sector banks are managing with their best efforts i.e. at 72 per cent reduction rate. But our public sector banks have reduced their cost of borrowing funds at a greater rate as compared to the cost of deposits. We can say that for public sector banks and private sector banks, it is more beneficial to borrow funds rather to get deposits, as the cost of borrowing funds is only 3.19 per cent (G-I), 5.45 per cent (G-II), 2.23 per cent (G-IV) whereas the cost of deposits is 6.59 per cent (G-I) & 6.01 per cent (G-II), 6.23 per cent (G-IV), which is almost double the cost of borrowing funds. But in case of foreign banks, it is more beneficial to collect deposits rather to borrow funds as the cost of deposits is 5.02 per cent whereas the cost of borrowing funds is 5.66 per cent with a minor difference. Overall, for Indian banks to it is cheaper to borrow funds as compared to collecting public deposits. Foreign banks and private sector banks with the highest variations show that they have much competitive environment amongst them and are at gain because more the competition more the opportunities to do business efficiently and hence, earn handsome income.

Return on Advances/Investments

In Table 3.4, all bank groups show a declining trend in their returns on advances during the study period. G-III shows the highest decline of 38 per cent in their returns whereas it is the least in G-IV that is 27 per cent. This decline is not a sign of sound system of credit control but the main reason is the increasing NPAs. On an average, return on investments is the highest in G-III that is 10.51 per cent whereas G-II &IV are in succession with 9.93 per cent and 9.76 per cent respectively.

Table 3.4: Return on Advances (X$_4$)

(Per cent)

Years	G-I	G-II	G-III	G-IV
2000-01	10.75	11.49	13.12	11.68
2001-02	9.72	10.56	11.64	8.75
2002-03	9.04	9.82	10.70	10.93
2003-04	7.93	8.72	8.96	9.78
2004-05	7.49	8.21	8.15	8.49
Overall Growth	-30.33	-28.54	-37.88	-27.31
Average	8.99	9.76	10.51	9.93
S.D.	1.32	1.33	2.01	1.37
C.V.	14.68	13.63	19.12	13.80

Source: Same as in Table 3.1.

Table 3.5 also shows a declining trend in the return on investments in all the bank groups as G-IV shows the highest decline at 45 per cent rate and G-III is in succession with 36 per cent rate of decline. On an average, return on investments is the highest in G-II that is 10.01 per cent whereas G-I is in succession with 9.69 per cent.

Overall, it may be concluded that return on investment is the highest in public sector banks whereas return on advances is the highest in foreign banks and private sector banks, mainly due to the reason that their priority sector lendings and lending to the poor poor are negligible and hence they reduce their NPAs and better control them also. In the case of public sector banks, their return on advances is low mainly because a large part of their advances goes to priority sector and the weaker sections at concessional rates. Secondly heavy NPAs due to the waiving of loans with the interference of political parties especially in case of agricultural, loans also affect their bottomline. Shri Montek Singh Ahluwalia, in a National Conference, had himself admitted that waiving of loans should be avoided and instead loans at concessional rates with greater flexibility should be provided.

Table 3.5: Return on Investments (X_5)

(Per cent)

Years	G-I	G-II	G-III	G-IV
2000-01	10.68	11.41	11.03	11.19
2001-02	10.77	11.02	10.36	9.18
2002-03	9.74	10.18	8.28	8.96
2003-04	8.87	9.22	8.26	7.62
2004-05	8.39	8.23	7.01	6.10
Overall Growth	-21.44	-27.87	-36.45	-45.49
Average	9.69	10.01	8.99	8.61
S.D.	1.06	1.30	1.66	1.90
C.V.	10.94	12.99	18.46	22.07

Source: Same as in Table 3.1.

Overall fluctuations are the highest in foreign banks and private sector banks which depicts a higher competition in their group thereby reflecting a positive market image. For the public sector banks, it is more beneficial to disburse their funds in investments which yield handsome returns rather than to advance loans as the return is lower. In the case of foreign banks, it is more beneficial to advance loans rather than to invest more elsewhere as their return from investments is not as much as from advances.

Deposits to Total Liabilities

Deposits are growing at a fast rate which is just imaginary due to attractive and innovative schemes provided by the banks to get competitive advantage. Table 3.6 shows that share of total deposits among the total liabilities decreased in all the bank groups with the highest decline of 12 per cent in private banks except in G-I, which shows an increase at 4 per cent. On an average, the share of deposits from the liabilities is the highest i.e. 85.79 per cent in G-II and G-I and IV are in succession with 78.84 per cent and 72.72 per cent respectively, whereas it is 58 per cent in G-III as observed in the last part. These banks are in a better position to get funds through borrowings rather to get deposits and therefore the share of deposits is less among the total liabilities.

Table 3.6: Deposits to Total Liabilities

(Per cent)

Years	G-I	G-II	G-III	G-IV
2000-01	77.47	87.30	58.13	83.65
2001-02	78.10	87.46	57.55	63.30
2002-03	79.16	86.99	59.56	70.11
2003-04	78.81	86.10	58.79	73.12
2004-05	80.64	81.11	56.13	73.42
Overall Growth	4.09	-7.09	-3.44	-12.23
Average	78.84	85.79	58.03	72.72
S.D.	1.20	2.67	1.30	7.34
C V	1.52	3.11	2.24	10.09

Source: Same as in Table 3.1

Overall liabilities of all the bank groups have more than 50 per cent share of deposits which depicts their tendency to prefer deposits over other liabilities. Here, G-IV shows the highest fluctuation i.e. 10 per cent in terms of C V among all bank groups.

Disbursement of Total Deposits in Advances, Investments and Total Funds

Table 3.7 exhibits that credit to deposit ratio is going on increasing in all the bank groups with the highest growth rate of

41.53 per cent in private sector banks (G-IV) whereas G-II holds second position with 26.91 per cent growth rate. On an average, credit to deposit ratio is the highest in G-III i.e. 77 per cent and G-IV is in succession with 63.80 per cent.

Table 3.7: Credit to Deposits

(Per cent)

Years	G-I	G-II	G-III	G-IV
2000-01	48.18	48.28	72.64	49.80
2001-02	46.88	51.17	75.39	68.71
2002-03	48.39	52.32	75.27	66.55
2003-04	50.94	51.92	75.50	63.45
2004-05	56.31	61.27	87.07	70.48
Overall Growth	16.96	26.91	19.87	41.53
Average	50.14	52.99	77.17	63.80
S.D.	3.75	4.89	5.66	8.25
C.V.	7.48	9.23	7.33	12.93

Source: Same as in Table 3.1.

Here, variation is maximum in G-III i.e. 13 per cent, which shows that there is much competition in this group as compared to others. In case of public sector banks, C-D ratio is only 50 per cent which again proves their preference to invest more funds in investments rather to advance loans and G-III has 77 per cent investment of their funds in credits which implies their preference for advances over investments, because their earning from advances is more than that of investments.

Table 3.8 shows that investments to deposit ratio has shown an increasing trend in G-I and II with just 2.38 per cent and 5.54 per cent growth rate respectively whereas, it is decreasing in G-III and IV at 18.65 per cent and 2.07 per cent respectively. On an average, it is the highest in G-III with 54.94 per cent share and G-I is in succession with 53.83 per cent share but variations in terms of CV are the highest in G-III with 11 per cent CV.

Table 3.9 shows that the share of total funds (credit and investments) in the total deposits is showing an increasing trend in all the bank groups with the highest growth rate of 20.73 per cent in G-IV and G-II is in succession with 16.79 per cent growth rate. On an average, it is the highest in G-III i.e. 132 per cent and G-IV and G-I are in succession with 113.84 per cent and 103.97 per cent share respectively.

Table 3.8: Investments to Deposits

(Per cent)

Years	G-I	G-II	G-III	G-IV
2000-01	50.36	43.29	60.42	45.39
2001-02	52.86	43.46	54.40	58.40
2002-03	57.12	46.82	58.86	51.53
2003-04	57.24	47.60	51.89	50.45
2004-05	51.56	45.69	49.15	44.45
Overall Growth	2.38	5.54	-18.65	-2.07
Average	53.83	45.37	54.94	50.04
S.D.	3.19	1.95	4.70	5.59
C.V.	5.93	4.30	8.55	11.17

Source: Same as in Table 3.1.

Overall, it can be concluded that G-III shows the highest share of total funds in deposits and even credits and investments separately have the highest share in this group - rather it also shows decline in investments to deposits ratio during the study period. Hence, it is proved that foreign banks prefer more credit rather than investments.

Secondly, G-I has the highest share of investments from the deposits i.e. 53.83 per cent as compared to share of credit which is 50 per cent. But G-II, III & IV have greater share of credits among their deposits, which ranges between 52 per cent and 77 per cent rather than the share of investments ranging between 45 per cent to 54 per cent. Overall, funds are more concentrated in advances rather in investments.

Correlation Co-efficient

Table 3.10 shows the rejection of all the hypotheses that test the correlation coefficient among the cost of funds and return there from is not significant which shows that cost and return of funds are significantly correlated with each other at different coefficients. In case of correlation between cost of deposits (X_1) and return on advance (X_4), it is positive and significant in all the bank groups except in G-IV that has a positive but insignificant correlation between both the factors. Correlation among cost of deposits (X_1) and return on investments (X_5) is also positive and significant in all the bank groups.

Table 3.9: Credit + Investments to Deposits

(Per cent)

Years	G-I	G-II	G-III	G-IV
2000-01	98.55	91.58	133.06	95.19
2001-02	99.74	94.63	129.79	127.12
2002-03	105.51	99.14	134.13	118.08
2003-04	108.18	99.52	127.39	113.90
2004-05	107.87	106.96	136.22	114.92
Overall Growth	9.46	16.79	2.37	20.73
Average	103.97	98.37	132.12	113.84
S.D.	4.54	5.83	3.52	11.65
C.V.	4.37	5.93	2.66	10.23

Source: Same as in Table 3.1.

Correlation between cost of borrowing funds (X_2) and return from advances (X_4) and return from investments (X_5) is positive and significant in all the bank groups except G-I and IV where they have a positive but insignificant correlation, which shows that the cost of borrowing funds and returns are not affecting each other at a significant rate but it may be due to other factors.

Similarly, all the banks show positive and significant correlation among their cost of funds (X_3) and return from investments and advances.

Overall, it can be concluded that cost and returns are positively and significantly correlated with each other which shows that with the increase in costs, returns also increase because more the funds will be generated either through deposits or borrowings more will be the investment either in terms of credits or securities. The main point to be noted here is that the decrease in returns of public sector banks is mainly due to the forced regulations that they have to adopt like waiving of deficit loans especially in agriculture sector which affects their financial conditions harshly.

Table 3.10: Correlation Coefficient Analysis

Factors	G-I	G-II	G-III	G-IV
X_1 & X_4	.935*	.980**	.992**	.600
X_1 & X_5	.977**	.995**	.935*	.961**
X_2 & X_4	.858	.971**	.949**	.629
X_2 & X_5	.789	.985**	.986**	.712
X_3 & X_4	.941*	.978**	.988**	.656
X_3 & X_5	.981**	.997**	.960**	.984**

Note: ** Correlation is significant at the 0.01 level (2 tailed)
* Correlation is significant at the 0.05 level (1 tailed)

Strategies for Efficient Fund Management

It is observed that return on advances of public sector banks is decreasing mainly due to their increasing NPAs. A paper 'Banking Sector Developments in India, 1980-2005: What the Annual Accounts Speak?' outlines that NPAs are reported more in non-priority sector, as NPAs in priority sector have declined over the past 25 years. The main reason for public sector banks investing a large portion of their deposits in investments and that too in approved securities is because they are their risk free and promise assured returns. Hence, they prefer to invest more in investments rather to advance loans.

Foreign Banks have attracted more funds of a short-term nature in the form of demand deposits because the business class is attracted towards better services of foreign banks. Hence, they prefer to advance loans rather than to invest in securities. In the case of private sector banks, they have invested more than 1/3rd of their total investments in non-SLR securities since 2000. Private and foreign banks prefer more to advance loans only in priority sector and to financially sound parties and secondly with the efficient management of NPAs and effective and attractive marketing strategies they get handsome returns. However, this is not the case of public sector banks since they have to bear losses of waiving loans by the government which affects their returns negatively and enhance their NPAs.

From the whole discussion, it is clear that foreign banks and private banks get their deposits at the least cost as compared to borrowing funds because they decide the interest rate of deposits themselves and in public sector banks, they have deposits more costly as compared to their borrowing funds which means they have to pay the interest at fixed rates except in some cases. If they are also given full autonomy, they can get opportunities to reduce their cost of deposits. In this light, following strategies are listed to make their fund management efficient.

- **Portfolio Management:** Portfolio for the funds that includes deposits, credits, investments and borrowings, should be so well planned that it gives productive results with efficient risk management. From deposits portfolio, current deposits should be the benchmark for private and foreign banks whereas fixed deposits are more beneficial for public sector banks which should be the benchmark for them. Similarly, among the investment instruments and advances, benchmark should be the same with more returns and less risks. The portfolio should be planned according to the survey of available and potential sources and means of funds.

- **NPAs' Management:** Public sector banks are always at gun point to bear deficit loans especially in the priority sector, just as it happened in 2006-07 when the government waived the farmers' loans just for political gains. But they don't bother about the results i.e. increased NPAs of public sector banks. These types of loans given at concessional rates and with easy installments can help to avoid NPAs to the maximum extent. Secondly, recovery rate should be increased along with the

ARC that has proved their strength to recover NPAs to the large extent.

According to a recent survey of RBI, NPAs are more in non-priority sector; hence special care should be taken while sanctioning loans to the concerned party, if he could be a probable defaulter or already included in the defaulters list provided by the RBI. The most important and effective step is to evaluate the security value as well as persons' financial condition and attitude for repayment of loan at regular intervals.

The Punjab government has recently announced to stop tractor loans to the farmers to reduce the substantial amount of NPAs of banks. In this light, the government with the collaboration of banks and expert committees should make sound and efficient policies to tackle these problems.

- **Information Technology:** IT plays a crucial role in managing funds. It provides detailed information for fund agencies that provide loans and other loan seekers like companies, institutions, individuals etc., areas under construction that need loans, various instruments of investments and companies that issue their securities. Credit rating agencies help to choose best performing investment instruments and companies with sound financial position etc. which further help banks to plan their portfolio. IT also helps to create and utilize funds that give handsome returns.

- **Risk Management:** Every bank should make his own policy to manage different types of risks. For this purpose Basel-II is the best offered international standards that provides risk management techniques. The best way to manage risk is firstly to examine the reasons and factors that give birth to particular risk and then find the various possible alternatives to solve these reasons so as to choose the best method to manage the risk.

- **Stop Political Interference:** In reality, most of the loans sanctioned are under the pressure of political parties, which either concentrate on rich parties or big industrialists and at the end they either refuse to repay or show their insolvency which again increases the burden for public sector banks to recover NPAs. Secondly, for political gains, they waive the loans of poor people like farmers etc. to capture good strength of votes, but who bear this burden ultimately is a big debate? One more thing to note is the increasing tendency of refusal to repay loans by political parties as observed in recent survey, where by most of the MPs take big amount of loans but at the end they never bother to repay.

How the banks, especially public sector banks would be able to reduce and manage their NPAs, if the political parties continue to interfere? Therefore, there is a dire need to stop political interference in these important decisions.

Implications of the Study

On the basis of the above analysis, it may be suggested that public sector banks and private sector banks would benefit if they mobilize funds through borrowings rather than through public deposits as the cost of borrowings is almost half as compared to deposits. Similarly, in the case of utilization of these funds, public sector banks are beneficiaries if they concentrate more on investments in different instruments rather disburse loans to their customers as return on investments is higher. However, foreign banks and private sector banks get more returns on their advances and hence are at an advantage.

Areas of Future Research

There are fewer studies related to cost-benefit analysis of banks with different portfolios. Hence, there is a need to study some important aspects in this context to make their fund management sound.

- Study of cost-benefit analysis for each and every aspect of bank funds i.e. deposits, borrowing, advances, investments and even capital at each bank level and group level.
- Study of best preferred mode of deposits, advances and investments among the customers especially in rural and semi-urban areas.

- Study for alternative portfolios to suggest optimum one for different banks.

Conclusion

We may conclude that foreign and private banks prefer deposits as a cheaper mode of funds mobilization and advances as more profitable utilization of funds, just because of their efficient marketing strategies and sophisticated risk management. But public sector banks prefer borrowing funds, that too from RBI and invest the maximum share of their funds in government securities as these are less risky with more returns. However, the main reason for more cost of deposits is the fixed rules of government which binds them not to make deposits at flexible rates of interest according to the market situation whereas low returns from advances is also due to more NPAs and that is again a reason of government interference in either way.

But for the efficient management of funds, banks should be given more autonomy and they should set their benchmarks for each type of portfolio separately according to the market conditions. The most successful banks will be those that combine visionary technology and competitive pricing with strong relationships and brands built on trust with previous in-depth experience of the client business. Banks should adopt effective, practical and competitive strategies to survive in the high-tech banking environment.

4

Globalisation and Competitive Banking

Introduction

Globalisation has been the most potent force in recent times, which has helped in integrating the world economies. Globalisation has transformed the entire world into a global village. It has softened or almost removed the hurdles of borders, distances and time and has provided a common integrated global market for all, for a free, deepened and broader flow of trade, finance and information. No country can live in isolation without being affected. Globalisation has emerged as irreversible process and the dark side of globalisation is that if someone does not want to play he will be ostracized. The phenomenon of globalisation has many aspects and implications. The globalisation has exposed the global competition. This is a great challenge as well as an opportunity.

Competition compels firms to explore new ways to increase their efficiency by extending their international reach to new markets. Survival and growth in such an environment requires achieving global competitiveness. Competitiveness i.e. the ability to compete successfully is determined by entrepreneurial and managerial competencies among others.

An organisation competes through creating the policy framework that encourage and enable its management to constantly upgrade themselves and keep on improving their productivity thereby enhancing the competitiveness and pursue competitive strategies for successful participation in the international markets. The organizational competitiveness is dependent on the nature of the major source of its present advantage over the competitors. Competitive advantage is sustained through constant improvement and continuous upgrading.

In this chapter our basic aim is to focus on the following aspects:

- To study the concept of competitiveness as a key challenge of globalisation.
- To study various factors affecting competitiveness.
- To suggest strategies to enhance the organizational competitiveness.

In order to achieve the above objectives, the chapter is organized into three Sections. Section I contains the conceptual framework of the globalisation and its challenges. Section II deals with the factors and strategies of organisational competitiveness. The conclusion and suggestions are incorporated in Section III.

Section I
Challenges of Globalisation

Globalisation is going on at a fast pace. This rapid move towards greater integration is fuelled by various factors like spreading political decisions to move towards liberalization and adoption of market economies for free flow of capital etc. These forces are creating new challenges. The expansion of global markets and dismantling of protective barriers to trade has enhanced the opportunities. The globalisation has brought global players in competition with the domestic players. Global players are very big and have the capacity to use their big size to establish monopoly and convert free competition into unfair competition. MNCs are more likely to compete out domestic players as MNCs have several advantages over the local players. There is a bigger challenge to keep the competition fair between local producers and global producers. Globalisation of an economy and the resultant liberlisation within the economic system of the country cannot be reversed. These forces have emerged due to the complex nature of the interaction between the growth of economies of most countries and the resultant trade and market pattern which are unfolding. Business organisations have to reap the benefits of their investments or otherwise the competitors would displace them out of market.

In this era of cutthroat competition, it is a great challenge for every management to think innovative and creative in order to ensure its existence. The survival of the fittest is the mantra of globalisation. It is possible only when an organisation is able to provide its services better than the competitors. The simple reason for this is that now the business is becoming global as compared to the national earlier. Developed countries have the capabilities to capture the market share in the global business as they have competitive advantages over the developing countries. Foreign enterprises are giving stiff competition to the enterprises of the developing countries. MNCs are able to deliver the products and services at lower prices and better quality. Moreover, the competition, which is an essential element of free economy, is unfair due to the anticompetitive practices of the MNCs. There is no level playing field for the developing countries. Global markets are exerting the pressure for economic efficiency in businesses and operations. Developing nations can face these pressures only with enhanced investments in R&D, superior management and easy access to finance. MNCs are accentuating merger and acquisition activities to consolidate and entrench themselves.

These challenges demand a well planned strategy to cope with the changing business environment. In a globalising economy there is a dire need for every management to develop the strategies to enhance competitiveness to become successful in the global competitive market.

Section II
Competitiveness: Factors and Strategies

With the spreading trade liberalization and deregulation, there is now closer integration of domestic and international markets. Thus, enterprises not only face increased competition in their export markets but even in the domestic markets. In open market competition, every organisation has to face stiff challenges and the success and survival of an organisation largely depends upon the competitiveness. Competitiveness has become a prominent business and government concern in the era of globalisation. The competitive environment has put burden on the corporate sector so as to play a crucial role as an engine of growth. There is an urgent need to inject much seeded vitality into the economic system. This could be achieved by making industry, corporate houses and ultimately the entire nation globally competitive. Competitiveness means the ability to constantly take the most advantageous position in the rapidly changing market environment. It can be defined as the relative standing of one competitor against other competitors. The concept of competitiveness implies:

- Production of goods and services based on new technologies;
- Capacity to increase market share in world trade; and
- A move towards surplus.

Competitiveness depends upon micro-economic fundamentals based on competition and the business environment as well as availability of quality and cheaper raw material, cheap labour, technological capabilities and marketing strategies. The ability to compete in the competitive market depends on the relative competitive strength. Management has to synchronize the efforts and focus the resources strategically in the right direction to enhance the competitiveness.

Factors Affecting Competitiveness
- Technological capabilities
- Managerial Skills
- Availability of Finance
- Quality of Human Resources
- Government Policies
- Infrastructure
- Nation-specific Factors
- Advertising
- Marketing Strategies

Globalisation has changed and opened up the world as a market place for us, be it for products, people or financial resources, so to capitalize on this opportunity, organizations have to be moulded to become globally competitive, be it, cost, quality, delivery or any other business parameters. The developing world is thus becoming increasingly polarized into those that have succeeded in becoming industrially competitive in open international economy and those that have not done so far. Competitiveness is the creation of industrial capacity in developing countries to cope with more intense global competition. This has drawn attention to mechanisms of technological advancement in developing economies, which lie well behind international technological frontiers.

Competitiveness results from the intimate interaction of the following factors at four levels:

1. Meta Level – Socio-cultural factors
2. Macro Level – Macro-economic policies.
3. Meso Level – Legal and regulatory framework
4. Micro Level – Entrepreneurial and managerial competencies.

Competition Strategies
*   Customer Orientation
*   Human Resource Management
*   Flexibility and Agility
*   Value Chain
*   Networking and Alliances

Competitiveness depends on strong domestic rivals, aggressive home-based suppliers and demanding home markets. It calls for domestic firms to adopt highly efficient and productive methodologies such as faster innovations, effective marketing strategies and most appropriate labour-capital-resource combinations in production activities. Sound macro economic conditions, trade liberalization and an emphasis on supply side factors such as FDI, technological effort, human capital and communications infrastructure are closely associated with better competitiveness performance in the developing world. Other policy measures include R&D, tax incentives and subsidies, initiatives for stimulating collaborative innovation, finance for innovation and technology foresight. The major determinants of the ability to sell products and services are no longer relative costs advantage alone but more and more, competitiveness is based on quality, speed, technical superiority and product differentiation. But the underlying determinant of competitiveness, whether at national, sectoral or enterprise level, remains raising total productivity, which combines the notion of efficiency and effectiveness.

Section III

Conclusion

Global competition is a complex dynamic process which could not characterize competitive capabilities amongst nations particularly when economic theory and logic rely in restrictive assumptions which have evaporated with open global economy, which today, is the reality of changing times. Globalisation has opened up the world as a market place for us, be it for products, people or financial resources. If we have to capitalize on this opportunity, we have to become globally competitive, be it, cost, quality, delivery or any other business parameter.

In the global market place, the competitiveness has been driven by the technology chain over time, which moved from high technology towards commodity classification. Survival in the global competitive market is to be planned through evolutionary process of differentiation and integration, which is further reinforced by the decreasing rigidity of national boundaries. Individual organisations need this dynamic perspective in the management of the global process. For global competitiveness we need global vision, exceptional human resource capital and consumer insight. Management has to be aware of the measures necessary to be taken for achieving and retaining global competitive edge. Systematic innovation requires a willingness to look on change as an opportunity. Innovations that succeed do so by exploiting change, and not attempting to force it.

For enhancing the organizational competitiveness, the following factors need due attention by the management:

• Increased investment in R&D.

- Identification of the growth opportunities.
- Management commitment.
- Customer delight.
- Market intelligence.
- Knowledge management.

The sustainability of the competitive advantage is dependent on the nature of the major source of its present advantages over the competitors. There is a hierarchy or level of sources of competitive advantage in terms of sustainability. Lower order sources of advantages such as low labour costs or cheap raw materials are relatively easy to imitate or acquire by the competitors. Higher order advantages such as proprietary process and technology, product differentiation based on unique product or services, brand reputation based on cumulative marketing efforts, and customer relationships protected by high costs to the customer of switching vendors, are more durable. These higher order advantages are created through sustained and cumulative investment in physical facilities, human resource development, R&D, and marketing activities. In order to sustain the competitiveness, an enterprise must become a moving target, creating new advantages at least as fast as competitors can replicate old ones. To remain competitive, an enterprise must constantly destroy old advantages to create new, higher-order ones.

5

Indian Banks and WTO

Introduction

One of the areas of the economy that has received renewed focus in recent times has been the financial sector. And within the broad ambit of the financial sector, it is the banking sector that has been the cynosure of academia and policymakers alike. Indian banking has come a long way since India embarked on the reforms path about a decade and a half ago in 1991-92. The reforms have unleashed tremendous changes in the banking sector. Today, Indian banks are as technology-savvy as their counterparts in developed countries. On the networking point, branch banking – the traditional forte, coupled with ATM networks – the new imperative, have evolved to place the banking services on a new trajectory. The competitive forces have led to the emergence of internet and mobile banking too, to let banks attract and retain customers.

In future, Indian banking is poised to face significant challenges with the continued deregulation of the sector, as competitive pressure would only increase. Also, with increased integration with world economy, international developments are going to a have strong influence on Indian banks' performance. Hence, adapting to such changes in the business environment would be crucial for their survival.

Globalization refers to extensive and liberal movements of goods, capital and people across nations. In India, the globalization process took off after 1991 in the shape of banking reforms, which can rightly be called a watershed event in our march towards globalization (S. Santhanakrishan). Globalization is both a challenge and an opportunity for Indian banks to gain strength in the domestic market and increase presence in the global market. According to Bhide, Prasad and Ghosh, the banking sector in most emerging economies is passing through challenging yet exciting times and India is no exception to this rule. Bhaduri, S. studied that the customer relationship management is a journey and not a 'one-shot' event and is probably the most critical ingredient for the successful implementation of CRM in global age. Knight, M. opined that over the past decade, India has emerged as one of the fastest growing economies on the globe. The rest of the world has been impressed to see that the reforms initiated in the early 1990s are bearing fruit.

Globalisation: Imperatives for Indian Banks

Globalization impacts the banking industry in one or more of the following ways:

- Greater and intensive competition
- Focus on efficiency, productivity and cost reduction
- Superior risk management system and practices
- Strengthening service quality and delivery and cross-selling of products/services
- Product innovation as an integral part of the retail banking revolution
- Up gradation of technology infrastructure
- Competency building and investment in human capital as a catalyst for transformation
- Consolidation within the financial system
- Opportunity to increase size and scale to gain dominance in the local market and penetrate into the global market
- Transparent, disclosure and market discipline

It is, therefore, imperative for Indian banks to address all the above issues, if they aspire to play a role in the global arena.

The present chapter is divided into six sections. After a brief introduction, section II fixes the objectives, hypothesis and database. Section III frames methodology and section IV discusses results. Section V discusses the strategies of globalization of Indian banks, where as the last part concludes the paper.

Objectives

The aim of the chapter is to evaluate the presence of Indian banks in global market and their presence in our country. Moreover, the following are the objectives:

- To study and evaluate the presence of Indian banks in the global market and foreign banks' presence in our country.
- To evaluate the comparative performance of Indian banks working abroad and foreign banks working in our country.
- On the basis of the comparative performance of banks, to work out the effective strategies for the globalization of Indian banks.

Hypotheses

- There is no significant difference between the presence of Indian banks in foreign countries and foreign banks in our country.
- The business per branch is significantly higher in foreign banks working in India as compare to Indian banks working outside India.

Methodology

The present chapter is concerned with the issue as to how Indian banks can be globalised. In this study we have taken only those Indian Public Sector banks (PSBs) and Indian private sector banks having their bank branches abroad. Similarly, we have taken only leading foreign banks namely Citibank, The Hong Kong and Shanghai Banking Corporation (HSBC), Standard Chartered Grindlay Bank (SCGB), Standard Chartered Bank (SCB), ABN Amro Bank, Bank of America (BOA), Deutsche Bank (DB) and BNP Paribas Bank.

The following ratios/parameters have been taken into consideration:

- Percentage share of Indian banks in global market
- Percentage share of Indian banks in foreign countries and Foreign banks in India (at group level)
- Business per Branch of Indian banks abroad
- Business per Branch of Foreign banks in India

- Deposits per Branch of Indian banks Abroad
- Deposits per Branch of Foreign banks in India
- Advances per Branch of Indian banks abroad
- Advances per Branch of Foreign banks in India

To evaluate the existence of Indian banks in foreign countries and foreign banks in India and their comparative performance, we calculated average, S.D. and C.V.

Results and Discussion

Presence of Indian Banks in Foreign Countries: Table 5.1 indicates that only 11 banks namely, SBI, Canara Bank (CB), Punjab National Bank (PNB), Bank of Baroda (BOB), Bank of India (BOI), Indian Overseas Bank (IOB), Syndicate Bank (SB), Indian Bank (IB), UCO, Bharat Overseas Bank (Bh.OB) & ICICI Bank have branches abroad out of 102 banks in India.

Among these SBI, BOB, BOI and Bh.OB occupy prominent place. PNB just entered the global market in 2004-05. Overall average of Indian banks in 1999-00 in global market was 0.55 which declined and became only 0.42 in 2004-05.

Table 5.2 shows the presence of Indian banks abroad at group level. Only SBI alone has an average of 0.37 branches in global market whereas Indian private sector banks (new and old) have only 0.02 branches. Bharat Overseas Bank and ICICI have little number of branches in foreign countries. Overall average share of Indian banks in foreign countries has declined from 0.24 in 1999-00 to 0.23 in 2004-05.

Overall, we may conclude that our banks (PSBs and private sector banks) have a very nominal place in the global market. They are not getting proper benefits of globalization. The data reveals that there is a need to make proper strategies for the globalization of Indian banks. If we will not workout proper strategies for our banks, foreign banks will capture our financial market and our financial system may become slave of foreign countries.

Table 5.1: Percentage Share of Indian Banks in Global Market (At Bank Level)

Banks	1999-00	2000-01	2001-02	2002-03	2003-04	2004-05
SBI	0.58	0.57	0.56	0.53	0.53	0.59
Canara	0.04	0.04	0.04	0.04	0.04	0.03
PNB	-	-	-	-	-	0.02
BOB	1.43	1.43	1.43	1.38	1.41	1.39
BOI	0.75	0.75	0.25	0.70	0.89	0.88
IOB	0.42	0.42	0.42	0.42	0.34	0.33
SB	0.06	0.06	0.06	0.06	0.06	0.65
IB	0.13	0.15	0.14	0.14	0.13	0.14
UCO	0.23	0.24	0.23	0.24	0.23	0.22
Bh. OB	1.31	1.29	1.27	1.25	000	000
ICICI	-	-	-	-	0.49	0.39
Average	0.55	0.55	0.49	0.53	0.41	0.42
S.D.	0.52	0.52	0.52	0.50	0.45	0.43
C.V.	94.54	94.54	106.12	94.34	109.76	102.38

Table 5.2: Percentage Share of Indian Banks in Foreign Countries and Foreign Banks in India (At Group Level)

Bank Groups	1999-2000	2000-01	2001-02	2002-03	2003-04	2004-05
G-I	0.39	0.38	0.37	0.35	0.35	0.39
G-II	0.22	0.22	0.21	0.21	0.22	0.22
G-I + II	0.03	0.27	0.26	0.25	0.26	0.27
G-III	0.02	0.02	0.05	0.02	000	000
G-IV	-	-	-	-	0.17	0.03
G-III+IV	0.02	0.01	0.01	0.02	0.04	0.03
G-V	0.32	0.36	0.38	0.39	0.42	0.52
Average	0.24	0.25	0.25	0.24	0.23	0.23
S.D.	0.16	0.16	0.16	0.17	0.16	0.23
C.V.	66.67	64.00	64.00	70.83	69.56	100.00

Prominent Foreign Banks Working in India: The presence of foreign banks in India is comparatively very high and it is continuously increasing day-by-day mainly because of attractive and effective marketing strategies. Table 5.3 shows that on an average, it was only 15.25 in 1999-00 and became 18.50 in 2004-05. Among the foreign banks working in India, prominent ones are, Citibank, HSBC, SCGB, SCB, ABN Amro, BOA, DB and BNP Paribas. Citibank, HSBC, SCGB and SCB are penetrating more in semi-urban, urban and metropolitan cities.

Table 5.3: Prominent Foreign Banks Working in India

Banks	1999-00	2000-01	2001-02	2002-03	2003-04	2004-05
Citibank	11	15	18	20	26	35
HSBC	26	28	30	33	36	39
SCG Bank	41	41	30	33	-	-
SCB	18	19	19	65	66	-
ABN Amro	8	9	13	15	15	19
Bank of America	4	4	5	5	5	5
Deutsche Bank	6	6	5	5	5	5
BNP Paribas	8	8	9	8	8	8
Average	15.25	16.25	16.12	18.88	23.00	18.50
S.D.	12.66	12.74	10.03	20.39	22.23	15.28
C.V.	83.02	78.40	62.22	108.00	96.65	82.59

Business per Branch of Indian Banks in Abroad: Table 5.4 exhibits that the average business per branch of Indian banks was only Rs. 1145.21 crore in 1999-00 which increased to Rs. 2052.79 crore in 2004-05 or so to say has become almost double in 6 years time. Among the Indian banks, prominent ones are CB and Syndicate Bank.

Business per Branch of Foreign Banks in India: Table 5.5 shows that although the branch network is increasing in India but their per branch business has declined from Rs. 1826.26 crore in 1999-2000 to Rs. 913.51 crore in 2004-05 on average basis.

Table 5.4: Business per Branch of Indian Banks in Abroad
(Rs. crore)

Banks	1999-00	2000-01	2001-02	2002-03	2003-04	2004-05
SBI	418.21	428.52	417.39	440.95	372.39	488.61
CB	1717.0	1869.0	2260.0	1843.0	9133.0	10932.0
PNB	-	-	-	-	-	26.17
BOB	245.46	266.03	337.34	352.63	395.13	546.55
BOI	808.58	829.63	1059.6	1202.88	961.95	1133.39
IOB	351.16	327.17	327.63	393.50	1126.40	629.00
SB	4569.0	3815.0	4870.0	2921.0	5632.0	5945.0
IB	1226.5	1189.0	1245.5	1020.0	947.50	867.50
UCO Bank	610.00	665.50	658.25	611.25	767.00	940.50
Total of PSBs	2581.5	507.88	563.37	585.08	641.05	648.50
Bh. OB	361.00	369.00	429.00	482.00	0	0
ICICI Bank	-	-	-	-	27.00	1072.00
Total Private Sector Banks	361	369	429	482	1337.5	1557.10
Average	1145.21	1084.32	1289.41	1029.69	1936.24	2052.79
S.D.	1371.10	1146.09	1481.05	862.66	3011.40	3369.02
C.V.	119.72	105.70	114.86	83.78	155.53	164.12

Table 5.5: Business per Branch of Foreign Banks in India
(Rs. crore)

Banks	1999-00	2000-01	2001-02	2002-03	2003-04	2004-05
Citibank	9929.82	1555.00	1479.28	1518.60	1374.00	1131.29
HSBC	507.31	578.46	672.57	636.45	719.39	759.85
SCG Bank	308.20	292.54	-	-	-	-
SCB	518.33	540.79	856.63	477.62	546.98	-
ABN Amro Bank	918.88	982.78	719.38	697.93	836.87	890.16
Bank of America	1549.50	1460.50	967.80	968.60	929.60	1042.40
Deutsche Bank	659.00	736.33	872.80	710.60	926.20	1233.20
BNP Peribas	219.00	346.00	351.22	375.25	381.50	424.13
Average	1826.26	811.55	845.67	769.29	816.36	913.51
S.D.	3300.83	481.45	343.42	380.29	318.16	293.22
C.V.	180.74	59.32	40.61	49.43	38.97	32.10

Among the foreign banks working in India, Citibank occupies a prominent place in it's per branch business. Recently, Citibank has started to penetrate in semi-urban and even rural sector of India. These banks are becoming popular among the young generation due to new products/services. Fortunately, these banks are fully computerized and based on latest information technology.

Deposits per Branch of Indian Banks Abroad: Table 5.6 shows that average deposits of public sector banks in foreign countries were only Rs. 31,269 crore in 1999-00 but in 2004-05 they became Rs. 47,076 crore. Among PSBs, BOI and SBI are prominent ones for deposits mobilization.

Similarly, an average deposit of Indian private sector banks was Rs. 3658.60 crore in 2004-05 up from Rs. 3496.33 crore in 1999-2000. ICICI and Bharat Overseas Bank are playing a vital role for deposit mobilization. But unfortunately, other new private sector banks and public sector banks are absolutely silent about globalization of their branches.

Table 5.6: Deposits of Indian Banks Working outside India

Banks	1999-00	2000-01	2001-02	2002-03	2003-04	2004-05
SBI	9182	7932	8011	7257	-	-
Canara	1285	1407	1544	1277	1968	2486
PNB	-	-	-	-	-	26
BOB	6351	6117	7272	6966	8621	10341
BOI	9218	8796	10353	10424	11288	13040
IOB	704	725	862	982	1104	1425
SB	1931	1417	1932	1542	2333	2589
IB	1162	1138	1009	703	811	727
UCO Bank	1435	1529	1625	1602	1777	2193
All PSBs	31269	29062	32609	30754	36727	47076
Bh. OB	199	197	226	259	284	319
ICICI Bank	-	-	-	-	1080	3440
Indian Private Sector Banks	199	197	226	259	1364	3759
Average	3496.33	3250.89	3648.22	3445.78	3251.78	3658.60
S.D.	3689.87	3368.50	3791.87	3726.41	3907.87	4413.51
C.V.	105.54	103.62	103.94	108.14	120.18	120.63

Advances of Indian Banks Working in Foreign Countries: Table 5.7 exhibits that average advances of public sector banks in foreign countries has increased from Rs. 28658 crore in 1999-00 to Rs. 52,899 crore in 2004-05. The average advances of Indian private sector banks increased from Rs. 162 crore in 1999-00 to Rs. 6,523 crore during the study period. Overall, there is an increase in advances of SBI, BOB and BOI dominates amongst the PSBs. Among Indian private sector banks, ICICI Bank has an edge over Bharat Overseas Bank.

Table 5.7: Advances of Indian Banks Working Outside India

Banks	1999-00	2000-01	2001-02	2002-03	2003-04	2004-05
SBI	12565	14351	13276	13909	15907	23899
Canara Bank	432	462	716	566	512	591
PNB	-	-	-	-	-	0.17
BOB	2984	3992	5547	6434	6404	7729
BOI	6145	8164	9779	11226	10837	13028
IOB	1403	1238	1375	1379	1505	1720
SB	2638	2398	2938	2392	3299	3356
IB	1291	1240	1482	1337	1084	1008
UCO Bank	1005	1133	1008	1043	1291	1569
All PSBs	28658	33398	36122	38285	40840	52899
Bh. OB	162	172	203	223	247	305
ICICI Bank	-	-	62	54	1064	6218
Indian Private Sector Banks	162	172	265	277	1311	6523
Average	3180.56	3683.33	3638.60	3856.30	4215.00	5402.11
S.D.	3957.87	4700.84	4528.29	4978.18	5283.81	7324.09
C.V.	124.44	127.62	124.45	129.09	125.36	135.58

Deposits of Selected Foreign Banks Working in India: Table 5.8 shows that more than 30 foreign banks are working in India but prominent banks are only 8. Their average deposits in India were Rs. 16751.75 crore in 1999-00 but declined to Rs. 10769.71 crore in 2004-05. Bank-wise analysis shows that Citibank (average deposits Rs. 31932.33 crore) has the maximum deposits in our country. Overall, average deposits of foreign banks are very high.

Advances of Foreign Banks Working in India: Table 5.9 exhibits that average advances of these banks were only Rs. 3703.13 crore in 1999-00 and become Rs. 9716.71 crore in 2004-05. Average advances of Citibank are the highest as this Bank has shown good performance in India and very fast it is penetrating in different cities with attractive facilities and products as compared to other banks.

Table 5.8: Deposits of Foreign Banks Working In India

Banks	1999-00	2000-01	2001-02	2002-03	2003-04	2004-05
Citibank	102608	14052	15242	17743	20465	21484
HSBC	8755	9951	12341	12801	16270	17013
SCG Bank	8478	8256	-	-	-	-
SCB	5011	5088	7244	18003	19949	22522
ABN Amro Bank	3423	4609	4865	5022	5856	7077
Bank of America	2512	2324	1906	1545	1589	1993
Deutsche Bank	2167	2322	2476	1945	2533	3625
BNP Peribas	1060	1706	1634	1580	1737	1674
Average	16751.75	6038.50	6529.71	8377.00	9771.29	10769.71
S.D.	34807.46	4371.47	5396.54	7587.88	8750.20	9276.64
C.V.	207.78	72.39	82.65	90.58	89.55	86.14

Table 5.9: Advances of Foreign Banks Working In India

Banks	1999-00	2000-01	2001-02	2002-03	2003-04	2004-05
Citibank	6620	9273	11385	12629	15259	18111
HSBC	4435	6246	7836	8202	9628	12621
SCG Bank	4158	3738	-	-	-	-
SCB	4319	5187	9032	13042	16152	19970
ABN Amro Bank	3928	4236	4487	5447	6697	9836
Bank of America	3686	3518	2933	3298	3059	3219
Deutsche Bank	1787	2096	1888	1608	2098	2541
BNP Peribas	692	1062	1527	1422	1315	1719
Average	3703.13	4419.50	5584.00	6521.14	7744.00	9716.71
S.D.	1789.62	2548.50	3850.60	4904.68	6150.53	7546.72
C.V.	48.33	57.66	68.96	75.21	79.42	77.67

Overall, we may conclude that foreign banks are penetrating fast in India with effective strategies to win the customers. The base of Indian public sector banks is very poor abroad. Similarly, Indian private sector banks except ICICI and Bharat Overseas

Bank have no base abroad. The need of the hour is to make different and effective strategies for the penetration of our banks in the global market. If our banks win the foreign market, the policy of LPG will also be strong and it will facilitate to enhance the global business.

Table 5.10: Comparative Number Branches per Bank

Bank Groups	1999-00	2000-01	2001-02	2002-03	2003-04	2004-05
Indian PSBs	4.55	4.55	4.51	4.37	4.48	4.78
Indian Private Sector Banks	0.03	0.03	0.03	0.03	0.07	0.07
Foreign Banks	4.31	4.52	4.29	5.11	6.61	4.55

WTO and Opportunities for Indian Banks

WTO has created a number of challenges and new opportunities for the Indian economy particular in the financial sector. If Indian banks, in the era of deregulation, explore possibilities in global markets, they will become very competitive. An empirical research regarding the tastes, habits, economic conditions of the global market, is needed and different policies and strategies will help to explore the possibilities of the expansion of Indian banks in the global market.

Strategies for Globalization of Indian Banks

The following are the possible strategies for the globalization of Indian banks:

- **Cadre of Experts:** A cadre of experts needs to be built up; personnel should have exposure in functioning in a truly global environment.
- **Information Technology:** Indian banks must build their expertise in rolling out technology as per Basel-II norms. IT can help in exploring newer possibilities in foreign countries.
- **International Capital Markets:** We should be active in international capital markets, approaching them off and on for trenches of capital subscription. Indian banks should try to capture at lower cost.

- **Linkages with other financial organization:** Indian banks have linkage with the rest of the financial infrastructure in India such as term lenders, investment banks, insurance ventures and credit rating agencies. Together they can face even tough competition at global level.
- **Strategic alliances:** Strategic alliances with national banks in oil rich countries can be very valuable, especially as Indian and China are becoming large consumers and there is an expectation of large India-related and Asia-related investments in this sector and these countries.
- **Acquisitions of Retail Banks:** Acquisitions should be of retail banks in selected markets. The selection will depend on the ability to implement technology, improve customer service and upgrade to Basel-II.
- **Research of Products and Services:** Indian banks should make comprehensive research in foreign countries regarding the financial requirements of the people and then they should enter in a big way.
- **Prices of Products and Services:** At the initial stages, Indian banks should provide products and services at comparatively lower prices to capture their market share.
- **Change in Mind-Set:** The bankers should change their own mindset to win the customers in other countries. A friendly customer environment would help to penetrate in other countries.
- **Alliance with Big Houses/Companies:** Indian banks should make some alliance with profit making big houses and companies to capture foreign market.
- **Effective Advertisements:** Indian banks should make effective and attractive advertisements according to the customer's tastes regarding their financial products.
- **Incentives:** Indian banks should provide allurement and incentives to the potential customers in the beginning.
- **Effective CRM:** Indian banks should make effective CRM in foreign countries. It will help to win potential customers.

Experiences and Lessons from Banks Which Went Global

Going global is the way forward for banks to gain size and scale. It is a natural progression for any organization. However, there are mixed experiences e.g.

i.   In India, Grindlays Bank sold its Indian operation to Standard Charted Bank and exited.

ii.   BNP Paribas, though, present in India for more than hundred years, decided to shut its Indian operations

iii. SBI, e.g. had to close its Panama branch for bad external relations.

iv.   Though there are 33 foreign banks operating in our country, only top four have a sizeable presence, others are only marginally present.

v.   SBI presently has planned to increase its presence in the global market from the present 54 to 75 branches.

Some of the lessons that can be drawn from the above could be that the management processes in the cross-border initiative should be aligned with the culture. There are two vital aspects every country should keep in mind:

• Differing national cultures, and

• Differing corporate cultures.

The failures of Japanese banks in US partly relates to the culture mismatch. It is necessary to announce at the time of acquisition itself as to what the approach/goals of the acquired entity will be post-acquisition.

i.   After acquisition, effective methods should be adopted for all the transactions.

ii.   Risk management needs maximum focus when expanding internationally.

iii. While entering new areas, especially internationally, there is a need for the top management to be aware of the emerging areas in finance.

The main finding of this chapter is that Indian banks should make effective and need based strategies for competing in the WTO regime. In the global age, it is not an option for Indian banks, but a compulsion to compete and survive in the global market. It is the question of survival of Indian banks in the changing scenario.

Conclusion

The present chapter concludes that the share of Indian banks is very little in the global market but foreign banks are entering in India with a cut throat competition. The performance of foreign banks is much better but we have discussed strategies for the globalization of Indian banks to get the fruits of the WTO which has thrown many new opportunities along with new challenges.

There is a need for comprehensive research related to the following areas:

• Feasibility and viability of Indian banks in the global market
• WTO and its impact on Indian banks
• Partnership of Indian banks with foreign companies
• Possibilities of merger of Indian banks to compete with foreign banks.

6

Second Generation Banking Reforms

Introduction

The financial system and Indian banking in the new millennium is facing emerging series of new challenges. The challenges' are manifold and multi-dimensional, under the influence of globalization, coupled with the adoption of new technology and stiff competition arising out of the changed situation.

The financial and banking sector reforms introduced in early nineties in Indian economy were primarily aimed at viable and efficient banking system in India. The recommendations made by Narsimaham Committee I (1991) and II (1998) for assets classification, asset-liquidity management, income recognition, capital adequacy, disclosure norms, risk management etc. in conformity with global standards have exposed the majority of our banks to quite tough, rather different situation at the initial stage of their implementation and a few of them are still in an uncomfortable phase.

In 1991, when Government of India introduced new economic policy, many reforms were introduced in the financial system particularly in the banking sector. These were:

A. For Strengthening:

- Introduction of capital adequacy standards and the Basel Norms,
- Prudential norms on asset classification, income recognition and provisioning,
- Introduction of valuation norms and capital for market risk for investments,
- Enhancing transparency and disclosure requirements for published accounts,
- Introduction of off-site monitoring system and strengthening

of supervisory framework for banks.

B. For Operational Flexibility: To provide more operational flexibility to the banks, the following important measures have been introduced during the decade of financial sector reforms:

- Statutory reserve requirement has significantly been brought down,
- The degree of autonomy to the Board of Directors of the banks has been substantially enhanced;
- Banks have been given the freedom to recruit specific staff as per their requirements,
- Besides deregulation of interest rates, the boards of banks have been given authority to fix their prime lending rates. Banks also have the freedom to offer variable rates of interest on deposits, keeping in view their overall cost of funds

C. For Competitive Efficiency: So far as increase in the competitive efficiency of banks is concerned, the following significant steps can be recommended:

- Opening up the banking sector for private participation, and
- Scaling down the shareholding of the Government of India in National Banks and of the RBI in State Bank of India.

D. For Legal Environment: Government of India has also taken the following measures to provide a more conducive legal environment for the recovery of dues of banks and financial institutions:

- Setting up of Debt Recovery Tribunals providing a mechanism for expeditious loan recoveries,
- Constitution of a High Power Committee under former Justice Sri Eradi to suggest appropriate foreclosure laws, and
- An appropriate legal framework for securities action of assets.

The whole chapter is divided into six sections. After the brief introduction the second section deals with review of literature, the third section is devoted for the objectives, methodology and database. Fourth section analyzes the impact of banking sector reforms in terms of some selected parameters and fifth section suggests some strategies to improve our banking sector. Last section concludes the paper.

Literature Review

Bhattacharya, et al (1997) examined the impact of partial liberalization during mid-eighties on the productive efficiency of 70 commercial banks using data envelopment method in the period 1986-91. They found that public sector banks had the highest efficiency followed by foreign banks. The private banks were found to be the least efficient. They also found a temporal improvement in the performance of foreign banks, virtually no trend in the performance of private sector banks and a temporal decline in the performance of public sector banks.

Das (1997a) examined the X-efficiency of public sector banks since nationalization using longitudinal data. The findings indicated that banks of SBI group are more efficient than the nationalized banks. The main source of inefficiency was found to be technical in nature, rather than allocative. It has been concluded that inefficiency in public sector banks is mainly due to underutilization or wasting of resources rather than incorrect input combination.

Das (1997b) utilized non-parametric frontier methodology to derive efficiency measures for 65 major banks using cross-section data for the year 1995. He found that, generally banks in India were more technically efficient as compared to their allocative efficiency. He also found that there is no significant difference in any of the efficiency measures between public and private sector banks. Except scale efficiency, foreign banks differed significantly from public and private banks.

Noulas and Ketkar (1996) analyzed the technical and scale efficiency of public sector banks using data envelopment analysis by utilizing cross-section data of 18 banks for the year 1993. It was observed that the overall technical inefficiency was approximately 3.75 per cent of which only 1.5 per cent is on account of pure technical inefficiency and 2.25 per cent is due to scale inefficiency and majority of the public sector banks were found to be operating under increasing returns to scale.

Saha & Ravisankar (2000) rated 25 public sector banks using data envelopment analysis for the period of 1991-92 to 1994-95. It was found that barring few exceptions, public sector banks have in general improved their efficiency over the study period. UBI, UCO Bank, Syndicate Bank and Central Banks of India were found to be at lower end of the relative efficiency scale. Also, Corporation Bank, OBC, SBI, Canara Bank, SBH, Bank of Baroda and Dena Bank were found to be consistently efficient banks.

Shanmugam & Lakshmanasamy (2001) utilized three approaches namely non-parametric approach, stochastic frontier function and random coefficient approach to measure efficiency and assess robustness of the efficiency measures using data on domestic banks in India for the year 1999. It was found that overall mean technical efficiency ranges between 52 and 80 per cent in different approaches. The high rank correlation among efficiency values computed in different approaches has also been observed and the results indicate that deposit is the dominant factor in determining the output of the banks in all the models.

Swami & Subrahmanyam (1994) utilized 'Taxonomic Method' for studying the inter-bank differences in the performance of public sector banks in India. It was found that many banks show wide disparities in their measures of performance especially with differential weighting of individual indicators of business activity. No bank has shown a measure of performance close to the ideal of respective groups of banks. Almost every bank in the study never attained even 50 pc efficiency measures in both periods (1971-73 and 1987-89).

Objectives

- To study and analyze the impact of banking sector reforms on the performance of banks.
- To give suggestions to improve the banking sector.

Methodology

The present chapter is concerned with performance of Indian commercial banks in the post-banking sector reforms period. The whole banking industry is divided into four groups excluding RRBs.

- G-I comprises Public Sector Banks (PSBs) - 28 (including

IDBI Bank in 2004-05)
- G-II comprises Old Private Sector Banks (OPSBs) - 21
- G-III comprises New Private Sector Banks (NPSBs) - 6
- G-IV comprises Foreign Banks (FBs) - 31

Parameters of the Study

The present study employs ratio analysis method to compare the performance of various bank groups. The ratios are:
- Business per Employee
- Profits per Employee
- Operating Cost as percentage of Total Assets
- Net Profits as percentage of Total Assets
- Net Interest as percentage of Total Assets
- Capital Adequacy Ratio
- Net NPAs as percentage of Net Advances

Impact of Banking Sector Reforms

In India banking sector reforms had significant impact on various activities of the banks. The second banking sector reforms (1997-98) had much more impact on performance of banking sector.

Analysis of Productivity of Commercial Banks

Productivity of banks can be gauged in terms of business per employee, profits per employee and ratio of operating costs to total assets. Productivity is directly related to profitability. It is interesting to note from Table 6.1 that new private sector banks have always been more productive especially in terms of business per employee as compared to their public and private sector counterparts.

Thus, business per employee in case of new private sector banks was Rs.785.94 lakh in 1997-98 as compared to Rs. 529.40 lakh in foreign banks. Business per employee in case of public sector banks was only Rs. 88.51 lakh and it is very low as compared to other bank groups. No doubt in 2005-06 productivity of public sector banks and old private sector banks increased but still it is very low as compare to foreign banks and new private sector banks.

Table 6.1: Productivity of Bank Groups

(in Rs. lakh)

Years	G-I		G-II		G-III		G-IV	
	B/E	P/E	B/E	P/E	B/E	P/E	B/E	P/E
1997-98	88.51	0.70	120.88	1.14	529.40	4.49	785.94	11.35
1998-99	100.09	0.61	144.87	0.81	553.02	5.61	759.29	7.35
1999-00	120.53	0.73	177.91	1.32	599.23	1.77	961.03	9.59
2000-01	152.88	0.69	202.35	-0.38	775.55	-4.86	837.26	6.85
2001-02	159.84	0.54	202.31	2.76	817.59	6.60	749.20	5.15
2002-03	191.37	1.10	227.43	4.22	959.87	5.90	906.20	3.88
2003-04	214.94	1.62	253.77	1.64	861.97	12.38	740.18	4.42
2004-05	247.08	2.20	313.88	6.26	877.91	11.79	728.10	6.17
2005-06	324.06	2.87	381.99	19.91	1012.79	26.49	728.89	6.27

Note: G-1, Public Sector Banks, G-11, Old Private Sector Banks, G-111, New Private Sector Banks, G-IV, Foreign Banks
Source: Report on Trend and Progress of Banking in India, (*various issues*)

The productivity of foreign banks was Rs. 1012.70 lakh in 2005-06 but it was only Rs. 728.89 lakh in new private sector banks. Similarly, per employee profit is the highest in new private sector banks and foreign banks. It was Rs. 11.35 lakh and Rs. 4.49 lakh respectively in new private sector banks and foreign banks in 1997-98 whereas it was only Rs. 0.70 lakh and Rs. 1.14 lakh in public sector banks and old private sector banks respectively. At the end of the study period, foreign banks were at the top among the various bank groups. The main reason for this gap is better use of IT, customer care, liberal policies of RBI and advanced mind set and commitment of employees towards their organization. No doubt now-a-days public sector banks are also in this race but it it will take a lot of time before they could change their image and style of operations. Structural changes and, change in mind set is needed in public sector banks for better efficacy. Among the public sector banks, banks like OBC, Corporation Bank, PNB are competing quite effectively with new private sector banks and foreign banks.

Inter-country comparison of operating costs as related to total assets shows that e-banks in India have had lower ratio of operating costs to total assets (1.1 per cent) as compared to Canada (2.8 per cent) and Spain (2.5 per cent), thus evidencing higher efficiency of Indian banks as compared to some of the advanced cities (Table 6.2).

Table 6.2: Operating Costs as Per cent of Total Assets of Commercial Banks in India

(per cent)

Bank Groups	1997-98	1998-99	1999-00	2000-01	2001-02	2002-03	2003-04	2004-05	2005-06
G-I	2.66	2.66	2.53	2.72	2.29	2.25	2.21	2.09	2.06
G-II	2.31	2.26	2.17	1.99	2.07	2.05	1.97	1.86	2.01
G-III	2.97	3.59	3.22	3.05	3.00	2.79	2.77	2.88	2.79
G-IV	1.76	1.74	1.42	1.75	1.10	1.96	2.04	2.06	2.00

Source: Same as Table 6.1

From the ongoing analysis, we may conclude that foreign banks and new private sector banks are much better in productivity as compared to their counterparts and these bank groups have thrown a challenge for the public sector banks as well as a new path for higher productivity. The only question is to what extent they compete with their counter parts.

Analysis of Profitability

Foreign banks operating in India as also private sector banks have been found employing their resources more efficiently and possessed greater capacity to generate income as compared to public sector banks. Thus, it may be noted from Table 6.3 that foreign banks had the highest ratio of net profits to total assets at 1.5 per cent in 2005-06 followed by public sector banks at 0.9 per cent, but it was only 0.5 per cent in old private sector banks and 0.8 per cent in case of new public sector banks.

Financial Soundness

From the perspective of regulatory and supervisory process, the CAR constitutes the most important indicator for evaluating soundness and solvency of banks. It is observed from Table 6.4

that among all the bank groups under study, the CAR of foreign banks was the highest at 13 per cent in 2005-06. Similarly, new private sector banks are also sound in this case.

Table 6.3: Net Profits as Percentage of Total Assets of Commercial Banks in India

(per cent)

Bank Groups	1997-98	1998-99	1999-00	2000-01	2001-02	2002-03	2003-04	2004-05	2005-06
G-I	0.77	0.42	0.57	0.42	0.72	0.96	1.12	0.87	0.82
G-II	0.81	0.48	0.81	0.59	1.08	1.17	1.20	0.33	0.59
G-III	0.97	0.69	1.17	0.93	1.32	1.56	1.65	1.29	1.52
G-IV	1.55	1.03	0.97	0.81	0.44	0.90	0.83	1.05	0.97

Source: Same as Table 6.1

Table 6.4: Capital Adequacy Ratio

(per cent)

Bank Groups	20001	2002	2003	2004	2005	2006
G-I	11.20	11.80	12.60	13.20	12.90	12.20
G-II	11.90	12.50	12.80	13.70	12.50	11.70
G-III	12.60	12.90	15.20	15.00	14.00	13.00
G-IV	11.50	12.30	11.50	10.20	12.10	12.60

Source: Same as Table 6.1

Quality of Assets

The better quality of the assets is the indicator of efficiency. The ratio of net NPAs to net advances declined in all the bank groups in 2005-06. This again shows the efficiency of Indian banking industry. However, foreign banks and new private sector banks managed their NPAs efficiently. This ratio was only 0.80 per cent for foreign banks and new private sector banks, whereas it was almost double for the old private sector banks and public sector banks (Table 6.5).

We may conclude that public sector banks and old private sector banks should improve their assets quality to compete with other bank groups.

Spread

The spread constitutes an important indicator of efficiency of banks since it is the most important driver of profitability of banks. The net interest as percentage of total assets of different groups of commercial banks in India is depicted in Table 6.6.

Table 6.5: Net NPAs as Percent of Net Advances of Commercial Banks in India

(per cent)

Bank Groups	1997-98	1998-99	1999-00	2000-01	2001-02	2002-03	2003-04	2004-05	2005-06
G-I	7.64	8.13	7.42	6.74	5.82	4.53	2.99	2.06	1.30
G-II	3.76	4.46	2.88	3.09	7.13	5.54	3.85	2.74	1.60
G-III	2.60	2.94	2.41	1.82	1.89	1.76	1.48	0.81	0.80
G-IV	3.76	4.46	2.88	3.09	4.94	4.63	2.36	1.85	0.80

Source: Same as Table 6.1

Table 6.6: Net Interest Margin as Percent of Total Assets of Commercial Banks in India

(per cent)

Bank Groups	1997-98	1998-99	1999-00	2000-01	2001-02	2002-03	2003-04	2004-05	2005-06
G-I	2.91	2.80	2.70	2.86	2.73	2.91	2.98	2.91	2.85
G-II	2.57	2.15	2.33	2.51	2.39	2.47	2.60	2.70	2.75
G-III	3.93	3.47	3.92	3.63	3.22	3.35	3.59	3.34	3.52
G-IV	2.23	1.98	1.95	2.14	1.13	1.70	2.03	2.17	2.14
All SCBs			2.73	2.85	2.57	2.77	2.88	2.83	2.78

Source: Same as Table 6.1.

From this table, it is observed that foreign banks had the highest interest margin in relation to their total assets at 3.5 per cent in 2005-06, whereas it was only 2.14 per cent in new private sector banks and 2.78 per cent in public sector banks.

The reason for higher spread of foreign banks as compared to their public sector banks and private sector counterparts was relatively lower interest cost on deposits. Persistently declining trend in interest spread of commercial banks in India during the last decade can be attributed to a slew of factors, such as competitive pricing, growing macro economic ability and healthy policy environment. Inter-country comparison of net interest margin reveals that net interest margin of Indian commercial banks at 2.8 per cent in 2003 was much higher than that of developed countries that ranged between 0.8 per cent to 2.4 per cent. Only US banks had moderately higher net interest margin at 3.0 per cent.

Customer Service and ATMs in Different Bank Groups

In their endeavor to ease customer's access to banking facilities, Indian banks, especially new private sector banks and foreign banks have, of late, begun offering bouquet of financial services to their clients. Some banks have embarked on customer relationship management not only to retain the existing customers but also to attract new ones (Table 6.7).

Table 6.7: ATMs of Scheduled Commercial Banks (As on March 31, 2006)

Bank Group	Number of ATMs			Percentage of Off-site to Total ATMs
	On-site	Off-site	Total	
G-I	4812	2353	7165	32.80
G-II	1775	3668	5443	67.40
G-III	1054	493	1547	31.90
G-IV	2255	3857	6112	63.10
G-V	232	648	880	73.60
Total	10128	11019	21147	52.10

Source: Same as Table 6.1.

However, these facilities remained confined to metro cities and urban areas and vast rural hinterland, where majority of the Indians reside, still remain deprived.

Adoption of latest technology and core banking solutions has enabled the banks to render anywhere and anytime banking facilities to the customers. Table 6.7 exhibits that for these services foreign banks and new private sector banks are on top.

Implications

The main implications of the chapter is that in the post-banking sector reforms period, the performance of all bank groups have improved but public sector banks still need some effective strategies to compete with their counterparts. Indian banks to expand their market base by penetrating into hitherto untapped but highly potential rural markets, should lay greater emphasis on boosting services and provide better customer satisfaction. They need to enhance their systems and procedures as per international standards and also simultaneously fortify their financial position.

Suggestions for the Improvement of Indian Banking Sector

Based on the above analysis and observation, we would like to suggest evolving suitable strategy in the days to come to improve the financial position of the banking sector:

1. For improving share of banks the low-cost deposit action plans should be prepared for those centers where there is adequate potential for deposit mobilization.
2. In order to involve all members in business development and build team at the branch level, regular staff meeting must be organized at least fortnightly or monthly.
3. Indian banking sector should stop copying western banking models and instead should take special care to understand the local ethos and cultural backdrops. Indian bankers should try to promote innovation and creativity taking into account the local ethos.
4. There should be a mechanism to review the working of the ARC at periodical intervals so that timely and adequate policy measures can be introduced.
5. Banks should estimate the profitability of default associated with borrowers in each of the rating grades.
6. With increasing competition among banks to meet customer expectation, banks should offer a broad range of deposits, investments and credit products through diverse distribution channels including upgraded branches, ATMs, telephone and internet. For this, banks should:

- become more customer centric, offering a wide range of products through multiple delivery channels,
- pay greater attention to profitability including cost-reduction and increasing fee-based income.
7. Domestic banks should begin to make them as competitive as possible.
8. The banks must look into wider issues and reap the overall economic benefits of free trading environment. There is dearth of adequate awareness in the banking industry about the implication of the agreement and several issues related to WTO.
9. In the emerging scenario, with more and more global players operating in India, there has been an urgent need to serve the customers promptly and efficiently.
10. VRS should continue and not be a one-time affair.
11. Autonomy in HRM areas such as deciding categorization of branches, vacancy, placements should be given to banks.
12. Use of technology should be increased substantially in banks to cope up with rising volumes and reducing transaction costs and processing time.

The main implication of the study is that no doubt there is a positive and upward effect in the performance of all the bank groups but, still nationalized banks should think about their present policies, strategies and modify these according to the customer needs.

Conclusion

The chapter concludes that banking sector reforms particularly second banking sector reforms have a significant effect on the performance of banking sector. The analysis shows that Indian banking sector is moving towards better tomorrow and highlights that banking sector reforms have created competitive environment and new private sector banks and foreign banks are much better than our public sector banks. There is a need to modify present policies and strategies of public sector banks to compete with their counterparts and to reap the fruits of globalization.

There is an urgent need of intensive research on the following key areas:

- To explore new possibilities of bank products/services in developing countries.
- New model for public sector banks.
- New retail activities of public sector banks in comparison to new private sector banks and foreign banks.
- Cost structure of rural and semi-urban branches.

7

Productivity of Various Bank Groups

Introduction

The Indian financial system, comprising of commercial banks, the financial institutions and capital markets, has undergone a very rapid transformation. The LPG is responsible for this rapid change in the banking sector. The Committee on financial system, well known as Narasimham Committee (NC) was set up in 1991, to recommend measures for bring out necessary reforms in the financial sector. The first Narasimham Committee found the following distortions in Indian commercial banking:

- Deterioration in the quality of the loan portfolio because of fixation of targets for specific sector lending
- Inadequate attention to quantitative aspects of lending
- Improper loan appraisal of credit applications
- No post-credit supervision and monitoring
- Growth of overdue and consequent erosion of profitability.
  The first NC had proposed wide ranging reforms for:
- Improving the financial viability of the banks
- Increasing their autonomy from government direction
- Restructuring unviable banks
- Allowing a greater entry to the private sector in banking
- Liberalizing the capital markets
- Setting up of proper supervisory system.

A number of reforms initiatives have been taken to remove or minimize the distortions impinging upon the efficient and profitable functioning of banks. These include the following:

- Reduction in SLR & CRR
- Transparent guidelines or norms for entry and exit of private

sector banks
- Direct access to capital markets
- Rationalization and regulation of regulated interest rate
- Liberalisation of the Branch licensing policy
- Merger of strong banks with weak unviable ones
- Strengthening of legal framework to accelerate credit recovery.

Overall, the main objective of the banking sector reforms was to improve the efficiency of the banks and prepare them to face global challenges. The post-banking scenario has shown that gap between the efficiency in various bank groups has been widened. No doubt Indian banks are improving their efficiency in the banking sector reforms period but the efficiency of foreign banks and new private sector banks is much higher than that of Public sector banks (PSBs).

Objectives
- To study and analyze the efficiency gap among the various bank groups in the post-banking sector reforms period.
- To find out some glaring reasons of lower efficiency in Indian nationalized banks and suggest ways and means to improve the efficiency of Indian nationalized banks.

Hypotheses
- Profitability per employee is significantly correlated with the expenses per employee and business per employee.
- Profitability per branch is significantly correlated with the expenses per branch and business per branch.

Methodology
The universe of the present study is Indian banking industry, which comprises five different ownership groups:
- G-I   Nationalized Banks (20),
- G-II   SBI and its Associates (8)
- G-III   Old Private Sector Banks (21)
- G-IV   New Private Sector Banks (8)
- G-V   Foreign Banks (31)

Parameters of the Study
The six parameters have been selected to analyze the bank

group's efficiency:
1. Per Employee Profitability X_1
2. Per Branch Profitability X_1
3. Per Employee Business Y_3
4. Per Branch Business Y_4
5. Per Employee Expenses Y_1
6. Per Branch Expenses Y_2

Time period of the study is related to second post-banking sector reforms (1999-2000 to 2004-05). This period has been chosen taking into consideration the following factors:

- The process of interest rate liberalization, which started in 1992, was fully liberalized (especially that of deposit rate) in 1998.
- New private sector banks started entering the banking business in a big way from 1998.

Also, the second phase of liberalization in the banking sector started in 1997-98 following the recommendations of the Second Narasimham Committee Report in 1998.

The ratio method is used to calculate the efficiency of the different bank groups. The average, correlation, coefficient of variation is calculated to know the variations in bank group's efficiency. The SPSS 10.0 version is used for the data calculation.

Results and Discussion

The present paper contributes to the banking efficiency literature by measuring efficiency of banks in five different bank ownership groups in India during the post-second banking sector reforms period i.e. from 2000 to 2005. The whole analysis is based on ratio analysis.

Profitability per Employee: The profit per employee is in the range of Rs. 0.41 to Rs. 2.32 lakh during the study period in G-I, similarly, it was between Rs. 0.77 to Rs. 2.04 lakh in G-II, Rs.1.08 to Rs. 6.15 lakh in G-III and Rs. 8.07 to Rs. 15.17 lakh in G-V (Table 7.1).

The G-I, II (public sector banks), even old private sector

banks (G-III) have shown poor efficiency in terms of profit per employee as compared to new private sector banks and foreign banks. But our new private sector banks are competing with the foreign banks whose average performance is higher (18.14) as compared to the foreign banks where average is only 11.68 at the end of the study period.

Table 7.1: Profitability per Employee - X_1

(in Rs. lakh)

Years	G-I	G-II	G-III	G-IV	G-V
1999-2000	0.44	0.85	1.08	7.75	8.07
2000-01	0.41	0.77	1.09	5.14	8.35
2001-02	0.65	1.21	1.89	4.56	12.12
2002-03	1.65	1.59	2.62	9.20	15.17
2003-04	2.32	2.00	5.09	5.20	14.89
2004-05	2.03	2.04	6.15	0.77	11.52
Average	1.26	1.42	2.98	5.44	11.68
S. D.	0.85	0.55	2.15	2.91	3.06
C.V. %	67.46	38.73	72.15	53.49	26.20

Source: Performance Highlights of 1999 to 2005, IBA, Mumbai

This overall trend of increasing employee profitability may be attributed to the reduction in the number of employees following the launch of VRS by some of the Indian banks as well as higher profits by the banks. On an average, new private sector banks enjoy a higher increase in their profitability per employee, as compared with their counter part public sector banks. This may be attributed largely to better technology which the new private sector banks employ, besides the advantage of carrying on historical baggage.

ICICI Bank and HDFC Bank in G-IV are dominating in profit per employee whereas Corporation Bank, OBC and PNB have the highest per employee profit in G-I whereas Punjab & Sindh Bank, UCO Bank and Dena Bank show lower profit per employee in G-1

Profitability per Branch: For Indian public sector banks, the profits per branch were in the range of Rs.6.39 to Rs. 41.08 crore during the study period. Among the Indian banks, new private sector banks displayed the highest profits per branch between Rs.19.09 to Rs. 174.34 crore. But overall, foreign banks depicted excellent results in this parameter (Table 7.2).

Table 7.2: Profitability per Branch - X_2

(Rs. lakh)

Years	G-I	G-II	G-III	G-IV	G-V
1999-2000	7.43	19.87	14.30	123.70	623.56
2000-01	6.39	16.39	14.24	76.44	637.06
2001-02	14.80	25.37	24.17	83.91	897.33
2002-03	23.50	33.12	35.32	174.34	1032.39
2003-04	32.70	41.08	61.12	123.96	1029.27
2004-05	27.98	41.06	71.87	19.09	1405.67
Average	18.80	29.48	36.84	100.24	937.55
S. D.	10.92	10.61	24.49	52.96	292.25
C.V. (%)	58.19	35.99	66.48	52.83	31.17

Source: Same as in Table 7.1.

The profitability per branch was in the range of Rs. 623.56 to Rs. 1405.67 crore. On an inter-temporal basis, per branch profits have been increasing gradually in the Indian banking sector.

The growth in branch profits for Indian banks is attributable to the overall increase in profitability in the banking industry. Hence, on an average, branch profitability of foreign banks is higher than that of G-I, II, III & IV. But, we can also say that G-IV is quite active and competing with foreign banks.

Expenses per Employee: On an average, Indian banks paid less as compared to foreign banks. Among Indian banks, new private sector banks pay on an average Rs. 59.83 lakh as compared to G-I, II & III which pay Rs.14.00, Rs. 14.43 and Rs. 18.07 lakh respectively. The highest expense per employee incurred by G-V (foreign banks) was Rs.79.84 lakh per employee (Table 7.3).

G-IV and G-V paid higher and attractive salary to the efficient employees; they also provide better facilities and incentives to their employees. Due to this reason, although per employee expenses are higher yet return per employee is much higher as compared to their counterparts.

Expenses per Branch: Amongst Indian banks, average per branch expenses incurred by new private sector banks (G-IV) was to the tune of Rs. 1169.06 lakh as compared to G-I, II & III with per branch expenses of Rs. 205.34, Rs. 303.38 and Rs. 228.74 lakh respectively. But branch expenses were the highest in G-V having amount of Rs. 6364.72 lakh for each branch (Table 7.4).

Table 7.3: Expenses per Employee - Y_1

(Rs. lakh)

Years	G-I	G-II	G-III	G-IV	G-V
1999-2000	9.76	9.93	13.80	44.76	76.33
2000-01	12.22	12.83	15.35	55.26	85.26
2001-02	14.30	14.55	18.34	50.76	92.99
2002-03	15.20	15.62	21.33	100.51	26.17
2003-04	15.85	16.48	19.88	60.91	74.21
2004-05	16.68	17.19	19.73	46.79	64.10
Average	14.00	14.43	18.07	59.83	79.84
S. D.	2.58	2.69	2.91	20.77	10.34
C.V. (%)	18.43	18.64	16.10	34.72	12.95

Source: Same as in Table 7.1

Overall, we may conclude that among the Indian bank groups, new private sector banks had shown excellent growth in their efficiency and this group is competing with foreign banks in terms of many parameters of efficiency. Many factors are contributing in their excellent efficiency performance like work culture, dedication, loyalty, technology, better facilities, new products/services, management, transparency etc.

Business per Employee: Since different employees in a bank contribute in different ways to the revenues and profits of a bank, it is difficult to come up with one universal metric that captures the business per employee accurately.

The business per employee is quite low in G-I, II & III as compared to G-IV & V. The average per employee business was the highest in G-IV i.e. Rs.905.83 lakh and G-V had an average of Rs. 901.50 lakh during the study period (Table 7.5).

Table 7.4: Expenses Per Branch - Y_2

(Rs. lakh)

Years	G-I	G-II	G-III	G-IV	G-V
1999-2000	166	232	182	747	5985
2000-01	189	274	200	820	6502
2001-02	206	304	234	934	6883
2002-03	217	326	288	1905	5866
2003-04	224	338	239	1450	5129
2004-05	230	346	230	1159	7824
Average	205.34	303.38	228.74	1169.06	6364.72
S. D.	23.99	43.43	36.52	441.82	931.51
C.V. (%)	11.68	14.32	15.97	37.80	14.64

Source: Same as in Table 7.1

Table 7.5: Business per Employee - Y_3

(Rs. lakh)

Years	G-I	G-II	G-III	G-IV	G-V
1999-2000	126	122	171	938	699
2000-01	160	160	202	749	817
2001-02	197	182	227	906	958
2002-03	222	205	299	1094	1014
2003-04	256	302	317	873	981
2004-05	308	379	355	875	940
Average	211.50	223.50	261.83	905.83	901.50
S. D.	65.69	93.83	72.32	112.31	119.83
C.V. (%)	31.06	41.98	27.62	12.40	13.29

Source: Same as in Table 7.1.

Thus, deposit mobilization and advances per employee are higher in G-IV & V.

These bank groups are providing a better interest on deposits and lower interest on advances and their market policies are quite effective as compared to Indian public sector banks.

Business per Branch: On an average, the per branch business is lower in G-I, II & III as compared to that of G-IV & V. It was only Rs.2704.17 lakh in G-I whereas it was Rs.17659.17 lakh in G-IV and Rs.73263.17 lakh in G-V (Table 7.6).

In this parameter, foreign banks had lion's share amongst all the Indian bank groups.

Hence, the new private sector banks in India have led the way in this regard, because of better use of technology and other infrastructure.

Co-efficient of Correlation: The co-efficient of correlation is positive and highly significant at 5 per cent level among per employee profitability (X_1) and expenses (Y_1) and per branch profitability (X_2) and expenses (Y_2) of G-I and G-II. Correlation among per employee profitability (X_1) and business (Y_3) is positive and significant only in G-II (0.92) at 1 per cent level and G-II (0.84) at 5 per cent significant level, whereas the correlation among per branch profitability (X_2) and business (Y_4) is positive and significant only in G-I at 5 per cent significant level and in G-II, III & V at 1 pc significant level. In other cases it is insignificant but positive (Table 7.7).

Table 7.6: Business per Branch - Y_4

(Rs. lakh)

Years	G-I	G-II	G-III	G-IV	G-V
1999-2000	2152	2860	2255	14989	54800
2000-01	2478	3411	2633	11131	62272
2001-02	2446	3793	2904	16673	70929
2002-03	1295	4260	4035	20733	69025
2003-04	3612	6196	3891	20776	67787
2004-05	4242	7454	4149	21656	114768
Average	2704.17	4662.17	3311.00	17659.17	73263.17
S. D.	1058.07	1782.03	812.63	4144.05	21155.42
C.V. (%)	39.13	38.22	24.54	23.47	28.88

Source: Same as in Table 7.1.

Table 7.7: Co-efficient of Correlation

Variables	G-I	G-II	G-III	G-IV	G-V
X_1 & Y_1	0.85*	0.90*	0.67	0.62	0.04
X_2 & Y_2	0.89*	0.89*	0.42	0.55	0.42
X_1 & Y_3	0.54	0.92**	0.84*	0.19	0.19
X_2 & Y_4	0.89*	0.93**	0.93**	0.61	0.92**

Note: *correlation co-efficient is significant at 0.05 level (2-tailed)
** Correlation co-efficient is significant at 0.01 levels (2-tailed)

From the ongoing analysis, we may conclude that nationalized banks i.e. G-1 & G-11 are moving in the right direction - as expenses per employees and branch increases, profitability per employee is also increasing and same is the case of business per employee. Similarly, profitability of per branch is increasing as expenses per branch increases. Both the hypothesis are accepted and positively correlated with each other.

Future Opportunities for Indian Banking Sector

The efficiency of public sector banks is quite low, when we compare them with foreign banks. The public sector banks are facing many severe challenges but at the same time there are many opportunities which are available. Here are a few issues that need to be addressed:

1. **High level of NPAs:** One of the challenges faced by the banking sector today is the high level of NPAs. To tackle with this critical problem, different options are available which includes:

*   Reducing the existing NPAs and curbing their further build-up;
*   Exploring avenues of recovering NPAs such as Lok Adalats etc. for recovering smaller loans;
*   Increasing the number of Debt Recovery Tribunals;
*   Complete ban on generalized loan waivers;
*   Setting up the Asset Reconstruction Fund (ARF) as recommended by the NC (1991) and reiterated in its Second Report (1998).
*   Reduce the recovery rate.
*   Shutting down loss making branches and slashing overstaffing. Another challenge is the large number of loss making branches which are highly overstaffed and use archaic methods of operations. All these factors have affected the efficiency of public sector banks negatively.

To cope up with this problem, public sector banks should close loss making branches and staff should be according to the branch requirements.

2. **Culture of blackmailing in public sector banks:** This is also another major area, which prevails in most of the public sector banks and adversely affects the efficiency of the employees. The Central Vigilance Commission (CVC) has said no action should be taken on anonymous/pseudonymous petition which would give confidence to the honest employees in the banking sector. CVC should ensure that the honest officers do not become victims of blackmail.

3. **Frauds committed by insiders:** Many a times, the insiders commit frauds. CVC recommends that high punishment should be given to win the customers back and to create more faith.

4. **Technology:** The public sector banks are not using technology aggressively. Only 80 pc of the business of all public sector banks have been computerized whereas new private sector banks and foreign banks have 100 pc of their operations computerized and they are providing e-banking services also. Public sector banks should now aim for computerization not only branch wise but bank wide too. Bank wise computerization with the capacity to focus on the customers and develop a culture of customer focus services mindset is perhaps needed in today's environment for facing the future.

5. **Innovative methods:** The foreign banks and new private sector banks are using innovative marketing methods but our public sector banks are lacking.

    In the emerging environment, two aspects have become important. One is the better corporate governance and the second is innovativeness and development of competitive edge through imagination. So for as better corporate governance is concerned, what is needed is ensuring that there is transparency in the system of decision making which leads to accountability.

6. **Poor Asset Quality of public sector banks:** Public sector banks should concentrate on asset quality and earnings.

7. **Autonomy in HRM:** Autonomy in HRM related decisions such as deciding categorization of branches, vacancy,

placements should be given to banks.

8. **WTO & Public Sector Banks:** Public sector banks must look into wider issues and reap the overall economic benefits of free trading environment. There is dearth of adequate awareness in the banking industry about the implications of the agreement and several issues related to WTO.

9. **More attention towards customer expectations:** With the increasing competition among banks, to meet customer expectations, banks should offer a broader range of deposits, investments and credit products through diverse distribution channels including upgraded branches, ATMs, telephone, Internet. For this purpose, banks should:

- become more customer centric, offering a wide range of products/services through multiple delivery channels;
- become proficient in managing assets and liabilities according to risk and returns:
- pay greater attention to efficiency including cost-reduction and increasingly fee-based income.

In brief public sector banks should follow these measures to make themselves up to date:

- Create a clear, simple, reality based customer-focused vision and should communicate the strategies to all the branches.
- Reach, set aggressive targets, recognize and reward progress, while understanding accountability and commitment.
- Possess a mindset that drives quality, cost and speed for a competitive advantage.

To make public sector banks world-class, five factors are important to consider and create:

- Vision
- Values
- Innovation
- Leadership and
- Social Commitment

The main finding of this chapter is that public sector banks have although improved their financial position but still these banks need many changes. To make them world-class in the era of competitive environment, five factors are important to consider - vision, values, innovations, leadership and social commitment which can convert the challenges of public sector banks into opportunities.

Conclusion

On the basis of important parameters of efficiency, the chapter concludes that among the Indian banks, efficiency of new private sector banks is quite high, but foreign banks have an edge over new private sector banks. Our new private sector banks are competing with foreign banks with continuous improvement in their performance. Hence, the public sector banks should make effective, innovative policies/strategies to compete with foreign banks if they want to survive in this emerging competitive environment. Vision, values, innovation, leadership and social commitment can convert the challenges of public sector banks into opportunities.

In the era of LPG and WTO regime, a comprehensive research is needed regarding:

- WTO regime and opportunities available for Indian banks
- A comprehensive study regarding the various dimensions of non-interest income in the era of deregulation of interest rates
- globalization of Indian banks in the global arena
- Recent partial privatization of Indian public sector banks and their performance.

8

Danger Zone Banks

Introduction

Financial sector is the backbone of every economy. The readiness of financial sector to adopt the objectives of economic and social development and to bring about a greater mobility of resources to meet the emerging challenges of the economy is a necessary concomitant of development. Financial sector comprises capital market, insurance and banking industry and contributes the maximum in the economic growth whereas banking industry is an important part of financial sector and contributes more than 25 pc in the growth of economy.

With the globalization trends allover the world, it is difficult for any nation, big or small, developed or developing, to remain isolated from what is happening around. For a country like India, which is one of the most promising emerging market, such isolation is nearly impossible. More particularly, in the time of these dynamic changes, India has also adopted liberalization, privatization and globalization policy, which has improved the performance of the banks to a large extent.

Due to these changes, the concept of banking has drastically changed from a business dealing with money transactions alone to a business related to information on financial transactions. It is so because with the entry of foreign and new private sector banks, competition has increased and banking business has become vast to a large extent that even education fee, bills payment, reservations and more particularly, security market and many non-banking transactions etc. are made through banks. It has become possible just because of the use of latest techniques of information technology in the regime of liberalized policies.

Due to liberalization and globalization, competition has intensified. Along with the new products, quality of services has also improved. Liberalization and globalization, where on the one hand has put pressure to face severe competition, on the other hand has opened new vistas of business for Indian banks in the global markets regards the qualitative and efficient services/products they should provide to the customers. Hence, Indian banks now should explore the new opportunities at a large scale to gain momentum in the global market.

Hence, liberalization as well as globalization has changed the ways of banking business and some banks are facing fierce competition to stay in the global market. They are facing number of new challenges to improve their performance on one hand and to serve the customers in new ways with greater efficiency and effectiveness on the other hand. Now-a-days, profitability and social objectives are two opposing considerations, which a bank is now required to keep in mind. Although, profits today are no longer the be-all and end-all of banking business; nevertheless any concern for healthy growth, long-term viability and lasting contribution of banks must accord due emphasis on profitability.

Profitability is an important criterion for determining the operational efficiency of banks. This has to be considered in relation to the growth of various selected variables. Raising profitability is one of the important ways by which a bank can vigorously expand its operations on a sustained long-term basis. The competitive profit is the very reason for the continued existence of every commercial organization. The rate of profitability is therefore, rightfully considered as an indicator of efficiency in the deployment of resources of banks.

In the last two decades, the circumstances prompted many countries to liberalize their financial sector through deregulation. Bhattacharya (1997) reported that deregulation and liberalization had a major impact on productivity and efficiency increases in various industries and banking sector in some eastern and central European countries as well as China. Although the primary goal of liberalization and deregulation is to improve efficiency, earlier results have been mixed, in particular, the short term effects of liberalization have been discouraging (Leightner & Lovel, 1998 &

Harker & Zenios, 2000). From these mixed reactions we can't conclude a final result but here in this chapter an attempt has made to study the behaviour of profitability in all Indian commercial banks in the post-liberalized and globalized era. The present chapter is mainly concerned with the analysis of profitability of Indian commercial banks in the post liberalized and globalized era.

Review of Literature

Arora & Verma (2005) studied the performance evaluation of PSBs in the post-banking sector reforms period on the basis of four parameters. They concluded that the performance of Corporation Bank in case of financial and operational parameters is higher as compared to other PSBs under study but Indian Bank scored poor in some parameters of operational performance. On the other side Vijaya Bank scored well in profitability parameters but UCO Bank scored negative growth in case of all parameters of profitability except operating profits as percentage of working funds. In case of productivity, Union Bank of India ranked good but UCO bank ranked lower. Overall they concluded that Indian Banking System is becoming increasingly mature in terms of transformation of business process and the appetite for risk management.

Bhattacharya, (1997) studied the impact of the limited liberalization initiated before the deregulation of the nineties on the performance of the different categories of banks, using data envelopment analysis. Their study covered 70 banks for the period 1986-91. They found PSBs with the highest efficiency among the three categories of bank groups whereas foreign and private sector banks had much lower efficiencies. However PSBs started showing a decline in efficiency after 1987, private banks witnessed no change and foreign banks disclosed a sharp rise in efficiency. The main results accord with the general perception that in the nationalized era, public sector banks were successful in achieving their principal objective of deposit and loan expansion.

Birla Institute of Scientific Research conducted a study to

evaluate the performance of nationalized banks in comparison with the private sector banks. The study reveals that the growth and development in banking after nationalization was not just because of transfer of ownership. It was rather because various incentives and punitive measures were implemented with more vigilance and care after 1969 by the Government and the Reserve Bank of India to make bank's fulfill their social responsibilities. The performance of private sector banks in the post-nationalization period was noteworthy, especially because of the odds they faced in securing the growth of the business.

Das, (1999) compares performance among public sector banks for three years in the post-reform period, 1992, 1995 and 1998. He finds a certain convergence in performance. He also notes that while there is a welcome increase in emphasis on non-interest income, banks have tended to show risk-averse behavior by opting for risk- free investments over risky loans.

Das, M R (2003) developed an objective method for ranking the nationalized banks. In this study, four aspects of banks' performance have been studied: (a) Business Performance, (b) Efficiency, (c) Safety and Soundness, and (d) Labour Productivity during 2000-01 and 1999-2000 for all 17 NBs. The study concludes that during 2000-01, Corporation Bank emerged as the topmost bank followed by Andhra Bank and OBC whereas in business performance, PNB was the topmost, followed by Bank of India and Union Bank of India. In terms of efficiency, Corporation Bank, in safety and soundness, Andhra Bank and in labour productivity, Corporation Bank, are the topmost. During 2000-01, the listed banks ranked higher than the unlisted ones.

Garg, Mohini (1994) compared the profitability of Indian scheduled commercial banks with foreign banks for the period of 1970 to 1990. The study reveals that Indian scheduled commercial banks have achieved remarkable progress in the last two decades under study, particularly in branch expansion in rural areas, deposits mobilization and credit deployment to priority sector and small borrowers. However, their profits have not kept pace their growth and hence, the share in profits has come down, whereas foreign banks with a much smaller geographical spread and resources base, earn almost as much by way of profits as 20 nationalized banks put together. It is concluded that there is a lot of difference in the pattern of advances and investments and even lending rates of Indian and foreign banks. The study suggests giving more autonomy to Indian commercial banks in their functioning.

Johri & Jauhari, (1994) also analyzed the importance of computers in banking industry. He also analyzed various issues related to computerization of banks in India. Whether banks use e-commerce & other IT systems to reinvest themselves, gain access to new markets or become extinct as dinosaurs or whether advances in technology create new opportunities for banks, or they become extinct remains to be seen in coming years.

Joshi, (1986) indicated various reasons for declining trends in profitability. His study is based on published data. He has suggested profits planning both at micro and macro levels for the banking industry to overcome the declining trends in profitability.

Kaushik, Sanjay (1995) examined why the productivity of banks is low and if whether due to social measures or not. He has studied the comparative productivity and profitability of public sector banks, nationalized banks and private sector banks with the help of various ratios through average, correlation, regression, and factor analysis. He concluded that the productivity of public sector banks shows greater decline as compared to that of private sector banks, which further reduces their profits. While analyzing the various parameters of cost, he concluded that lack of proper cost control measures in public sector banks is a major factor adversely affecting their profitability.

Kulkarni, (2000) in his article attempts to review the various seminal changes which have taken place at an astonishing pace today which is likely to change the pace of banking like never before. The traditional brick and mortar bank is giving way to the virtual bank with e-banking leading the way. He also discussed the future scenario for banking. As the brick-and-mortar edifice of banks starts crumbling and banks enter an era of virtual banking, the barriers of geography and time would crumble and communication would just be a click away. In the above scenario the role of the traditional bank branch of the 20th century would almost be non-existent.

Murty, (1996) analyzed various factors which can be helpful to improve the profitability of public sector banks. The study examine the impact of monetary policy and market interest rates on the bank profitability and also suggest various measures to improve the profitability of the public sector banks in India.

Nayar, Anita (1992) studied the profitability of nationalized banks for the period 1970 to 1986 in case of first category and from 1980 to 1986 in case of second category of nationalized banks. The study examined the factors leading to the deterioration in profitability and then suggests some measures for better profit planning. The study concluded that in terms of performance indicators viz. deposits, advances to priority sector and number of branches, Central Bank of India ranked first followed by BOI, BOB, and PNB. In case of second category, Andhra Bank ranked at the top. Overall profitability of banks has been under constant strain during the study period except during 1970-74 when a downfall was experienced. In case of first category, operating cost to total cost, liquid assets to total assets and priority sector advances to total advances have been found to be the major cause of low profitability whereas in case of second category, operating costs and rural and semi-urban branches have been found to be the cause of low profitability of banks.

According to Roger, (2000) a set of principles can actually prevent most fires in business. Pretty much everyone acknowledges that business is being completely reinvented because transaction costs are much lower on the Internet than in traditional channels. The banks are rapidly shifting their business functions and customers relationships on to the Web.

Sarker and Das, (1997) compared performance of public, private and foreign banks for the year 1994-95 by using measures of profitability, productivity and financial management. They found PSBs comparing poorly with the other two categories.

However, they caution that no firm inference can be derived from a comparison done for a single year.

Satyamurty, (1994) clarified the concepts of profits, profitability and productivity applicable to the banking industry. It is organized by the bank managements that the pressure on the profitability is more due to the factors beyond their control. He suggested the technique of ratio analysis to evaluate the profit and profitability performance of banks. He opined that endeavors should be made to improve the spread performance through better funds management.

Singh, Inderjeet & Parmod Kumar (2006) analyzed the liberalization–efficiency in relation to Indian banking system by using data envelopment analysis and production function approach to measure technical and allocative efficiency during the period 1991-92 to 2002-03. The study concluded that ROA is the highest in FBs, ROE and spread are the highest in PSBs whereas Net Profits are the highest in NPSBs. In regard to production function, deposits is a major determinant of spread followed by borrowings and labour. The study again concluded that average technical and allocative efficiency are the highest in foreign banks, while in PSBs it is although lower than FBs but much better than private sector banks. Overall, efficiency is a product of technical and allocative efficiency which is again the highest in FBs (0.70966) whereas PSBs had 0.633157 which is much better than private banks having 0.39987.

Singla and Arora (2005) studied the comparative performance of Canara Bank and Indian Bank for 4 year from 2000-01 to 2003-04 with the help of various profitability and productivity ratios. Their study reveals that both the banks have improved their financial performance during the study period whereby Canara Bank had an upper hand in growth of deposit, advances and average working funds. In the case of net NPAs to net advances ratio, it is decreasing in both the banks but more in Indian Bank where it is decreased from 10.60 pc in 2000-2001 to 2.71 pc in 2003-04 where it was 2.89 pc in Canara Bank in 2003-04. In case of productivity it is rising in both the banks but remained much higher in Canara Bank.

Swamy, (2001) studied the comparative performance of different bank-groups since 1995-96 to 1999-2000. He studied the impact of financial sector reforms on the structure of the Indian banking system, the advantages reaped by some of the new Indian private and foreign banks vis-à-vis PSBs and effect of new competition on the overall efficiency of the banking system. An attempt is made in this chapter, in the context of financial sector reforms, to identify factors which could have led to changes in the position of individual banks in terms of their share in the overall banking industry. He concludes that in many respects NPSBs are much better than PSBs and even they are better than foreign sector banks.

T. Padamasai (2000) studied the profitability, productivity and efficiency of five Indian public sector banks i.e. SBI, PNB, BOB, BOI and Canara Bank as these are the big five among the Indian nationalized commercial banks and are also listed in world's top 40 banks. The study concluded that productivity and profitability of these five big banks increased throughout the post-reforms period in terms of selected ratios of each parameter, but on account of efficiency, the performance of the top five banks was dismal as inefficiency in these banks increased during the study period. He suggested that if the government sells its share in the profit making banks, it would be able to bail out the weak banks.

There have been a number of studies on liberalization programmes and its impact on efficiency in industrialized countries and transition economies. However, a limited number of studies have been undertaken in this context in mixed developing economies where liberalization and globalization programmes have been introduced. The relation of liberalization and efficiency of banking sector in the context of developing and transitional economies is still a relatively inclusive and unexplored area of research.

Hence, there is a need to explore this area for research in detail as review of the literature on the subject indicated that changes due to liberalization and globalization are very vital for the present banking system. This study is an attempt to examine the profitability of Indian commercial banks in the post-liberalized and globalized era along with the analysis of its impact in terms of twelve selected factors of profitability.

Objectives of the Study
- To study, analyze and compare the profitability of three major bank groups.
- To suggest possible measures to improve the profitability of danger zone banks.

Methodology

Research Design: The present study is mainly concerned with the profitability analysis of commercial banks in India. The present study evaluates the profitability of Indian banking industry in the liberalized and globalized environment. Further, from the Indian banking industry, commercial banks of only three major bank groups have been chosen to study whereas RRBs are excluded from the study.

Sample Design: The whole Indian banking industry is taken in terms of three major bank groups as given below:

G-I comprises Nationalized Banks - 19

G-II comprises SBI & Associates - 8

G-IV comprises New Private Sector Banks - 7

Profitability Analysis

The performance of a bank can be measured by number of indicators. Profitability is the most important and reliable indicator as it gives a broad indication of the capability of a bank to increase its earnings. For measuring the profitability of commercial banks, the present study employs two methods viz., trend analysis and ratio analysis. The analysis of profitability is made at bank level in all commercial banks of three major bank groups.

Profitability of commercial banks is analyzed with the help of following three ways:

- Trend Analysis
- Ratio Analysis

Trend Analysis: Trend indicates the direction of operations over a period of time. It also predicts the historical developments in the banks' operations. Trend analysis in this study is used to predict the trends in profitability of all commercial banks and of five major bank groups from 1998-99 to 2005-06.

Here, overall growth rate is also calculated with the help of following formula:

$$G = \frac{Y(t) - Y(t_0)}{Y(t_0)} \times 100$$

Where;

G = simple percentage growth rate over the base year

Y (t) = value of the given parameter in the current year i.e. 2005-06

Y t_0 = value of the given parameter in the base year i.e. 1998-99.

Overall growth rate helps to know increase or decrease in parameters under study and it further helps to know the extent of increase/decrease in that parameter so that appropriate action can be taken to make improvement in case of any deficiency. Growth rate is calculated for profitability and its twelve selected parameters.

Further the study seeks to classify the banks with regard to their profitability level in three different variation ranges viz. very poor performance (negative profitability), good performance banks (0.01 – 1.00 pc), and excellent performance banks (above 1.50 pc).

Ratio Analysis: Ratio provides a convenient means of analysis and expression of the various operational aspects of banks. Ratio analysis is important due to its comparability and direct relevance in the relationships established with various earning capabilities of the banks. These sets of ratios have been employed for assessing the profitability of commercial banks. In this paper profitability of commercial banks is calculated in terms of following ratio:

Net Profit as a percentage of Total Assets

Time Period for the Study

Time period for the study is taken from post second banking sector reforms i.e. from 1998-99 to 2005-06. This time period is taken because the true impact of liberalization and globalization can be studied after second banking sector reforms period came into force and competition increased, IT Act, 2000 was implemented, free entry of foreign and private sector banks was allowed and the implementation of WTO with new facilities etc. took place. The effect of these mixed factors on the banking industry is studied in the selected time period.

Findings

Profitability of Nationalized Banks (G-I): Table 8.1 shows that among the nationalized banks, 13 banks recorded an increasing trend in their profitability during the study period, where United Bank of India witnessed the highest growth almost 6 times (588.89 pc) with just 0.62 pc average profitability, Indian Overseas Bank, with 473.91 pc growth followed the United Bank of India whereas it has higher average profitability i.e. 0.76 pc than Union Bank of India. UCO Bank, although having only 0.38 pc average profitability, has shown an excellent growth of 196.97 pc as the bank was bearing losses (-0.33 pc) in 1998-99 but improved its profitability to 0.32 pc at the end of 2005-06. Similarly, Indian Bank also recorded growth of 129.12 pc to improve its profitability from -3.64 pc losses in 1998-99 to 1.06 pc profits in 2005-06 and witnessed an excellent growth. Canara Bank also witnessed growth at 114.89 pc rate in its profitability.

Other 6 banks depicted a declining trend in their profitability, whereby Dena Bank recorded the highest decline with 63.51 pc rate having 0.23 pc average profitability. It is interesting to note that average profitability was the highest in Corporation Bank i.e. 1.37 pc although it recorded a decline of 14.73 pc. In the same way, Oriental Bank of Commerce followed the Corporation Bank with 1.18 pc average profitability but showed a decline of 22.76 pc. From loss point of view, it was the highest in the case of Indian Bank - although it recorded a 129.12 pc growth to improve from losses in 1998-99 to profits in 2005-06. It is interesting to note that Indian Bank was the only bank that has recorded average loss during the study period otherwise, all other banks had profits although variations were the highest in Indian Bank i.e. 482.86 pc in terms of C.V. but it affected its profitability badly. Year-wise, average profitability was the highest during 2003-04 i.e. 1.18 pc whereas it was the least i.e. 0.27 pc in 2000-01 and variations were the highest i.e. 302.94 pc in 1998-99 meaning there was much competition among the nationalized banks in 1998-99 as compared to other years.

Overall, average profitability of all nationalized banks was good except some banks who recorded a decline in their profitability as all nationalized banks recorded an excellent growth of 118.92 pc in its group level average profitability.

Profitability of SBI Group (G-II): Table 8.2 shows that among the SBI Group, all 8 banks except 3 banks has shown an increasing trend in their profitability, whereby State Bank of Mysore witnessed the highest growth of 128.57 pc with 0.83 pc average profitability during the study period. State Bank of Travancore followed with 102.50 pc growth and 0.74 pc average profitability whereas SBI has shown 93.48 pc growth with 0.75 pc average profitability.

State Bank of Bikaner & Jaipur has shown the highest decline of 41.11 pc in its profitability and State Bank of Saurashtra has the lowest average profitability i.e. 0.68 pc. It is interesting to note that State Bank of Patiala, even recorded decline of 21.51 pc but has the highest average profitability (1.15 pc) and State Bank of Saurashtra witnessed the highest variations i.e. 66.187 pc in terms of C.V. Overall, the entire SBI Group has shown 0.79 pc average profitability with 68.63 pc growth in 2005-06 over the period of 1998-99.

Year-wise, average profitability was the highest (1.33 pc) in 2003-04 but it was the least in 1998-99 i.e. 0.63 pc and variations were the highest in 2000-01 i.e. 48.44 pc which means it was the year in which competition was at the peak whereas the year 2003-04 witnessed the least competition having 21.05 pc value of C.V. but recorded the highest profitability.

Table 8.1: Net Profits/Loss as Percentage of Total Assets (Nationalized Banks)

(Per cent)

Banks	1998-99	1999-00	2000-01	2001-02	2002-03	2003-04	2004-05	2005-06
ALB	0.77	0.35	0.18	0.32	0.59	1.34	1.20	1.28
AB	0.78	0.76	0.59	0.97	1.63	1.72	1.59	1.19
BOB	0.81	0.86	0.43	0.77	1.01	1.14	0.71	0.73
BOI	0.34	0.31	0.42	0.73	1.12	1.19	0.36	0.62
BOM	0.43	0.59	0.24	0.68	0.89	0.95	0.54	0.16
CNB	0.47	0.43	0.43	1.03	1.24	1.35	1.01	1.01
CBI	0.41	0.36	0.10	0.31	0.54	0.98	0.52	0.34
COB	1.29	1.39	1.33	1.31	1.58	1.73	1.19	1.10
DB	0.74	0.37	-1.49	0.06	0.57	1.04	0.25	0.27
IB	-3.64	-1.81	-1.03	0.11	0.53	1.04	0.93	1.06
IOB	0.23	0.15	0.38	0.65	1.01	1.08	1.28	1.32
OBC	1.23	1.14	0.75	0.99	1.34	1.67	1.34	0.95
PSB	0.53	0.52	0.10	0.17	0.03	0.06	-0.45	0.57
PNB	0.80	0.75	0.73	0.77	0.98	1.08	1.12	0.99
SYB	0.65	0.79	0.83	0.79	1.00	0.92	0.77	0.88
UCOB	-0.33	0.16	0.12	0.52	0.59	0.99	0.63	0.32
UBI	0.51	0.29	0.40	0.71	1.08	1.22	0.99	0.76
UDBI	0.09	0.16	0.09	0.52	1.26	1.22	1.03	0.62
VB	0.27	0.41	0.50	0.81	1.03	1.71	1.30	0.40
All NBs	0.37	0.44	0.33	0.69	0.98	1.19	0.89	0.81
Average	0.34	0.42	0.27	0.64	0.95	1.18	0.86	0.77
S.D.	1.03	0.64	0.63	0.33	0.4	0.39	0.48	0.36
C.V. %	302.9	152.3	233.3	51.56	42.11	33.05	55.81	46.75

Note: ALB- Allahabad Bank, AB- Andhra Bank, BOB-Bank of Baroda, BOI - Bank of India, BOM - Bank of Maharashtra, CB - Canara Bank, CBI - Central Bank of India, COB - Corporation Bank, DB - Dena Bank, IB - Indian Bank, IOB - Indian Overseas Bank, OBC - Oriental Bank of Commerce, PSB - Punjab & Sindh Bank, PNB - Punjab National Bank, SB - Syndicate Bank, UCOB - UCO Bank, UBI - Union Bank of India, UDBI - United Bank of India, VB - Vijaya Bank

Source: Performance Highlights, Various Issues, 1998-99 to 2005-06

Overall, profitability of SBI Group was sound but here it is interesting to note that even two or three banks, although recorded a decline in their profitability but still have the highest average profitability among other banks with increasing profitability such as State Bank of Patiala and State Bank of Bikaner & Jaipur.

Table 8.2: Net Profits/Loss as Percentage of Total Assets (SBI Group)

(Per cent)

Banks	1998-99	1999-00	2000-01	2001-02	2002-03	2003-04	2004-05	2005-06
SBI	0.46	0.78	0.51	0.70	0.83	0.90	0.94	0.89
SBBJ	0.90	0.97	0.76	1.06	1.13	1.50	0.88	0.53
SBH	0.85	0.82	0.82	1.02	1.15	1.24	0.72	1.05
SBOI	0.63	0.72	0.78	1.27	1.76	1.73	0.79	0.67
SBM	0.49	0.58	0.27	0.64	1.02	1.28	1.25	1.12
SBP	0.93	1.06	1.12	1.34	1.51	1.60	0.91	0.73
SBS	0.40	1.18	0.16	0.88	0.81	1.38	0.27	0.36
SBT	0.40	0.53	0.67	0.73	0.90	1.02	0.86	0.81
Total of SBI & its Associates	0.51	0.80	0.55	0.77	0.91	1.02	0.91	0.86
Average	0.63	0.83	0.64	0.96	1.14	1.33	0.83	0.77
S.D.	0.23	0.23	0.31	0.26	0.34	0.28	0.27	0.25
C.V. (%)	36.51	27.71	48.44	27.08	29.82	21.05	32.53	32.47

Note: SBI – State Bank of India, SBBJ – State Bank of Bikaner & Jaipur, SBH - State Bank of Hyderabad, SBIR- State Bank of Indore, SBM- State Bank of Mysore, SBP- State Bank of Patiala, SBS – State Bank of Saurashtra, SBT – State Bank of Travancore
Source: Same as in Table 8.1

Profitability of New Private Sector Banks (G-III): Table 8.3 shows that all new private sector banks except Kotak Mahindra and Yes Bank have shown fluctuating trend in their profitability during the study period. 4 among 8 new private sector banks have recorded improvement and 4 witnessed decline in their profitability during the study period. Overall, growth was the highest i.e. 558.62 pc in Yes Bank having an average profitability 0.13 pc. It is pertinent to note that Yes Bank has started its business in 2004-05 with 0.29 pc losses but gained top position with excellent growth in profitability as it was improved to 1.33 pc in just one year. UTI Bank followed with 40 pc growth having 0.90 pc average profitability.

Table 8.3: Net Profits/Loss as Percentage of Total Assets (New Private Sector Banks)

(Per cent)

Banks	1998-99	1999-00	2000-01	2001-02	2002-03	2003-04	2004-05	2005-06
BOP	1.53	1.04	0.93	0.92	-0.74	0.76	-1.25	-
CBL	0.69	0.66	0.12	-2.26	-0.75	-2.96	0.54	0.77
HDFC	1.89	1.02	1.35	1.25	1.27	1.20	1.29	1.18
ICICI	0.91	0.87	0.82	0.25	1.13	1.31	1.20	1.01
IIB	0.60	0.70	0.47	0.50	0.91	1.74	1.35	0.21
KMB	-	-	-	-	2.09	1.35	1.30	1.16
UTI	0.70	0.76	0.80	0.93	0.98	1.15	0.89	0.98
YB	-	-	-	-	-	-	-0.29	1.33
All NPSB	0.94	0.85	0.76	0.39	1.08	1.21	1.17	1.00
Average	1.05	0.86	0.76	0.29	0.72	0.67	0.68	0.95
S.D.	0.48	0.16	0.38	1.18	0.98	1.5	0.89	0.34
C.V. %	45.71	18.60	50.00	406.90	136.11	223.88	130.88	35.79

Note: BOP – Bank of Punjab Ltd., CB – Centurion Bank Ltd., HDFC- HDFC Bank Ltd., ICICI – ICICI Bank Ltd., IIB – IndusInd Bank Ltd., KMB – Kotak Mahindra Bank Ltd., UTI – UTI Bank Ltd., YB – Yes Bank Ltd.
Source: Same as in Table 8.1

On the other hand, HDFC Bank, the top most bank, Bank of Punjab, IndusInd Bank and Kotak Mahindra Bank have recorded decline in their profitability where IndusInd Bank recorded the highest decline at 65.00 pc rate. Kotak Mahindra Bank was following with 44.49 pc rate of decline as started its business in 2002-03 with 2.09 pc profitability and it further declined to 1.16 pc in 2005-06 but still had good amount of profitability.

HDFC Bank has shown 37.57 pc decline although it has the highest average profitability i.e. 1.31 pc among all new private sector banks whereas ICICI Bank and UTI Bank followed with 0.94 pc and 0.90 pc average profitability respectively. Centurion Bank of Punjab (emerged as new bank as a result of merger of Bank of Punjab and Centurion Bank), has shown average losses of 0.40 pc. Variations were the highest in Yes Bank (384.62 pc in terms of C.V.) which has contributed to their higher profitability as more the competition more will be the profitability in terms of various improved activities. Year-wise, average profitability was the highest in 1998-99 i.e. 1.05 pc and the least i.e. 0.29 pc in 2001-02 but recorded the highest variations i.e. 406.90 pc in terms of C.V.

Overall, average profitability of new private sector banks was 0.93 pc with 6.38 pc growth rate and reflected good efforts to improve their profitability as new banks are entering the banking industry with attractive and high quality products/services and gaining good position in Indian banking industry. Here, the major issue was deterioration in profitability of some commercial banks that has to be improved by adopting some effective strategies.

Changes in the Profitability of Various Banks under Study

From Table 8.4, it is evident that among the total 19 nationalized banks, 10.53 pc banks such as Indian Bank and UCO Bank have shown poor performance in profitability during 1998-99 while in 2005-06, these 2 banks improved their profitability whereby Indian Bank succeeded in improve its profitability to an excellent level i.e. above 1 pc. Also, a majority of other banks (78.95 pc) such as Allahabad Bank, Andhara Bank, Bank of Baroda etc. showed good performance with profitability ranging between 0.01 pc and 1 pc. The banks having excellent performance i.e. profitability above 1 pc were only 2, namely, Corporation Bank and Oriental Bank of Commerce in 1998-99 and increased to 6 in 2005-06 including Allahabad Bank, Andhra Bank, Canara Bank, Indian Bank and Indian Overseas Bank.

From the SBI Group, not even a single bank has shown poor performance during the study period as all the 8 banks had a good performance with their profitability ranging between 0.01 pc and 1 pc in 1998-99 while in 2005-06, 25 pc banks (State Bank of Hyderabad and State Bank of Mysore) were having excellent profitability performance and 75 pc were having profitability ranging between 0.01 pc and 1 pc.

Overall, from the all public sector banks, 7.41 pc had poor performance and 7.41 pc had excellent performance in 1998-99 while in 2005-06 not even a single bank has shown losses and 29.63 pc witnessed excellent performance at the end of the study period.

Table 8.4: Profitability Performance Levels of Indian Bank Groups

Bank Groups	Profitability Variation Ranges							
	Total Banks		Poor Performing Banks		Good Performance Banks		Excellent Performance Banks	
	1998-99	2005-06	1998-99	2005-06	1998-99	2005-06	1998-99	2005-06
G-I	19	19	2 (10.5)	0	15 (78.9)	13 (68.4)	2 (10.5)	6 (31.5)
G-II	8	8	0	0	8 (100)	6 (75.0)	0	2 (25.0)
G-I+II	27	27	2 (7.41)	0	23 (85.1)	19 (70.3)	2 (7.41)	·8 (29.6)
G-III	6	7	0	0	4 (57.1)	3 (42.8)	2 (28.5)	4 (57.1)

Note: Values in parenthesis shows percentage of banks from total banks of concerned group

Source: Computed from above tables

From the new private sector banks, all banks have shown good profitability performance as not even a single banks witnessed poor performance. In 1998-99, majority of the banks i.e. 57.14 pc (Centurion Bank, ICICI Bank, IndusInd Bank & UTI Bank) have shown good performance in terms of profitability while in 2005-06, majority of these banks i.e. 57.14 pc (HDFC Bank, ICICI Bank, Kotak Mahindra Bank & Yes Bank) witnessed excellent performance which means the profitability of many new private sector banks has improved from good to excellent level in terms of performance.

Comparatively, only 2 banks from 2 nationalized bank group showed poor performance in 1998-99 but from other two bank groups not even a single bank witnessed poor performance and in 2005-06, not even a single bank from any bank group has shown poor performance since majority of them had profitability ranging between 0.01 pc and 1 pc. In 1998-99, 10.53 pc of nationalized banks and 28.57 pc of new private sector banks had excellent profitability and these banks in 2005-06 witnessed excellent profitability. In this regard, profitability of nationalized banks increased form 10.53 pc to 31.58 pc and for the new private sector banks it increased form 28.57 pc to 57.14 pc at the end of the study period. In case of SBI Group 25 pc banks recorded excellent profitability performance in 2005-06. From this analysis, it may be concluded that majority of the banks from all the banks groups have shown good profitability performance whereas among new private sector banks, the banks having excellent profitability were more as compared to other two banks groups.

Top Banks among Five Banks from each Bank Group under Study

Table 8.5 shows the list of five top banks from all three bank groups under study who have the highest average profitability along with their growth rate. From this table, it is evident that from the nationalized banks, Andhra Bank, Canara Bank, Corporation Bank, Oriental Bank of Commerce & Punjab National Bank, from SBI group, State Bank of Bikaner and Jaipur, State Bank of Hyderabad, State Bank of Indore, State Bank of Mysore and State Bank of Patiala and from new private sector banks HDFC Bank, ICICI Bank, InduaInd Bank, Kotak Mahindra Bank and UTI Bank are the top five banks from three bank groups. Also, top most bank was chosen from these three bank groups.

Table 8.5: Top Five Banks on the Basis of Average Profitability

G-I			G-II			G-III		
Banks	AP	Growth Rate	Banks	AP	Growth Rate	Banks	AP	Growth Rate
AB	1.15	52.56	SBBJ	0.97	-41.11	HDFC	1.31	-37.57
CB	0.87	114.89	SBH	0.96	23.53	ICICI	0.94	10.99
COB	1.37	-14.73	SBIR	1.04	6.35	IIB	0.81	-65.00
OBC	1.18	-22.76	SBM	0.83	128.57	KMB	0.74	-44.49
PNB	0.90	23.75	SBP	1.15	-21.51	UTI	0.90	40.00

AP = Average Profitability

From nationalized banks, Corporation Bank was the top most bank recording the highest average profiotabilit i.e. 1.37 pc whereas State Bank of Patiala from SBI Group got top position with 1.15 pc average profitability which was much lower as compared to Corporation Bank. HDFC Bank from the new private sector banks' group was at third position with 1.31 pc average profitability. Again from these three banks, Corporation Bank was the top most bank among all the bank groups which recorded 1.37 pc average profitability ad HDFC was at second position with a minor difference having an average profitability 1.331 pc.

On the other hand, if we analyze the growth rates of these top five banks of three banks groups, State Bank of Mysore is at the top position with the highest rate growth i.e. 128.57 pc where Canara Bank follows with 114.89 pc growth in their profitability and UTI Bank shows a 40 pc growth which is almost three times less than the State Bank of Mysore.

Overall, it may be concluded that on the basis of profitability, Corporation Bank is at the top position follows by HDFC Bank, although these banks recorded a decline in their profitability.

Strategies

Although a lot of reforms have been made for Indian banks, still there is a need to modify the policies of public sector banks. At present, they are facing many internal and external challenges, which are hindering their performance, but these banks can convert the current challenges into opportunities with some modifications in accordance with the globalization and changes in the technology as financial markets, world over have become closely integrated. Customers can access their accounts anywhere anytime. Deregulation and liberalization has opened up new opportunities for banks but at the same time the pressure of competition has led to narrowing spreads, shrinking margins, consolidation and restructuring. With the winds of change sweeping across the world, the banks should equipped to handle large. There some suggestions are given, which may be helpful to the banks with poor performance, to improve their performance.

Planning for Future: To manage the whole business, planning should be the first step as it helps to complete every task especially to provide customer services at the right time at right price and place, by the right person and ultimately to the right person. It also helps to evaluate the performance of the bank employees by comparing with the fixed standards and results in timely action to improve deficiencies, if any. To capture and survive in such a competitive market, it is necessary to plan every move accordingly and then take important decisions.

Knowledge Management: Knowledge management is an important aspect for today's banking business as the way of business is changing at every hour and the customers demand for new information immediately. To satisfy the customers, it is necessary to update the knowledge of every employee. Only those organizations addressing every enquiry of the customers promptly are successful and ultimately gain momentum in the market. It is evident that new private sector banks provide training and make their employees aware about new concepts through various ways, and that's why they are far ahead of the public sector banks. For the public sector banks, it is necessary to adopt knowledge management as a part of their policy environment to compete in the market.

Innovations: New private sector banks are far ahead of public sector banks because they are providing innovative products/services through advanced technology. The public sector banks lag behind because their employees are not ready to adopt the changing environment and never take initiatives to provide innovative services and uses of advanced technology. To compete and survive in the market, they should also make efforts to adopt new technologies and provide services/products according to the customer needs.

Regulatory Body: The government/RBI should make public sector banks free from all bindings so that they can also take important decisions immediately and timely explore the opportunities. Because, in the time of getting permission for major decisions from RBI, they loose the opportunity and hence, lag behind to gain benefits from these opportunities.

Training and Development: Senior employees should be trained to face new technical challenges. These people should be given training according to their needs. It is need of the hour to make all the employees of public sector banks adaptable to the changing environment so that every new opportunity can be explored at the right time.

Adopt IT: IT advancement is a major and important tool for new private sector banks and foreign banks to attract more and more potential customers because through the appropriate use of these techniques, they serve their customers in the shortest possible time and at lower costs and at any place convenient to them. Public sector banks should also make their all branches fully computerized and start providing customer services electronically so that they can also survive in the markets. Now-a-days, IT has become a necessity to survive

All the banks which recorded poor performance in their profitability should make competitive strategies and explore all the opportunities with innovative ways to improve their profitability.

Since no study is complete in itself, the following areas can be explored for further study in this area of research:

1. Comprehensive study of comparative profitability behaviour of all individual banks in urban, semi-urban and rural areas.
2. Comprehensive study for SWOT analysis for banks with poor performance in profitability.
3. Feasibility and viability of e-banks in rural areas and semi-urban areas.
4. In-depth study for profitability analysis of banks at branch level.
5. Profitability behaviour of banks in the post-merger and acquisition era.

Conclusion

India is now Asia's third largest economy and has the world's fourth largest foreign exchange reserves. Technology, competition and benchmarking to the best international practices have to be the driving forces of India's development efforts. The country is making rapid strides in all these areas. Technology is getting upgraded rapidly and competition in the market place has become fierce. The vibrant IT industry is contributing immensely by providing information about latest technology and international business practices. Hence, all banks should adopt the latest technology with customer friendly and innovative products and services to explore the global opportunities.

9

Comparative Efficiency of Banks in India

Introduction

In a highly competitive and uncertain globalized environment, the banks are facing a number of challenges to endure and achieve sustainable competitive edge over their rivals. They need to be efficient, resilient and evolve strategies to face the emerging global challenges. They must work together to achieve competitive efficiency by utilizing resources, introducing innovative products and delivering high quality services to the bank customers at an affordable price. In India, at present, potential customers of traditional banks are shifting towards e-banks (foreign banks and new private sector banks) who have thrown many new challenges for public sector banks to retain their share in the market. Globalization and WTO also added fuel to the fire and at the same time, all these emerging changes have created new opportunities for Indian public sector banks, the only need is to explore these opportunities in a proper and dynamic way. In the coming years, only those banks will survive which are innovative, vigilant and dynamic.

Objective of the Study

- To examine the comparative efficiency in various bank groups in post-second banking sector reforms era.

Methodology

The present paper is concerned with comparative efficiency of Indian banking in the post-second banking sector reforms period. The whole banking industry is divided into four major bank groups and this paper excludes RRBs.

G-I: comprises Public Sector Banks - 28 (Including IDBI Bank in 2004-05)

G-II: comprises Old Private Sector Banks - 21

G-III: comprises New Private Sector Banks - 7
G-IV: comprises Foreign Banks - 31
Selected Efficiency Parameters
A. Productivity Ratios
* Business per Employee
* Profits per Employee
B. Profitability Ratios
* Interest Income as percentage of Total Assets
* Interest Expended as percentage of Total Assets
* Net Interest as percentage of Total Assets
* Operating Expenses as percentage of Total Assets
* Provisions and Contingencies as percentage of Total Assets
* Net Profits as percentage of Total Assets
C. Financial Soundness
* Capital Adequacy Ratio
D. Quality of Assets
* Net NPAs as percentage of Total Assets
* Net NPAs as percentage of Net Advances

The present study analyzes these selected ratios to compare the competitive efficiency of various bank groups.

Database
* Report on Trends and Progress of Banking in India, Reserve Bank of India, Mumbai, Various Issues, From 1997-98 to 2005-06
* Performance Highlights, Indian Banking Association, Mumbai, Various Issues, From 1997-98 to 2005-06

Major Findings

Efficiency: The present chapter examines the efficiency of banks in terms of productivity, profitability, financial soundness and quality of assets.

Productivity: Productivity of banks can be gauged in terms of business per employee, profits per employee. Productivity is directly related to profitability. It is interesting to note from Table 9.1 that new private sector banks have always been more productive especially in terms of business per employee as compared to that of public and private sector banks.

Business per employee in case of foreign banks was Rs. 785.94 lakh in 1997-98 as compared to Rs. 529.40 lakh in new private sector banks. Business per employee in case of public sector banks was only Rs. 88.51 lakh which was very low as compared to other bank groups. No doubt in 2005-06 productivity of public sector banks and old private sector banks increased but still it is very low in comparison to foreign banks and new private sector banks.

Table 9.1: Productivity of Bank Groups

(lakh)

Years	G-I		G-II		G-III		G-IV	
	B/E	P/E	B/E	P/E	B/E	P/E	B/E	P/E
1997-98	88.51	0.70	120.88	1.14	529.40	4.49	785.94	11.35
1998-99	100.09	0.61	144.87	0.81	553.02	5.61	759.29	7.35
1999-00	120.53	0.73	177.91	1.32	599.23	1.77	961.03	9.59
2000-01	152.88	0.69	202.35	-0.38	775.55	-4.86	837.26	6.85
2001-02	159.84	0.54	202.31	2.76	817.59	6.60	749.20	5.15
2002-03	191.37	1.10	227.43	4.22	959.87	5.90	906.20	3.88
2003-04	214.94	1.62	253.77	1.64	861.97	12.38	740.18	4.42
2004-05	247.08	2.20	313.88	6.26	877.91	11.79	728.10	6.17
2005-06	324.06	2.87	381.99	19.91	1012.79	26.49	728.89	6.27

Sources: 1. Report on Trends and Progress of Banking in India, Reserve Bank of India, Mumbai, Various Issues, From 1997-98 to 2005-06
2. Performance Highlights, Indian Banking Association, Mumbai, Various Issues, From 1997-98 to 2005-06

The productivity of new private sector banks was Rs.1012.70 lakh in 2005-06 but it was only Rs. 728.89 lakh in foreign banks. Similarly, per employee profit was the highest in foreign banks and new private sector banks. It was Rs. 11.35 lakh and Rs. 4.49 lakh respectively in foreign banks and new private sector banks in

1997-98 whereas it was only Rs. 0.70 lakh and Rs. 1.14 lakh in public sector banks and old private sector banks respectively. At the end of the study period, new private sector banks group was at the top among the various bank groups. The main reason for the increasing gap in productivity of new private sector banks and foreign banks is mainly because new private sector banks use more IT and are more customer-centric, having liberal policies and mind set and commitment of employees towards their organization.

No doubt, now-a-days public sector banks have also joined this race but it will still take a lot of time to cover the distance and move ahead of all. Structural changes and change in mind set is required in public sector banks. Among the public sector banks, some banks like OBC, Corporation Bank, PNB are competing vigorously with new private sector banks and foreign banks.

From the ongoing analysis, we may conclude that overall, foreign banks and new private sector banks are much better in productivity as compared to their counterparts and these bank groups have thrown a challenge for the public sector banks as well as a new path to improve their productivity.

Profitability: Interest Income as a Percentage of Total Assets: Interest deregulation was responsible for the decline in the share of interest income of the commercial banks. The severe competition in inter and intra-bank groups further accelerated down trend in this ratio. The reason for higher spread of new private sector banks as compared to public sector banks, old private sector banks and foreign banks was the relatively lower interest cost on deposits. Persistently declining trend in interest spread of commercial banks in India during the last decade could be attributed to a slew of factors, such as competitive pricing, growing macro economic stability and healthy policy environment.

Inter-country comparison of net-interest margin revealed that net interest margin of Indian commercial banks at 2.88 per cent in 2003 was much higher than that of developed countries which ranged between 0.8 per cent and 2.4 per cent and intra-bank groups further accelerated down trend in this ratio. This ratio adversely affected the profitability of the bank groups. Table 9.2 exhibited that old private sector banks and foreign banks were comparatively more efficient even during the period of deregulation of interest rates.

Table 9.2: Interest Income as Percentage of Total Assets

(per cent)

Bank Group	1997-98	1998-99	1999-00	2000-01	2001-02	2002-03	2003-04	2004-05	2005-06
G-I	9.10	9.01	8.92	8.85	8.72	8.34	7.45	6.79	6.83
G-II	10.00	9.92	9.66	9.53	9.36	8.50	7.56	6.95	6.92
G-III	9.27	9.19	7.60	8.17	4.48	8.13	6.71	5.77	5.76
G-IV	10.42	10.27	9.93	9.27	8.56	7.68	6.74	5.97	6.07
All SCBs	9.27	9.18	8.97	8.88	8.26	8.28	7.31	6.61	6.62

Source: Same as for Table 9.1.

Interest Expended as Percentage of Total Assets: Normally, private sector banks pay higher interest to attract the new customers and retain old bank customers.

As interest income declined in all bank groups, similarly, interest paid also declined in all bank groups and due to this, net margin also declined. Table 9.3 indicates that the maximum interest was paid by G-II and G-I i.e. 4.16 per cent and 3.98 per cent respectively while it was the least (2.55 per cent) in case of G-IV in 2005-06.

Table 9.3: Interest Expended as Percentage of Total Assets

(per cent)

Bank Group	1997-98	1998-99	1999-00	2000-01	2001-02	2002-03	2003-04	2004-05	2005-06
G-I	6.19	6.21	6.22	5.99	5.99	5.43	4.67	3.88	3.98
G-II	7.72	7.43	7.33	7.02	6.97	6.03	4.96	4.25	4.16
G-III	7.26	7.04	5.64	6.03	3.33	6.43	4.68	3.60	3.62
G-IV	6.49	6.79	6.01	5.64	5.34	4.33	3.15	2.63	2.55
All SCBs	6.32	6.41	6.25	6.03	5.70	5.51	4.44	3.78	3.84

Source: Same as for Table 9.1.

Spread: The spread constitutes an important indicator of efficiency of banks since it is the most important driver of profitability of banks. The net interest as percentage of total assets of different bank groups in India is depicted in Table 9.4. From this table, it was observed that new private sector banks had the highest interest margin in relation to their total assets i.e. 3.52 per cent in 2005-06, whereas it was only 2.14 per cent in foreign banks and 2.75 per cent in old private sector banks.

Table 9.4: Net Interest Margin as Percent of Total Assets of Commercial Banks in India

(per cent)

Bank Groups	1997-98	1998-99	1999-00	2000-01	2001-02	2002-03	2003-04	2004-05	2005-06
G-I	2.91	2.80	2.70	2.86	2.73	2.91	2.98	2.91	2.85
G-II	2.57	2.15	2.33	2.51	2.39	2.47	2.60	2.70	2.75
G-III	3.93	3.47	3.92	3.63	3.22	3.35	3.59	3.34	3.52
G-IV	2.23	1.98	1.95	2.14	1.13	1.70	2.03	2.17	2.14
All SCBs	NA	NA	2.73	2.85	2.57	2.77	2.88	2.83	2.78

Source: Same as for Table 9.1.

The reason for higher spread of new private sector banks group as compared to other bank groups was the relatively lower interest costs on deposits of new private sector banks. Persistently declining trend in interest spread of commercial banks in India during the last decade can be attributed to a slew of factors, such as competitive pricing, growing macro economic stability and a healthy policy environment. Inter-country comparison of net interest margin revealed that net interest margin of Indian commercial banks at 2.88 per cent in 2003 was much higher than the developed countries that ranged between 0.8 per cent and 2.4 per cent. Only US banks had moderately higher net interest margin at 3.0 per cent. Thus, score of interest spread of banks in India has fared better than those of other countries.

Operating Expenses as Percentage of Total Assets: This ratio affects the efficiency of the commercial banks i.e. how they manage the expenditure. From Table 9.5, it is clear that this ratio was the highest in foreign banks i.e. 2.79 per cent in 2005-06 whereas it was only 2.06 pc in public sector banks. New private sector banks recorded the least operating cost level i.e. 2.00 per cent in 2005-06.

Table 9.5: Operating Expenses as Percentage of Total Assets

(per cent)

Bank Group	1997-98	1998-99	1999-00	2000-01	2001-02	2002-03	2003-04	2004-05	2005-06
G-I	2.66	2.66	2.53	2.72	2.29	2.25	2.21	2.09	2.06
G-II	2.31	2.26	2.17	1.99	2.07	2.05	1.97	1.96	2.09
G-III	1.76	1.74	1.42	1.75	1.10	1.96	2.04	2.06	2.00
G-IV	2.97	3.59	3.22	3.05	3.00	2.79	2.77	2.88	2.79
All SCBs	2.63	2.63	2.50	2.64	2.19	2.24	2.21	2.21	2.11

Source: Same as for Table 9.1.

Provisions and Contingencies as Percentage of Total Assets: Every bank has to maintain some provisions and contingencies to secure their future uncertainties. In this case foreign banks were much efficient as compared to public sector banks. Table 9.6 indicates that this ratio was 1.78 pc in foreign banks in 2005-06 whereas it was only 1.12 pc in the case of public sector banks. Hence, foreign banks and new private sector banks were much efficient as compared to their counterparts.

Table 9.6: Provisions and Contingencies as Percentage of Total Assets

(per cent)

Bank Group	1997-98	1998-99	1999-00	2000-01	2001-02	2002-03	2003-04	2004-05	2005-06
G-I	0.81	0.95	0.89	0.92	1.16	1.36	1.55	1.31	1.12
G-II	1.16	0.73	1.01	1.15	1.62	1.50	1.45	1.35	1.00
G-III	1.32	0.75	1.14	0.93	0.78	1.41	1.26	0.80	1.01
G-IV	2.94	1.64	2.08	2.12	1.78	1.63	2.02	1.69	1.78
All SCBs	0.98	1.00	1.00	1.03	1.19	1.39	1.54	1.28	1.15

Source: Same as for Table 9.1.

Net Profits as Percentage of Total Assets: Foreign banks operating in India and new private sector banks have been found employing their resources more efficiently and possessed greater capacity to generate income as compare to public sector banks. Thus, it may be noted from Table 9.7 that new private sector banks had the highest ratio of net profits to total assets (1.52 per cent) in 2005-06 followed by foreign banks at 0.97 per cent, but it was only 0.59 per cent in old private sector banks and 0.82 per cent in case of public sector banks.

Table 9.7: Net Profits as Percentage of Total Assets of Commercial Banks in India

(per cent)

Bank Groups	1997-98	1998-99	1999-00	2000-01	2001-02	2002-03	2003-04	2004-05	2005-06
G-I	0.77	0.42	0.57	0.42	0.72	0.96	1.12	0.87	0.82
G-II	0.81	0.48	0.81	0.59	1.08	1.17	1.20	0.33	0.59
G-III	0.97	0.69	1.17	0.93	1.32	1.56	1.65	1.29	1.52
G-IV	1.55	1.03	0.97	0.81	0.44	0.90	0.83	1.05	0.97

Source: Same as Table 9.1.

Financial Soundness: From the perspective of regulatory and supervisory process, the CAR constitutes the most important indicator for evaluating soundness and solvency of the banks.

It is observed from Table 9.8 that among all the bank groups under study, the CAR of new private sector banks was the highest i.e.13 per cent in 2005-06. Similarly, foreign banks were also sound in this case.

Table 9.8: Capital Adequacy Ratio

(per cent)

Bank Groups	2001	2002	2003	2004	2005	2006
G-I	11.20	11.80	12.60	13.20	12.90	12.20
G-II	11.90	12.50	12.80	13.70	12.50	11.70
G-III	12.60	12.90	15.20	15.00	14.00	13.00
G-IV	11.50	12.30	11.50	10.20	12.10	12.60

Source: Same as for Table 9.1.

Quality of Assets: Net NPAs as Percentage of Total Assets: Non-performing assets adversely affected the profitability of commercial banks. From Table 9.9 it is observed that in 2005-06, the ratio was the highest (0.91 per cent) in case of old private sector banks but it was only 0.40 per cent in case of foreign banks. No doubt, net NPAs were declining in all bank groups, but private sector banks, particularly new private sector banks and foreign banks were much efficient to manage the NPAs as compared to other bank groups.

Table 9.9: Net NPAs as Percentage of Total Assets

(per cent)

Bank Group	1998-99	1999-00	2000-01	2001-02	2002-03	2003-04	2004-05	2005-06
G-I	3.14	2.94	2.72	2.42	1.93	1.28	0.95	0.72
G-II	3.56	3.27	3.28	3.22	2.61	1.77	1.39	0.91
G-III	1.59	1.08	1.18	2.10	2.16	1.10	0.80	0.43
G-IV	1.10	1.03	0.77	0.81	0.79	0.66	0.42	0.40

Source: Same as for Table 9.1.

Net NPAs as Percent of Net Advances: The better quality of the assets is an indicator of better efficiency. The ratio of net NPAs to net advances declined in all the bank groups in 2005-06. Although it showed the efficiency of Indian banking industry but foreign banks and new private sector banks were more efficient in managing their NPAs. Table 9.10 indicates that this ratio was only 0.80 per cent in foreign banks and new private sector banks, whereas it was almost double in case of old private sector banks (1.60 per cent).

Table 9.10: Net NPAs as Percent of Net Advances of Commercial Banks in India

(per cent)

Bank Groups	1997-98	1998-99	1999-00	2000-01	2001-02	2002-03	2003-04	2004-05	2005-06
G-I	7.64	8.13	7.42	6.74	5.82	4.53	2.99	2.06	1.30
G-II	3.76	4.46	2.88	3.09	7.13	5.54	3.85	2.74	1.60
G-III	2.60	2.94	2.41	1.82	1.89	1.76	1.48	0.81	0.80
G-IV	3.76	4.46	2.88	3.09	4.94	4.63	2.36	1.85	0.80

Source: Same as for Table 9.1.

We may conclude that public sector banks and old private sector banks should improve their assets' quality to compete with other bank groups. This ratio shows inefficiency of old private sector banks and public sector banks to manage their NPAs level.

Implications

The main inference of this chapter is that in the post-banking sector reforms period, the performance of all bank groups have improved but public sector banks lag behind the new private sector banks and still need to make some effective strategies to compete with their counterparts. Indian banks, to expand their market base by penetrating into untapped but highly potential rural markets, should lend greater support to boost production and provide better customer satisfaction. They need to enhance their systems and procedures to international standards and simultaneously fortify their financial position also.

Enhancing Comparative Competitive Efficiency

Indian public sector banks have low competitive efficiency as compare to new private sector banks and foreign banks. To increase the comparative competitive efficiency of banks, the following significant steps are recommended.

- Opening up the banking sector for private sector participation.
- Scaling down the shareholding of the government of India in nationalized banks and the RBI in State Bank of India.
- Steps should be taken to reduce the present level of NPAs.
- On the basis of perceptions and expectations of the customers, banks should try to increase the C-D ratio.
- Further liberalization is required for banks particularly for public sector banks.

Issues for Future Research

- Mergers and acquisition of public sector banks
- New strategies of banks in the global market
- Feasibility and viability of e-banking services in rural and semi-urban markets

- IT and changing behaviour of bank employees
- Customer relationship management
- Business process re-engineering
- Empowering of banks through technology.
- Study of external factors of efficiency.

Conclusion

The study reveals that comparative efficiency of new private sector banks and foreign banks was much better as compared to public sector banks. In some aspects, the new private sector banks perform better than the foreign banks. Productivity of foreign banks was the highest, although they had the highest costs whereas new private sector banks followed these banks with excellent growth and recorded the highest profitability with lower operating costs and the maximum provisions for contingencies. Although public sector banks had the lowest level of costs but there was greater decrease in their interest income and expenditure mainly due to deregulation that created competition in the market and these banks had to change the interest rates to retain in the market. The decline in interest income and expenditure further resulted in decrease in their spread and bring down their profitability lower as compared to new private sector banks and foreign banks. From liquidity point of view, new private sector banks and foreign banks were much stronger than public sector banks and old private sector banks. Hence, the poor performance of public sector banks lagged them behind other banks and it is challenging for them to survive and retain their share in the market. To gain sound position and compete in the global market, these banks have to change their ways of working and dealing with customers and hence need to adopt competitive strategies along with the latest technology and change in mind set. Indian public sector banks should explore new opportunities created by this new changing environment.

10

Non-interest Income of Banks

Introduction

The traditional financial intermediation role of banking, whereby banks make loans that are funded by deposits, which in the era of liberalization and emerging competition, it appears, is loosing its importance globally and this trend is also observed in our country. Due to liberalization measures in the area of banking industry and the soft interest regime prevalent globally, banks have started diversifying their activities from purely traditional banking to providing various financial and other services to its customers. This trend is very much seemed in the Indian context as well, as banks have started providing many other services in order to earn more income and reduce risks.

It is now important for banks to thrust themselves into each and every profit-earning segment of business and pleasure that caters to customers. The banks have turned increasingly to non-interest income deployment of funds for their survival. The non-interest income accounts for over 45 pc of operating income in the US commercial banking industry. In India, non-interest income is currently near about 20 pc of their total income. It is evident that there is a big scope for the spread of fee-based activities. For the very survival of banks, it will be determined by way of fee-based income and income on non-fund based business income in future.

Non-fund based income traditionally comes from fee on corporate services like financial and performance guarantees, letter of credit, bank's acceptance, cash management services, forex, remittances etc. The retail services include issue of drafts, pay orders/bank's cheques, commission/exchange, collection charges, service charges, handling charges, inspection charges and even attestation charges. There are utility services like lockers, depository services, ATMs, credit and debit cards, Internet banking, tele-banking, mobile-banking and web-banking.

The present chapter attempts to study the behaviour of interest and non-interest income of scheduled commercial banks and the variability of each source of income.

Review of Literature

Economic forces have led to financial innovations that have increased competition in the financial markets. As such, the traditional business of banking is on the declining trend at global level. The present scenario has encouraged banks to diversify into new activities that bring higher returns. It was conventionally believed that expansion of bank's activities into new fee-based products and services reduced earnings volatility, via diversification efforts. However, non-interest income co-exists with, rather replaces interest income from the intermediation activities that continue to remain bank's core financial services function [De Young & Rice, 2003]. Some studies indicate that fee-based income stabilizes profitability [Saunders & Walters, 1994]. Some studies concluded that non-interest income stabilizes total income [De Young & Roland, 1999]. In a study on the variability of interest and non-interest income and their correlation for the banking system of EU countries for the years 1994-98, it was found that the increased importance of non-interest income did, for most, but not all categories of banks, stabilize profits [Smith, 2003].

The average non-interest income ratio of banks has risen around the world over the past decade, yet for Australian banks it has declined [Hawtrey, 2003]. New sources of non-interest income like e-delivery channels are affecting non-interest income and ultimately total income [Ramachandran, 2005]. Non-interest income is a crucial segment for the stability of total bank income; banks should follow new strategies in the era of competition [Uppal & Rimpi, 2004]. Another study reveals that while net interest income of the banks rose by 12 pc over the period 1992-97, the bigger in bank earnings came from non-interest income. Non-interest income grew by 34 pc in this period-nearly three times fast as interest income [Aggeler and Feldman, 1998]. A Study on European Banks found that EU banks have not been able to increase their non-interest income sufficiently to offset the falling interest income and gave some suggestions to improve it and concluded that relation of non-interest income to profitability tends to be positive [Davis and Tuori, 2002].

Some major changes in the banks business occurred during the financial reforms period, affecting the profitability [Mahadevan, 2002]. It was found that credit card lending specialization gave higher and more volatile returns than achieved by banks with conventional product mixes [Nash, 1993]. One working paper studied the income structure of European Banking Sector with the help of time series and cross-sectional analysis and concluded that non-interest income has increased but does not fully offset the reduction in the interest margin and non-interest income is much more volatile than interest income [Rosie & Wood, 2002].

From the above review it may be concluded that non-interest income is playing a significant role in stabilizing the total income. The banks, who do not diversify their fee-based activities, will not survive in the emerging competition.

Objectives

- To study and analyze the trends in interest and non-interest income in the post second banking sector reforms period.
- To examine the trends in major components of interest and non-interest income.
- To analyze the stability of bank's income through interest and non-interest income.
- To suggest some strategies to increase non-interest income in all bank groups.

Methodology

The present chapter is concerned with Indian banking industry. In the present chapter, co-operative banks and RRBs are excluded. In this study, the return possibilities of a bank have been measured with the help of arithmetic mean and risk is measured with the help of standard deviation. In order to measure the volatility of interest and non-interest income of commercial banks, the co-efficient of variations is made use of. C.V. is used for measuring the fluctuations around the trend. The study covers the second half of the post-reform period from 1997 to 2005. This period has been chosen taking into consideration the following factors:

a. The process of interest rate liberalization, which started in 1991, was fully liberalized (especially that of deposit rates) in 1997.

b. New private sector banks started entering the banking business in a big way from 1997.

c. Also, the second phase of liberalization in the banking sector started in 1997-98 following the recommendations of the Second Narasimham Committee Report in 1998.

Interest income comprises of:

• Interest/discount on advances/bills
• Interest on investments
• Interest on balances with RBI

We have studied only first and second components of interest income, which constitutes a large portion of interest income.

Non-interest income comprises of:

• Commission, exchange and brokerage
• Profit on sale of investments
• Profit on revaluation of interest
• Profit/loss on sale of land, building and other assets
• Profit on exchange transactions
• Miscellaneous

In the present paper only first two and last two components are analyzed because these contribute significantly towards non-interest income.

A. Pattern of Interest and Non-Interest Income in the Second Post Banking Sector Reforms

All Scheduled Commercial Banks: An analysis of the interest and non-interest income of scheduled commercial banks since 1997-98 indicates that interest income has fallen from 85.89 pc of total income in 1997-98 to 81.99 pc in 2004-05. On the other hand, non-interest income was in the range of 14.11 pc and 18.01 pc during the study period.

It is due to financial liberalization that banks have diversified their fee-based activities. This is welcome trend as it may reduce the risks arising out of the sole dependency on interest as the source of income. This trend/change also indicates that banks have started to move towards globalization process.

Components of Interest Income: The components of interest income of all scheduled commercial banks shows that average interest income on advances/discount and interest on investments increased to a large extent. In 1997-98 it was only 96.26 pc (average) and became 203.36 pc in 2004-05. Similarly, average ratio of non-interest income to total income increased from 74.92 pc to 164.26 pc during the study period. Major part of these investments is in the form of government securities.

Components of Non-Interest Income: It is seen that income earned in the form of commission/exchange/brokerage, which formed the major chunk on non-interest income of banks increased from 16.28 pc to 37.02 pc from 1997-98 to 2004-05. Another important component of non-interest income gaining greater importance in recent years is the income from profits on sale of investments, which increased from 2.39 pc to 21.49 pc during the study period.

B. Bank Group-Wise Analysis: Bank group-wise interest income and non-interest income shows that in the case of public sector banks, income from interest as a percentage of total income is maximum i.e. an average of 85.40 pc whereas non-interest income ratio is 14.61 pc. The private sector and foreign banks are also seen to be increasingly dependent upon non-interest income sources of income. Non-interest income of new private sector banks forms an average of 20.18 pc and in the case of foreign banks it forms 24.32 pc of their total income.

C. Bank-wise Analysis: Bank-wise frequency distribution on non-interest income as a percentage of total income in 2005 shows that in respect of 23 banks, non-interest income as a percentage of total income falls in the range of 15 to 20 pc and for 18 banks in the range of 20 to 25 pc. In the case of six banks, their share of non-interest income from the total income falls in the range of 1 to 10 pc. 13 bank's income is greater than 30 pc, and among these 13 banks, one is from old private sector banks and 12 banks falls in the category of foreign banks (Table 10.1).

Table 10.1: Bank Group-Wise Frequency Distribution of Non-Interest Income of All Scheduled Commercial Banks (As Percentage of Total Income)

(per cent)

Range of Change	PSBs	OPSBs	NPSBs	FBS	All SCBs
Less than 0	-	-	-	1**	1
Up to 0	-	-	1*	-	1
1 to 10	1	-	-	5	6
10 to 15	9	4	-	4	17
15 to 20	14	6	2	1	23
20 to 25	4	6	1	6	18
25 to 30	-	4	4	2	10
More than 30	-	1	-	12	13
Total	28	21	8	31	88

Note: *Yes Bank, **Bank International Indonesia

D. Bank Group-wise Variations: Bank-wise frequency distribution of variations in percentage of non-interest income to total income in 2005 over the year 1997 depicts that in respect of 24 banks, non-interest income share from total income has declined. The 8 banks whose non-interest income as a percentage of total income declined by more than 10 pc in 2005 over the year 1997, belonged to the old private sector banks and 4 banks to foreign banks (Table 10.2).

Non-interest income as a percentage of total income in 2005 over the year 1997 has increased in the case of 53 banks and declined in respect of 12 banks.

Return, Risk and Stability of Income Sources
A. Return and Risk of Income Sources: All Scheduled Commercial Banks: Net interest income is considered by taking

the difference between interest income and interest expenses. The average return on interest income as a proportion of total assets of all scheduled commercial banks declined gradually from 3.17 pc in 1997-98 to 2.5 per cent in 2004-05. The decline could be attributed to the liberalization measures adopted in the banking sector and the resultant competition among banks. This could also be due to the soft interest rate regime followed in recent years (Table 10.3).

Table 10.2: Bank Group-Wise Frequency Distribution of Variation in Non-Interest Income to Total Income of All Scheduled Commercial Banks in 2005 over the Year 1997

(per cent)

Range of Change	PSBs	OPSBs	NPSBs	FBS	All SCBs
More than -20	-	-	-	3	3
-20 to -10	-	4	-	1	5
-10 to 0	1	8	3	4	16
0 to 10	26	3	3	6	38
10 to 20	-	1	-	4	5
More than 20	-	2	-	8	10
Total	27	18	6	26	77

Due to the declining return possibilities from interest income sources, banks are switching over to non-interest income earning sources. It can be seen that the average return on non-interest income has increased from 1.69 pc in 1997 to 2.41 pc in 2005. The standard deviation of net income declined from 1.86 pc 1997 to 0.73 pc in 2005, indicating that net interest income has slowly stabilized over the period 1997 and through 2005. The co-efficient of variation in net interest income as a percentage of total assets and non-interest income as percentage of total assets declined from 58.68 pc and 56.62 pc in 1997 respectively to 29.20 pc and 42.74 pc in 2005 respectively.

Bank Group-Wise Analysis: Bank GroupWise analysis indicates that the average interest income of all bank groups has declined over the years from 1997-98 to 2004-05 (Table 10.4).

Table 10.3: Return and Risk of Income Sources of All Scheduled Commercial Banks

Statistics		Net Interest Income % Total Assets	Non-Interest Income % Total Assets
1997-98	Average	3.17	1.69
	S.D.	1.86	0.94
	C.V.	58.68	56.62
1998-99	Average	2.62	1.65
	S.D.	0.69	0.57
	C.V.	25.65	30.04
1999-00	Average	2.69	1.81
	S.D.	0.85	0.56
	C.V.	31.60	40.52
2000-01	Average	2.73	1.53
	S.D.	0.66	0.62
	C.V.	24.18	30.04
2001-02	Average	2.33	1.91
	S.D.	0.88	0.74
	C.V.	37.77	38.74
2002-03	Average	2.63	2.28
	S.D.	0.67	0.45
	C.V.	25.48	19.74
2003-04	Average	2.74	2.04
	S.D.	0.63	0.11
	C.V.	22.99	5.39
2004-05	Average	2.50	2.41
	S.D.	0.73	1.03
	C.V.	29.2	42.74

The maximum decline is observed in foreign banks and new private sector banks 9.5 pc to 5.73 pc and 10 pc to 5.31 pc in 2005 respectively. As regards the proportion of non-interest income to total assets, it increased in public sector banks and foreign banks from 1.1 pc to 1.37 pc and 2.2 pc to 2.64 pc in 2005 respectively.

As regards the stability of interest income, it is evident from the measure of standard deviation and co-efficient pf variations (C.V.) that the non-interest income of foreign banks is more volatile as compared to the income of other bank groups.

B. Stability of Income Sources: In case of interest income, C.V. is the highest in new private sector banks, which indicates that interest income of this group is more instable whereas maximum stability is found in old private sector banks (C.V. 29.04 pc) and foreign banks (C.V. 30.99 pc). Non-interest income is more stable in public sector banks and as compared to other groups (33.48 pc C.V), maximum instability is found in foreign banks (C.V. 82.71 pc) and in case of new private sector banks it was 80.80 pc in terms of C.V (Table 10.5).

Table 10.4: Bank Group-Wise Return and Risk of Income Sources

(per cent)

Statistics		PSBs		OPSBs		NPSBs		FBs	
		II/TA	NII/TA	II/TA	NII/TA	II/TA	NII/TA	II/TA	NII/TA
1997-98	A	9.6	1.1	10.70	1.40	9.5	1.90	10.00	2.20
	S.D.	0.8	0.2	0.90	0.60	2.5	0.90	3.80	2.20
	C.V.	8.0	19.5	8.10	39.90	26.30	47.50	38.20	100.00
1998-99	A	9.1	1.2	10.20	1.60	9.10	2.30	10.50	3.20
	S.D.	0.7	0.2	1.10	0.70	1.60	0.80	3.00	2.70
	C.V.	7.5	20.0	10.40	42.20	17.00	34.30	28.00	85.40
1999-00	A	9.15	1.33	9.76	1.63	7.90	1.58	7.78	2.57
	S.D.	0.45	0.34	1.03	0.54	1.20	0.43	4.23	2.16
	C.V.	4.92	25.56	10.55	33.13	15.19	27.22	54.37	84.05
2000-01	A	9.12	1.23	9.76	1.27	8.71	1.39	8.16	2.40
	S.D.	0.49	0.29	0.79	0.43	1.31	0.24	2.37	2.47
	C.V.	5.37	23.58	8.09	33.86	15.04	17.27	29.04	102.92
2001-02	A	8.87	1.79	9.25	2.40	7.92	2.31	8.27	2.67
	S.D.	0.49	0.40	0.68	0.86	2.63	1.17	2.33	2.40
	C.V.	5.52	22.35	7.35	35.83	33.21	50.65	28.17	89.89
2002-03	A	8.44	2.01	8.51	2.26	8.03	2.44	7.65	2.56
	S.D.	0.52	0.43	0.64	0.72	1.27	0.68	2.99	2.61
	C.V.	6.16	21.39	7.52	31.86	15.82	27.87	39.08	101.95
2003-04	A	7.97	2.01	8.50	1.99	7.86	1.42	6.40	2.84
	S.D.	1.61	0.39	0.77	0.84	1.46	1.08	1.93	3.44
	C.V.	20.20	19.40	9.06	42.21	18.58	76.06	30.16	121.13
2004-05	A	7.00	1.37	7.17	0.89	5.73	1.33	5.31	2.64
	S.D.	0.41	0.38	0.88	0.60	1.50	0.64	1.74	3.21
	C.V.	5.86	22.74	12.27	67.42	26.18	48.12	32.77	121.59

A = Average

Emerging Issues

Major issues, arising from the above analysis, which need to be considered immediately include:

1. Decreasing share of interest income from total income due to fall in interest rate.

2. Tremendous increase in non-interest income from total income.
3. Profitability of public sector banks declined due to decrease in the interest income but not the increase in non-interest income as is the case of new private sector and foreign banks
4. How to increase the non-interest income in the regime of falling rate of interest to maintain the profitability in the liberalized and globalized environment?

Table 10.5: Volatility of Interest & Non-Interest Income (C.V. in per cent) Bank Group-Wise Comparison

Bank Group	C.V. (Interest Income)	C.V. (Non-Interest Income)
PSBs	37.33	33.48
OPSBs	29.04	43.53
NPSBs	73.03	80.80
FBs	30.99	82.71

Strategies to Enhance the Share of Non-Interest Income

The banks should reduce the CEB fee to attract more and more customers. As this source comprises various services and help to earn fee, they should make some attractive policies, which may help to convince the customers to avail these services. Side by side, they can earn more from other activities except CEB, if banks can attract customers to avail of other services of the banks also.

If policies of the banks are poor, it may be harmful for them because rather to earn more it may result in losses. For earning more from CEB and other sources of non-interest income, following strategies are suggested separately for possible sources of non-interest income.

Remittance of Funds

Banks are suitable for remittance of funds from one place to another through mass instruments like mail transfer, telegraphic transfer, bank drafts, travelers cheques, EFT etc. Customers are required to pay a small fee for utilizing these facilities that become a source of income for banks either in the form of commission or any other fee based source.

Strategies for Increasing Remittance of Business

1. Offer excellent customer service at the counter.
2. Appoint tellers in heavy draft business branches for receiving cash and issuing draft. They may be authorized even to sign the drafts.
3. Open branches in areas having large inflow and outflow of drafts.
4. Create links with educational institutions to accept their bank drafts for fee collection, donation etc. also with hotels, restaurants and supermarkets to motivate them to accept their traveler cheques.
5. Issue and encash bank drafts electronically to save the time and to provide accurate results.
6. Extend business hours in the selected branches for issuing drafts.
7. Obtain standing instructions from customers to issue mail transfers/drafts.
8. Charge higher commission for issuing drafts of larger amounts.
9. Give concessions to the customers who give sizeable draft business during the year.

Safe Custody of Valuables

Banks, well equipped with safe and strong rooms, can accept valuables for safe custody and can earn good income.

Strategies to enhance this business

1. Increase rent for lockers – as this will never affect their customers because the rich class mostly uses lockers and normally utility of money is less for the rich class.
2. To use the locker facilities, banks should fix minimum amount required to be maintained in their saving accounts.
3. Banks should advertise the availability of lockers and safe custodies.
4. Banks should provide concession for the lockers and safe custody to those customers who have more deposits in their

current accounts.
5. Lockers can be installed at extension counters also.
6. Vacant lockers to be hired out and rent to be collected within the stipulated date.
7. Facility of nominations, use of lockers in the off time should be given to the customers.

Merchant Banking

It offers tremendous scope for the banks to increase their income, as today it is a core competitive activity.

Strategies to enhance this business

1. Recruit persons having requisite skills.
2. Identify existing staff and give specialized training on merchant banking.
3. Merchant banking cells can be introduced in related branches having potential for such business.
4. More power to zonal offices/regional offices to decide the fee to be charged for holding merchant banking activities.

Letter of Credit and Letter of Guarantee

Banks lend their creditworthiness to the beneficiaries by issuing LCs and LGs to get commission from the customers for these facilities. These facilities add to risk exposure, so should be extended to effective/potential parties only.

Strategies to enhance this business

1. Loan powers for granting the above facilities should be enhanced at the field level. It will fulfill the needs of the borrowers and will save time.
2. Banks should offer PLR to borrowers to give the banks substantial non-fund business.
3. A bank officer may be posted at commercial centers to exclusively canvass non-fund business.
4. Banks should create links with intermediaries to convince/attract the potential customers to use LCs and LGs.

Bill Business

Collection of outstation and inward cheques and bills is an

important source of non-interest income. If a bank purchases the bills, it can earn a substantial non-interest income.

Strategies to enhance this business

1. Branches, situated in mandi areas (business centers), should approach the traders to canvass bill business.
2. Bill and cheque clearance should be made timely, safely and immediately.
3. Regular follow-up is required with their sister branches for quick realization of the procedures of the bills.
4. In this e-age, banks should obtain standing instructions from the customers for bill/cheque clearance electronically.

Government Business

When a bank holds government business, it gets commission from the RBI. Government business may be in the form of payment of pensions, collection of taxes etc. Many banks are providing such facilities and getting a substantial income from this source.

Strategies to enhance this business

1. List of retiring persons should be collected from government departments/railways/defense departments and efforts should be made to canvass their pension accounts. Respect the old citizens and provide some attractive facilities. Recently some state governments are providing old-age pension - banks should try to offer such facilities to get commission.
2. The efficient staff should be appointed to provide facilities of pension.
3. The banks should create their links with various departments to get income from this source.

Exchange Transactions

Remuneration from exchange transaction is a major source of non-interest income for the banks. It depends upon the quantum of export profits which further depends on the export and import turnover along with the exchange rates of the currencies.

Strategies to enhance this business

1. Branches should encourage the exporter/importers to book

forward contracts, which gives ample scope for improving this income.

2. All the potential officers should be given permission for trading in currencies.
3. Bank should create links with DGFT/ECGC to ascertain the list of importers/exporters in their command areas.
4. Bank should give concession to the importers/exporters in issuing drafts, LCs, LGs etc. and some other concessions.

Issuance of Stock Investment

Stock investment is the non-negotiable instrument used to subscribe capital in the primary capital market. The investor deposits the application money in his demat account and gets interest till the allotment of shares/debentures by the company.

Strategies to enhance this business

1. Banks should distribute the pamphlets to popularize the demat services.
2. Banks should give concession in the fee charged for the demat services to potential customers.
3. Banks should create links with the stock brokers to procure the list of investors who can directly contact the banks to sell their stock invest.
4. More branches should be added to provide facilities of these services.

Miscellaneous Non-Interest Income

1. Service charges for credit cards should be increased at least to the bearable extent.
2. Banks should collect ledger-folio charges from current account holders.
3. Banks should collect processing fee for fresh/enhancement/renewal of limits.
4. Banks should collect incidental charges for not maintaining minimum balance in current and saving accounts.
5. Banks should charge nominal fee for the collection of local cheques to at least cover the cost incurred for clearing

business.

Conclusion and Policy Implications

- Interest income as a percentage of total income of all scheduled commercial banks declined, whereas non-interest income as a percentage of total interest income increased during the study period.
- The maximum increase in non-interest income as a percentage of total income was found in new private sector banks and foreign banks.
- Interest on advances and interest on investment increased for all scheduled commercial banks and is a major component of interest income.
- Commission, exchange and brokerage contributed maximum to non-interest income during the study period.
- Net interest income as a percentage of total assets declined where as non-interest income as a percentage of total assets increased from 1.69 pc to 2.41 pc during the study period.

Due to the liberalization of the banking sector, the resultant competition and soft interest rates prevalent in the Indian economy, risks arising out of the traditional banking business are on an increase. The non-interest income activities of banks are also on the increase in recent years. This has helped to stabilize the total income of banks. Increase in the non-interest income, as a source of funds for banks, would be greatly helpful in maintaining the financial soundness of banks.

11

Impact of Banking Sector Reforms

Introduction

The banking system in India has undergone significant change during the last 17 years. There have been new banks, new instruments, new windows, new opportunities and along with that new challenges. Prior to 1991, commercial banks in India were functioning in a highly regulated environment - there was insufficiency in the functioning of banks, and productivity and profitability was low. In consonance with the liberalization and privatizations wave sweeping across the world, the Government of India decided to review the banking policies in early 1990's. With this background in view the Narsimham Committee worked out the road map for banking sector reforms. The successful implementation its various recommendations has given a new dynamism to the banking sector since 1992.

The objective of the chapter is:

- To study and evaluate the banking sector reforms, and
- To explain the impact of these reforms on the productivity of various banks.

This chapter portrays how these banking sector reforms affected the banking industry in India and the challenges that they have to face after the implementation of these reforms.

Banking Sector Reforms

Although there is some debate whether the reforms of 1991 were a single point of departure for the reforms process with in India. There is no doubt that measures that were announced then, had a preformed impact.

Raja Raman; 1991: Industrial licensing was effectively dismantled and entrepreneurs were essentially free to set up any capacity, subject only to obtaining some minimum clearance.

However, there were few business houses and even they have very little capital - the only real constraint became the availability of finance from the DFIs. Manners in which banks and DFI were being regulated and industrial licensing combined with fix interest rate were the most important form of implicit "credit insurance" available to the financial system. The commercial banks were permitted to participate only in working capital finance. The reforms of 1990s permitted them entry in to project and other long term financing.

First Banking Sector Reforms: In 1991, the Government of India appointed a committee to examine the structure, organization and functions of the financial system under the chairmanship of Sh. M. Narsimham. Main recommendations of Committee-I were:

SLR and CRR: SLR should not be used for financing public sector. It should be used as was originally intended. It should be reduced to 25 per cent in a phased manner over five years. The Committee was also in favour of reduction in CRR.

High Interest Rates on SLR and CRR: The rate on SLR should get linked with market rates while the rate of interest on CRR should be broadly related to banks' average cost of funds.

Phasing out of Directed Credit: Directed credit should be phased out. Priority sector should be refined to include marginal farmers, small-scale industries, and other weaker sections. Credit target for these sectors should be fixed at 10 percent.

Deregulate Interest Rates: The Committee favoured deregulation of interest rates. Recommendations regarding interest rates were:

1. Deregulate interest rates to reflect emerging market conditions.
2. Link deregulation with reduction in fiscal deficits.
3. Ceiling of bank deposit rates be increased with progressive reduction of SLR.

Capital Adequacy Norms: The Committee recommended Bank of International Standards (BIS) norms in a phased manner. A capital adequacy ratio of 4 per cent should be achieved by banks and financial institutions by March 1993 and BIS norm of 8 per cent also. Profitable banks may raise funds from the capital market immediately.

Uniform Accounting Standards: The banks and financial institutions should adopt uniform accounting standards. This is particularly related to income recognition and provisioning against doubtful debts.

Income Recognition

- In banks and financial institutions which are following accrual system of accounting, no income should be recognized in respect of non-performing assets (NPA's).
- An asset would be considered NPA if interest on such assets in part is due for a period exceeding 180 days on balance sheet. This time of 180 days was shifted to 90 days and at present the time limit is 90 days.

Provisioning

- The Committee recommended that the assets should be classified into four categories - Standard, sub-standard doubtful and loss assets.
- There should be a provision of 10 per cent in case of sub-standard assets and 100 per cent of security shortfall in case of doubtful debts. In case of secured debts in doubtful category, a further provision of 20 to 50 per cent should be created. Loss assets should either be fully written off or surely 100 per cent should be created.

Transparency: The balance sheet of banks and financial institutions should be made as per international standards. Full disclosure should be made as per international accounting standards committee norms and this may be done after implementing the income reorganization and provisioning norms.

Assets Reconstruction Funds

- The need is that as ARF with special power be set up which should take off bad and doubtful debt from the balance sheets at a discount.
- Special tribunals as recommended by Tiwari Committee be set up to speed up process.

Structure of Banking System

- Regarding structure of the banking system it should be evolved towards a pattern of 3 or 4 large banks (including SBI) which could be international in character.
- Local banks, (including RRBs) should be confined to rural areas concentrating on agriculture finance.

Branch Licensing

- Branch licensing should be abolished.
- Opening and closing of branches (other than rural) be left to the judgment of individual banks.
- Government should be more liberal with opening of branches of foreign banks. They should be treated at par with domestic banks.
- The internal organization be left to the bank. In case of national banks a three tier of structure of head office, zonal office and branch is favoured. Local banks may be two-tiered and SBI may have four tiers.

Computerisation

The Committee favoured Rangarajan Committee on computerisation. Computer is indispensable for enhanced customer services.

Control

The Committee favoured less regulated and administrated system. Duality of control over banks between RBI and Banking Division of Ministry of Finance should be ended and only the RBI should have control. The supervisory function of banks and financial institutions be given to an autonomous body working under the RBI.

Development Financial Institutions (DFIs)

- They should be granted operational flexibility, measure of competition and adequate internal autonomy.
- A system of syndication or participation in lending should be evolved.
- Commercial banks should be encouraged to provide term finance and core working capital.

- Cross equity holding amongst DFIs should be done away with.
- Regulatory framework should be developed for new institutions like merchant banks, mutual funds, leasing companies, venture capital companies etc. A new agency under RBI should be set up for this purpose.
- Prudential guidelines relating to capital adequacy, debt equity ratio, income recognition, provisioning, sound financial and accounting policies, disclosures and valuation of assets should be laid down.

Implementation of the Reforms: In a phased manner, most of the recommendations have been implemented or are being implemented. Up to April 1998, following aspects of implementation can be noticed.

Interest Rate Deregulation: The interest rates for deposits and loans almost completely deregulated in April 1998. All advances from RBI are now linked to bank rate. Lending rates of banks have been linked with prime lending rate (PLR) from 1997.

Reduction in CRR and SLR: CRR has been brought down to 10 per cent and SLR to 25 per cent. Interest rates on CRR increased in 4 per cent w.e.f. Oct.1997. The CRR rates has further been reduced to 8.00 per cent in May 2008.

Directed Credit: Number of credit categories and interest rate subsidy element has been substantially reduced. Weaker sections under priority sectors have been redefined. Return on loans to SSI units has been increased.

Capital Adequacy Ratio: All banks are required to attain capital to risk weighted assets ratios as per BIS norms by March 1997. All banks except (UCO & Indian Bank) have attained the norms.

Prudential Accounting Standards: Prudential accounting norms regarding income recognition, assets classification and provisioning have been implemented in a phased manner and further strengthened. Banks has been instructed to classify advances into four categories w.e.f. 1998-99.

Private and Foreign Banks: Setting up of new private sector banks and entry of foreign banks have been allowed. Numbers of private sector banks have come up.

Branch Licensing: Branch licensing has been liberalized. Domestic banks satisfying capital adequacy requirements are free to start branches.

Banks Access to Capital Markets: Nationalized banks have been permitted to raise capital from the markets up to 49 per cent of their authorized capital.

Customer Services: Baking Ombudsman Scheme 1995 has been introduced for speedy settlements of customer disputes.

Recommendation of Narsimham Committee –II (1998)

The Report of the Second Committee was submitted in April 1998. The important recommendations are:

Capital Adequacy and Recapitalization of Banks: Out of the 27 public sector banks, 26 PSBs achieved the minimum capital to risk asset ratio of 9 per cent by March 2000. Of this, 22 PSBs had CRAR exceeding 10 per cent. To enable the PSBs to operate in a more competitive manner, the Government adopted a policy of providing autonomous status to these banks, subject to certain benchmarks. As on end March 1999, 17 PSBs became eligible for autonomous status.

Need for a Strong Banking System: The Committee wants a strong banking and financial system in view of implementing the Capital Account Convertibility (CAC). CAC will result in large inflows and outflows of foreign exchange. Only a strong system can cope with it.

Merger of Strong Banks: The Committee has recommended merger of strong banks with strong banks. However it is against merger of weak banks with strong banks.

Narrow Banking for Weak Banks: Narrow banking may be tried to rehabilitate weak banks. This means, these banks should narrow down their operations for safer securities.

Confine Area of Local Banks: Small local banks should confine to state or districts to serve local trade, industry and agriculture.

Review Government's Role in Public Sector Banks: The Government's role in public sector bank has become an instrument of micro management. This is not good for their autonomy and flexibility.

Review Legislations: It has recommended review of various legislations like RBI Act, Banking Companies Regulation Act, Nationalization Act, SBI Act, Sick Industrial Undertaking and Banking Book Evidence Act etc.

Speeding up Computerisation: There is an urgent need of computerisation, especially in large banks.

Review Personnel Policies: There should be a review of recruitment procedures, training and remuneration policies of public sector banks.

Asset Liability Management: In February 1999, the Reserve Bank advised banks to put in place the proper system of asset liability management and risk management.

Money Market Rates: The Committee has favoured a money market reference rate on the pattern of LIBOR i.e. London Inter Bank Overnight Rate to enable issuing of floating rate instruments and deposits.

Impact of Banking Sector Reforms in India

Banks have been accorded greater discretion in sources and utilization of resources, albeit in an increasingly competitive environment. The outreach of the Indian banking system has increased in terms of expansion of branches/ATMs in the post reform period and assets/liabilities of banks have grown consistently at a high rate. The financial performance of banks also improved as reflected in their increased profitability. Net profit to assets ratio improved from 0.49 per cent in 2000-01 to 1.13 per cent in 2003-04. Although it subsequently declined to 0.88 per cent in 2005-06, it was still significantly higher than that in the early 1990s. Banks have been successful in weathering the impact of upturn in interest rate cycle through increasing diversification of their income, though banks had to incur huge expenditure on upgradation of information technology and the restructuring of the workforce on public sector banks helped them cut down the staff cost and increase business per employee.

Another welcome development has been the sharp reduction in non-performing loans (NPLs). Both gross and net NPLs started to decline in absolute term since 2002-03. Gross NPLs as percentage of gross advances, which were above 15 percent in early 1990s, are now less than 3 per cent.

The distinct improvement in asset quality may be attributed to the improved recovery climate underpinned by strong macroeconomic performance as well as several institutional measure initiated by the Reserve Bank and the Government, such as debt recovery tribunals, Lok Adalats, scheme of corporate debt restructuring in 2001 and the SARFAESI Act in 2002.

Since 1995-96, the banking sector, on the whole, has been consistently maintaining CRAR well above the minimum stipulated norms. The overall CRAR for scheduled commercial banks increased from 8.7 percent as on end March 1996 to 12.3 percent as on end march 2006. The number of banks not complying with the minimum CRAR also declined from 13 as on end march 1996 to just 2 by end March 2006. Improved capital position stemmed largely from the improvement in profitability and raising of capital from the market, though in the initial stages the Government had to provide funds to recapitalise weak public sector banks.

Even though public sector banks continue to dominate the Indian banking system, accounting for nearly three-fourths of the total assets and incomes, the increasing competition in the banking system has led to the failing share of public sector banks, and increasing share of new private sector banks, which were set up around mid 1990s. It is clear that we are at the beginning of this new phase in the Indian banking with competitive pressure, both domestic and external, catching up and the need for banks to continuously reassess and reposition themselves in their business plans.

Future Challenges for Indian Banks

Few broad challenges facing the Indian banking industry are -

threats of risks from globalization; implementation of Basel II; improvement of risk management systems, implementation of new accounting standards; enhancement of transparency and disclosures, enhancement of customer services, and application of technology.

Globalization: A Challenge as Well as an Opportunity: The wave of globalization sweeping across the world has thrown up several opportunities accompanied by concomitant risks. Integration of domestic market with international market has been facilitated by tremendous advancement in information technology. There is a growing realization that the ability of countries to conduct business across national borders and ability to cope with the possible downside risks would depend, inter alia, on the soundness of the financial system. This has necessitated convergence of prudential norms with international best practices as well consistent refinement of technological and institutional framework in the financial sector through a non disruptive and consultative process.

Opening up of the Capital Account: The Committee on fuller capital account capital account convertibility (Chairman Sh. S.S. Tarapore) observed that under a full capital account convertibility regime, the banking system would be exposed to greater market volatility and this necessitated enhancing the risk management capabilities in the banking system in view of liquidity risk, interest rate risk, currency risk, counter party risk and country risk that arise from international capital flows. The potential dangers associated with the proliferation of derivatives instruments, credit derivatives and interest rate derivatives also need to be recognized in the regulatory and supervisory system. The issues relating to cross-border supervision of financial intermediaries in the context of greater capital flow are just emerging and need to be addressed.

Basel II Implementation

The Reserve Bank of India and commercial banks have been preparing to implement Basel II, and it has been decided to allow banks some more time in adhering to new norms. As against the deadline of March 31, 2007 for compliance with Basel II, it was decided in October 2006 that foreign banks operating in India and Indian banks having presence outside India would migrate to the standardized approach for credit risk and the basic indicator approach for operational risk under Basel II with effect from March 31, 2008, while all other scheduled commercial banks are required to migrate to Basel II by March 31, 2009.

It is widely acknowledged that implementation of Basel II poses significant challenge to both the banks and the regulators. Basel II implementation may also bring opportunities for banks, in terms of refinement of risk management systems and improvement in capital efficiency. The transition from Basel I to II essentially involves a move from capital adequacy to capital efficiency.

The reliance on the market to assess the risk of banks would lead to increased focus on transparency and market disclosure, critical information describing the risk profile, capital structure and capital adequacy, besides, making banks more accountable and responsive. These processes would enable banks to strike the right balance between risks and rewards and to improve the access to markets, improvement in market discipline and also call for greater coordination between banks and regulators.

Improvement Risk Management System

Basel II has brought into focus the need for more comprehensive risk management framework to deal with various risks, including credit and market risk and their interlinkage. Banks in India are also moving from individual silo system to an enterprise wide risk management system. While the first milestone would be the risk integration across the entity, the next step would entail risk aggregation across the risks. Banks would therefore be required to allocate significant resources towards this endeavor. In India, the risk-based approach to supervision is also serving as a catalyst to banks migration to the integrated risks management system. However, taking into account the diversity in the Indian banking system, stabilizing the RBS as an effective supervisory mechanism is another challenge.

Corporate Governance

To a large extant, many risk management failures reflect a breakdown in corporate governance whish arises due to poor management of conflicts of interest and inadequate understanding of key banking risks, and poor board oversight of the mechanism for risk management and internal audit. Corporate governance is therefore, the foundation for effective risk management in banks and thus the foundation for a sound financial system. The choice that banks make when they establish their risk management and corporate governance systems have important ramifications for the financial stability. Banks may have to cultivate a good governance culture building in appropriate checks and balance in their operations. There are four important forms of oversight that should be included in the organizational structure of any bank in order to ensure appropriate checks and balances, namely (i) oversight by the board of directors of supervisory board (ii) oversight by individuals not involved in the day to day running of various business areas; (iii) direct line supervision of different business areas and (iv) independent risk management, compliance and audit functions. In addition, it is important that key personnel are fit and proper for their job.

Implementation of New Accounting Standards

Derivatives activity in banks has been increasing at a brisk pace. While the risk management framework for derivatives trading which is a relatively new area for Indian banks is an essential pre-requisite, the absence of clear accounting guidelines in this area is a matter of significant concern. The Accounting Standard Board of the Institute of Charted Accountants of India is considering issue of accounting standards in respect of financial instruments. These will be the Indian parallel to International Accounting Standards 32 and 39. The proposed accounting standards would have considerable significance for financial entities, and could, therefore, have implications for financial institutions. The formal introduction of these accounting standards by the ICAI is likely to take some time in view of the process involved. In the meanwhile, the RBI is considering the need for banks and financial institutions to adopt the broad underlined principles of IAS 39. Since this is likely to give rise to some regulatory prudential issues, all relevant aspects are being comprehensively examined. The proposal in this regard would, as is normal, be discussed with the market participants before introduction. Adoption and implementation of these principles are likely to pose a great challenge to both the banks and The Reserve Bank of India.

Supervision of Financial Conglomerates

The financial landscape is increasingly witnessing entry of some bigger banks into other financial segments like merchant banking, insurance etc. Emergence of several new players with diversified presence across major segments makes it imperative for supervision to be spread across various segments of the financial sector. In this direction, an inter-regulatory working group was constituted with members from RBI, SEBI and IRDA. The framework proposed by the group is complementary to the existing regulatory structure wherein the individual entities are regulated by the respective regulators and identified financial conglomerates are subjected to focus regulatory oversight through a mechanism of inter regulatory exchange of information. As a first step in this direction, an inter agency working group on financial conglomerates (FC) comprising the above three supervisory bodies identified 23 FC's and a pilot process for obtaining information from these conglomerates has been initiated. The complexity involved in the supervision of financial conglomerates are a challenge not only to RBI but also to other regulatory agencies which need to have a close and continued coordination on an ongoing basis.

In view of the increased focus on empowering supervisors to undertake consolidated supervision of bank groups and the core principles for effective banking supervision issued by Basel Committee, new norms on banking supervision have been introduced as an initial step with consolidated accounting and their quantitative methods to facilitate consolidated supervision. The components of consolidated supervision includes consolidated financial statements intended for public disclosures, consolidated prudential reports intended for supervisory assessment of risk and application of certain prudential regulations on group basis.

Application of Advanced Technology
The role of technology in increasing new business models and processes, in initiating competitive advantages, in enhancing quality of risk management system in banks and in revolutionizing the distribution channel cannot be overemphasized. A case in point is the implementation of core banking solution by some banks by assessing its scalability or adaptability to meet Basel II requirements.

Financial Inclusions
While banks are focusing on methodologies of meeting the increasing demands placed on them, there are legitimate concerns with regards to banking practices that tend to exclude rather than attract vast sections of population, in particulars pensioners, self employed and those employed in unorganised sectors. While commercial considerations are no doubt important, banks have been bestowed with several privileges, especially of seeking public deposits, on a highly leveraged basis and consequently they should be obliged to provide banking services to all segments of the population on an equitable basis. Further experience has shown that consumers' interests are at times not accorded full priority and their grievances are not properly attended. It is in this context that Governor, Reserve Bank of India had mentioned in the Annual Policy Statement 2005-06 that RBI will initiate to encourage greater degree of financial inclusions in the country by setting up mechanisms for ensuring fair treatment of consumers,

and effective redressal of customer grievances.

Conclusion

With increasing level of globalization of the Indian banking industry, evolution of universal banks and building of financial services, competition of banking industry will intensify further. The banking industry has a potential and ability to rise to the occasion as demonstrated by the rapid pace of automation, which already had a profound impact on raising the standard of banking services. The financial strength of individual banks, which are major participants in the financial system, is the first line of defence again financial risks. Strong capital positions and balance sheets place banks in a better position to deal with and absorb the economic shocks.

12

Privatisation of Indian Public Sector Banks

Introduction

The Indian financial sector underwent a radical change during the nineties. From the relatively closed and regulated environment in which agents had to operate earlier, the sector was opened up as part of the efficiency enhancing structural policies to bring about high sustainable long-term growth of the economy. The banking sector was also not an exception to this rule. New measures were undertaken to induce efficiency and competition into the system. Accounting and provisioning norms, capital adequacy rules, proper risk management measures, partial privatization of public sector banks etc. were brought in place and entry regulations were also relaxed. It is believed that private ownership helps to improve efficiency and performance. Accordingly, the Indian government started diluting its equity in public sector banks from early 1999 in a phased manner. Table 12.1 indicates the share of the Government /RBI and the private sector.

Has the partial privatization of Indian banks really helped to improve their efficiency and financial performance? International evidence on impact of privatization is mixed, though the issue is important in the Indian context.

A healthy banking system, besides undertaking the role of financial intermediation also serves as an engine of growth. Indian banking is presently in the process of completing one full circle. Initially, it was in private sector and moved to public sector with the nationalization of banks in two stages in 1969 and 1980. Now with the proposal to reduce government's stake in banks from 51 pc to 33 pc, public sector banks are again moving in the direction of partial privatization.

**Table 12.1: Details of Public Equities by Public Sector Banks
(Amount in Rs. crore)**

Bank	Date of Issue	Equity Capital Before Public Issue	Equity Capital After Public Issue	Post-Issue Shareholding	
				GOI/RBI	Others
State Bank of India	December, . 1993	200.00	474.00	314.34 (66.3)	159.67 (43.7)
State Bank of Bikaner & Jaipur	November, 1997	36.40	50.00	37.50 (75.0)	12.50 (25.0)
Oriental Bank of Commerce	October, 1994	128.00	192.54	128.00 (66.5)	64.54 (33.5)
Dena Bank	December, 1996	146.82	206.82	146.82 (71.0)	60.00 (29.0)
Bank of Baroda	December, 1996	196.00	296.00	196.00 (66.2)	100.00 (33.8)
Bank of India	February, 1997	489.00	639.00	489.00 (77.0)	150.00 (23.0)
Corporation Bank	October, 1997	82.00	120.00	82.00 (68.3)	38.00 (31.7)
State Bank of Travancore	January, 1998	35.00	50.00	37.50 (75.0)	12.50 (25.0)
Syndicate Bank	October, 1999	346.97	471.97	346.97 (73.5)	125.00 (26.5)
Vijaya Bank	December, 2000	259.24	359.24	259.24 (72.2)	100.00 (27.8)
Andhra Bank	February, 2001	347.95	450.00	299.98 (66.6)	150.03 (33.4)
Indian Overseas Bank	February, 2001	333.60	444.80	333.60 (75.0)	112.20 (25.0)

Source: Report on Trends and Progress of Banking in India, 2001-02.

Different Phases of Indian Banking

- Foundation Phase: 1950-1969
- Expansion Phase: 1970-1984
- Consolidation Phase: 1985-1990
- Reforms, Liberalization & Privatization Phase: 1991 till date.

There is substantial difference in the competitive strengths of various bank groups, which affects their performance and efficiency (Table 12.2).

The present chapter is significant due to many reasons and mainly because enhancing efficiency and performance of the public sector banks has been the key objective of the reforms in many countries, including India. Talwar (2001) states that "as a part of financial sector reforms and with a view to giving the public sector banks operational flexibility and functional autonomy, partial privatization has been authorized as a first step, enabling them to dilute the stake of the Indian government to 51 pc." Anderson (1997) considers a firm as privatized when more than one-third of the shares stand transferred to the private investors. The RBI (2003) stated "dilution of government stake could provide greater operational freedom to banks which could have a positive impact on their efficiency".

Table 12.2: Competitive Strengths of Banks

Banks	Strengths	Weaknesses
Public Sector Banks	• Branch Network • Market Coverage • Product Differentiation • Technology Adoption • Knowledge of Local Environment • Expertise in Niche Segment	• Poor HRD • Delayed Decision Making • Poor Risk Management Systems
Old Private Sector Banks	• Knowledge of Local Environment • Personalized Services • Reasonable Branch Network • Technology Absorption	• Poor Risk Management • Poor Product Innovations • Poor Branch Network
New Private Sector Banks & Foreign Banks	• Automation & Latest Technology • Product Innovations • Strong Risk Management • Speedy Decision Making • Personalized Services • Progressive HRD Policies • Expertise in niche Market	• Small Branch Network • Poor Coverage

Literature Review

The development theories emphasize that government ownership helps channelise savings for long-term projects of strategic interest. The "political theorists" oppose this view and state that government ownership leads to misallocation of resources and inefficiencies of government enterprises and that there are political motives behind such public ownership. It has long been argued that privatization of firms make them efficient and perform better. Galal (1994), World Bank (1997) and La Porta and Lopez-de-Silances (1997) support the view that privatization helps to improve performance.

However, recent studies in transition economies, for example, by Carlin & Landesman (1997), Frydman (1998) and Jones an Mygrind (1999) found that post-privatization performance of the firms was poor. The RBI (2003) stated, "as regards the linkage between ownership and performance, international evidence suggests that ownership has limited impact on economic efficiency". Studies that support this position include those of Tulkens (1993), Altunbus, Evans & Molynenx (2000) and Denizer, Tarimcilar & Dinc (2000).

Against this background, Indian banking sector provides, particularly interesting setting to examine the impact of privatization on the banking. The banking sector in India comprises of domestic banks (privately-owned, partially privatized and fully public sector banks) as well as foreign banks. In the beginning, it was proposed to reduce the government stake in the public sector banks to 51 pc. Accordingly, 12 out of 27 public sector banks have issued capital reducing the government share, though it still continues to be 66 pc at the minimum. The government is now considering a legislation that allows its stake to be reduced to 33 pc.

Objectives

- To study and analyze the impact of privatization on Indian Public Sector Banks.
- To compare the financial performance and efficiency of partially privatized Indian Public Sector Banks with fully government owned banks.
- To compare the financial performance and efficiency of partially privatized Indian Public Sector Banks with the banks already in the private sector.
- To highlight the challenges and opportunities available for partially privatized Indian Public Sector Banks.

Our analysis is related to only five out of 12 partially privatized banks. We have selected these five banks, which were partially privatized after 1997 from the 12 partially privatized Indian public sector banks. These are:

- State Bank of Travancore (SBT) – January, 1998
- Syndicate Bank – October, 1999
- Vijaya Bank – December, 2000
- Andhra Bank – February, 2001
- Indian Overseas Bank – February, 2001

Similarly, five fully government-owned and five fully privatized banks have been selected on the basis of business per employee in 2003-04.

Fully Government Owned Banks:

- Allahabad Bank
- Bank of Maharashtra
- Canara Bank
- Central Bank of India
- Punjab & Sindh Bank

Banks already in private sector:

- ICICI Bank
- HDFC Bank
- IndusInd Bank
- UTI Bank
- Bank of Punjab

Time period for the study is dived into two categories:

- Pre-privatized period – 4 years earlier than partial privatization
- Post-privatized period – later years till current financial year

Time period for the fully government owned and fully privatized banks is six years from 1999-2000 to 2004-05.

Conceptual Framework

We used the ratio analysis method to compare the financial performance and efficiency of the selected banks.

Financial Performance Ratios:

- Return on Assets (ROA)

- Establishment Expenditure as percentage of Total Expenditure (EE/TE)
- Spread as percentage of Working Funds (S/WFs)
- Net Non-Performing Assets as percentage of Net Advances (NPAs/NA)
- Credit as percentage of Deposits Ratio (C/D)
  Efficiency Ratios:
- Profits Per Employee (P/E)
- Deposits Per Employee (D/E)
- Credits Per Employee (C/E)

The data is calculated on the basis of various statistical tools like simple average, combined average, standard deviation and co-efficient of variations with the help of SPSS 10.00 version.

Analyzing Financial Performance and Efficiency of SBT: This bank comes under SBI and its associate bank group. The average financial performance from 1994-95 to 1997-98 i.e. pre-privatization period is quite poor when compared with post-privatization period that is 1998-99 to 2004-05. The average ROA ratio was only 0.45 pc in the pre-privatization period and it became almost double in post-privatization period i.e. 0.73 pc (Tables 12.3 (a) and 12.3 (b)).

Similarly, efficiency of the all the selected partially privatized public sector banks increased to a large extent in the post-privatized period. The average P/E was only 0.29 lakh, which further increased to 1.24 lakh during 1998-2005 (Table 12.3 (c)).

Table 12.3 (a): State Bank of Travancore

(percent)

Pre-Privatization Period					
Years	ROA	EE/TE	S/WFs	NPAs/NA	C/D
1994-95	0.32	16.30	2.63	7.20	65.27
1995-96	0.37	16.06	3.29	6.50	61.75
1996-97	0.47	16.83	3.18	8.82	56.61
1997-98	0.64	14.20	3.58	12.21	53.57
Average	0.45	15.85	3.17	8.68	59.30
S.D.	0.14	1.14	0.40	2.54	5.22
C.V.	31.11	7.19	12.62	29.26	8.80

Table 12.3 (b): State Bank of Travancore

(percent)

		Post-Privatization Period			
Years	ROA	EE/TE	S/WFs	NPAs/NA	C/D
1998-99	0.40	15.35	2.20	10.80	49.11
1999-00	0.53	17.20	2.27	8.58	50.39
2000-01	0.67	19.61	2.73	7.75	55.28
2001-02	0.73	15.67	2.57	5.77	55.24
2002-03	0.90	15.72	2.75	3.06	57.58
2003-04	1.02	16.12	2.85	1.39	56.45
2004-05	0.86	15.56	3.10	1.81	61.53
Average	0.73	16.46	2.64	5.60	55.08
S.D.	0.22	1.52	0.32	3.62	4.23
C.V.	30.14	9.23	12.12	64.64	7.68

Financial Performance and Efficiency of Syndicate Bank:
This bank was nationalized in 1969. The financial performance of
this bank in the five ratios ROA, EE/TE, S/WFs, NPAs/NA and
C/D, has shown excellent improvement in post-privatized period
e.g. in the pre-privatized period ROA was 0.40 pc and became
1.07 pc in the post-privatized period and C/D ratio increased to
52.57 pc from 42.40 pc [Tables 12.4 (a) and 12.4 (b)].

Table 12.3 (c): State Banks of Travancore

(per cent)

Pre-Privatization Period				Post-Privatization Period			
Years	P/E	D/E	C/E	Years	P/E	D/E	C/E
1994-95	0.17	37.63	24.56	1998-99	0.35	65.42	32.13
1995-96	0.20	42.19	26.05	1999-00	0.54	78.61	39.61
1996-97	0.31	49. 76	28.17	2000-01	0.85	95.08	52.56
1997-98	0.48	57.23	30.66	2001-02	1.06	110.90	61.26
Average	0.29	46.70	27.36	2002-03	1.51	132.66	76.39
S.D.	0.14	8.62	2.65	2003-04	2.16	164.25	92.72
C.V.	48.27	18.46	9.69	2004-05	2.21	204.03	125.54
				Average	1.24	121.56	68.60
				S.D.	0.74	49.26	32.57
				C.V.	59.68	40.52	47.40

Source: Performance Highlights of IBA (Various Issues)

Similarly, efficiency in terms of P/E, D/E & C/E increased to
a large extent in the post-privatization period for Syndicate Bank.

Profit per employee became 1.15 lakh in the post-privatized period from 0.33 lakh of pre-privatized period [Table 12.4 (c)].

Table 12.4 (a): Syndicate Bank

(percent)

Pre-Privatization Period				
Years	ROA	EE/TE	S/WFs	NPAs/NA	C/D
1995-96	0.12	28.15	3.20	9.80	42.44
1996-97	0.37	28.63	3.17	7.53	39.02
1997-98	0.41	27.50	2.85	5.78	41.39
1998-99	0.71	26.81	2.94	3.93	46.76
Average	0.40	27.77	3.04	6.76	42.40
S.D.	0.24	0.79	0.17	2.50	3.24
C.V.	60.00	2.84	5.59	36.98	7.64

Financial Performance and Efficiency of Vijaya Bank: This bank was nationalized in 1980. Its average financial performance is quite better and improved to a large extent in the post-privatized period. ROA was only 0.28 pc in the pre-privatized period and increased to 1.18 pc in the post-privatized period. Similarly, other financial performance ratios are also showed improved results in the post-privatization period [Tables 12.5 (a) and 12. 5 (b)].

Table 12.4 (b): Syndicate Bank

(percent)

Post-Privatization Period				
Years	ROA	EE/TE	S/WFs	NPAs/NA	C/D
1999-00	0.89	26.47	3.04	3.17	51.60
2000-01	0.91	31.05	3.87	4.05	52.27
2001-02	0.79	28.05	3.49	4.52	52.14
2002-03	1.31	28.08	3.51	4.29	53.18
2003-04	1.67	25.43	3.03	2.58	48.48
2004-05	0.82	24.53	3.25	1.59	57.74
Average	1.07	27.27	3.70	3.70	52.57
S.D.	0.35	2.53	0.32	1.14	3.00
C.V.	32.71	9.28	8.65	30.81	5.71

Table 12.4 (c): Syndicate Bank

(per cent)

Pre-Privatization Period				Post-Privatization Period			
Years	P/E	D/E	C/E	Years	P/E	D/E	C/E
1995-96	0.50	34.06	14.45	1999-00	0.66	68.41	35.30
1996-97	0.18	40.50	15.80	2000-01	0.81	81.71	42.71
1997-98	0.23	46.37	19.19	2001-02	0.98	111.65	58.21
1998-99	0.42	55.71	26.05	2002-03	1.30	120.46	64.06
Average	0.33	44.16	18.87	2003-04	1.62	159.22	77.20
S.D.	0.15	9.20	5.17	2004-05	1.53	186.42	107.63
C.V.	45.45	20.83	27.40	Average	1.15	121.31	64.18
				S.D.	0.39	45.03	26.03
				C.V.	33.91	37.12	40.56

Table 12.5 (a): Vijaya Bank

(per cent)

Pre-Privatization Period					
Years	ROA	EE/TE	S/WFs	NPAs/NA	C/D
1996-97	0.23	24.66	2.91	9.56	36.26
1997-98	0.23	23.10	2.76	7.56	39.25
1998-99	0.28	20.43	2.86	6.72	38.88
1999-00	0.38	21.61	3.03	6.62	40.88
Average	0.28	22.45	2.89	7.62	38.82
S.D.	0.01	1.83	0.11	1.36	1.91
C.V.	3.57	8.15	3.81	17.85	4.92

Table 12.5 (b): Vijaya Bank

(per cent)

Post-Privatization Period					
Years	ROA	EE/TE	S/WFs	NPAs/NA	C/D
2000-01	0.53	22.92	3.23	6.22	45.28
2001-02	0.81	19.16	3.01	6.02	42.21
2002-03	1.13	23.57	3.37	2.61	46.32
2003-04	1.91	16.14	3.48	0.91	52.56
2004-05	1.43	15.42	3.36	0.59	55.96
Average	1.18	19.44	3.39	3.27	48.47
S.D.	0.53	3.75	0.32	2.71	5.63
C.V.	44.91	19.29	9.44	82.87	11.61

Table 12.5 (c): Vijaya Bank

(per cent)

Pre-Privatization Period				Post-Privatization Period			
Years	P/E	D/E	C/E	Years	P/E	D/E	C/E
1996-97	0.13	47.85	17.35	2000-01	0.53	93.77	42.46
1997-98	0.16	58.11	22.81	2001-02	1.11	124.13	52.39
1998-99	0.22	68.53	26.64	2002-03	1.76	145.18	67.32
1999-00	0.36	80.93	32.73	2003-04	3.73	180.79	95.02
Average	0.22	63.86	24.88	2004-05	3.48	222.94	124.76
S.D.	0.10	14.17	6.47	Average	2.12	163.36	76.39
C.V.	45.45	22.19	26.00	S.D.	1.42	53.03	33.53
				C.V.	66.98	32.46	43.89

Table 12.5 (c) shows that efficiency in terms of P/E, D/E & C/E has witnessed an excellent improvement in their performance and efficiency in the post-privatized period.

Financial Performance and Efficiency of Andhra Bank: This bank was nationalized in 1980. The financial performance changed in the post-privatized period. Among the selected five financial ratios, the average ROA was only 0.73 pc during 1997-98 to 2000-01 and became 1.48 pc during 2001-02 to 2004-05. Similarly, the average of S/WFs, C/D ratio also improved in the post-privatized period [Tables 12.6 (a) and 12.6 (b)].

In the same way, Table 12.6 (c) shows that the average efficiency increased in the post-privatized period. The average ratio of P/E, D/E & C/E was 0.72, 91.34 and 37.22 lakh respectively in the pre-privatized period, which increased to 3.05, 172.96 and 99.05 lakh in the post-privatized period showing almost 2 to 3 times increase.

Financial Performance and Efficiency of Indian Overseas Bank: This bank was nationalized in 1969 and comes under the group of public sector banks since that year. The financial performance and efficiency ratios are much better in the post-privatized period. The average ROA from 1997-98 to 2000-01 was only 0.32 pc and became double i.e. 0.63 pc during 2001-02 to 2004-05 (Tables 12.7 (a) and 12.7 (b)).

Table 12.6 (a): Andhra Bank

(per cent)

	Pre-Privatization Period				
Years	ROA	EE/TE	S/WFs	NPAs/NA	C/D
1997-98	0.78	20.72	3.37	2.92	41.62
1998-99	0.78	21.60	2.91	4.26	43.34
1999-00	0.76	16.81	2.68	3.47	38.66
2000-01	0.59	17.30	2.45	2.95	40.58
Average	0.73	19.11	2.85	3.40	41.05
S.D.	-1.59	2.41	0.39	0.63	1.96
C.V.	217.81	12.61	13.68	18.53	4.77

Table 12.6 (b): Andhra Bank

(per cent)

	Post-Privatization Period				
Years	ROA	EE/TE	S/WFs	NPAs/NA	C/D
2001-02	0.97	14.63	2.75	2.45	52.34
2002-03	1.63	16.56	3.05	1.79	54.66
2003-04	1.72	16.77	3.37	0.93	56.17
2004-05	1.59	21.52	3.27	0.28	63.58
Average	1.48	17.36	3.11	1.35	56.84
S.D.	0.34	2.93	0.27	0.96	4.85
C.V.	22.97	16.88	6.68	71.11	8.53

Table 12.6 (c): Andhra Bank

(per cent)

Pre-Privatization Period				Post-Privatization Period			
Years	P/E	D/E	C/E	Years	P/E	D/E	C/E
1997-98	0.50	53.03	22.07	2001-02	1.58	144.32	75.54
1998-99	0.61	70.67	30.63	2002-03	3.10	162.13	88.62
1999-00	0.82	98.73	38.17	2003-04	3.54	175.19	98.40
2000-01	0.95	142.92	58.00	2004-05	3.97	210.18	133.63
Average	0.72	91.34	37.22	Average	3.05	172.96	99.05
S.D.	0.20	39.20	15.34	S.D.	1.04	27.86	24.88
C.V.	27.78	42.92	41.21	C.V.	34.10	16.11	25.12

Similarly, Table 12.7 (c) shows that efficiency in terms of P/E increased almost more than 6 times in the post-privatized period as compared to that in the pre-privatized period.

A Comparative Average Financial Performance and

Efficiency in the Post-Privatized Period: Among the five selected partially privatized banks, Vijaya Bank has shown excellent financial performance in terms of ROA, while in case of Spread ratio, Syndicate Bank has shown excellent performance after their partial privatization.

Table 12.7 (a): Indian Overseas Bank

(per cent)

Pre-Privatization Period				
Years	ROA	EE/TE	S/WFs	NPAs/NA	C/D
1997-98	0.50	19.63	2.31	6.26	44.84
1998-99	0.23	20.39	2.31	7.30	46.17
1999-00	0.15	21.15	2.46	7.65	47.59
2000-01	0.38	22.46	2.91	7.02	47.77
Average	0.32	20.91	2.50	7.06	46.59
S.D.	0.16	1.21	0.28	0.59	1.37
C.V.	50.00	5.79	11.20	8.36	2.94

Table 12.7 (b): Indian Overseas Bank

(per cent)

Post-Privatization Period				
Years	ROA	EE/TE	S/WFs	NPAs/NA	C/D
2001-02	0.65	19.00	2.74	6.32	47.67
2002-03	0.01	20.05	2.97	5.23	47.54
2003-04	1.08	18.92	3.38	2.85	48.92
2004-05	0.28	21.41	3.65	1.27	56.97
Average	0.63	19.85	3.19	3.92	50.28
S.D.	0.64	1.16	0.41	2.28	4.51
C.V.	1.02	5.84	12.85	58.16	8.97

Table 12.7 (c): Indian Overseas Bank

(per cent)

Pre-Privatization Period				Post-Privatization Period			
Years	P/E	D/E	C/E	Years	P/E	D/E	C/E
1997-98	0.40	68.19	30.58	2001-02	0.93	128.91	61.45
1998-99	0.20	77.34	35.71	2002-03	1.70	151.04	71.81
1999-00	0.14	86.19	41.02	2003-04	2.10	170.14	83.24
2000-01	0.45	105.05	50.35	2004-05	2.66	181.57	103.44
Average	0.30	84.19	39.42	Average	1.85	157.92	79.99
S.D.	0.15	15.73	8.44	S.D.	0.73	23.08	17.99
C.V.	50.00	18.68	21.41	C.V.	39.46	14.61	22.49

In the efficiency parameters, Vijaya Bank and Andhra Bank are at the top among the five selected banks.

Overall, we may conclude that partially privatized banks have performed better in the post-privatized period in the different financial performance and efficiency ratios.

A Comparative Analysis

The partially privatized public sector banks show a significant positive difference in their financial performance and efficiency when compared with the fully public sector banks. Interestingly, the financial performance and efficiency in the pre-privatized period was very low but on the other hand, the financial performance of banks already in the private sector is not significantly different from those public sector banks that are partially privatized. With the partial privatization of banks showing encouraging results, this study suggests that the current proposal of the government of India to bring down its stake further to 33 pc of the capital may help in improving the performance and efficiency of these banks [Table 12.8 (a)].

It can be seen from Table 12.8 (b), the ROA of the partially privatized public sector banks is almost three times more i.e. 1.02 pc in the post-privatized period than that of pre-privatized period which is only 0.44 pc. It is even more than the fully public sector banks i.e. 0.55 pc but it is marginally higher in new private sector banks i.e. 1.03 pc.

The EE/TE (which refers to salary, wages and other benefits to the staff) is not significantly different, possibly because even though these banks introduces VRS, still they have to carry the burden of VRS-related expenditure in either form.

This fact is also borne out by the efficiency ratios. All the three efficiency ratios of the partially privatized public sector banks presented in Table 12.8 (b) are significantly greater than that of the fully public sector banks. The superior efficiency and performance can be attributed due to 'marketization shock', which seems to have geared the staff of the partially privatized public sector banks for better productivity.

The S/WFs ratio is also better in partially privatized public sector banks in the post-privatized period i.e. 3.17 pc where it was only 2.89 pc in pre-privatized period where it is 2.94 pc in fully public sector banks and important point to note here is that it is much higher than that of new private sector banks having 2.11 pc only.

Table 12.8 (a): Statistical Analysis of Financial Performance

(per cent)

Ratios	Partially Privatized-PSBs in Pre-Privatized Period	Partially Privatized-PSBs in Post-Privatized Period	Fully Govt. Owned Banks (FPSBs)	Fully Privatized Banks (NPSBs)
ROA	0.44	1.02	0.55	1.03
EE/TE	21.22	20.24	19.68	4.82
S/WFs	2.89	3.17	2.94	2.11
NPAs/NA	6.70	3.80	6.26	2.95
C/D	45.63	52.76	46.76	60.09

Source: Derived from the Earlier Tables

Table 12.8 (b): Statistical Analysis of Efficiency

(per cent)

Ratios	Partially Privatized-PSBs in Pre-Privatized Period	Partially Privatized-PSBs in Post-Privatized Period	Fully Govt. Owned Banks (FPSBs)	Fully Privatized Banks (NPSBs)
P/E	0.37	1.76	0.96	7.90
D/E	44.03	154.50	134.27	597.51
C/E	19.70	75.52	63.45	355.62

Source: Derived from the Earlier Tables

In terms of quality of loans and advances, though on an average, the ratio of NPAs/NA is lower in the partially privatized public sector banks as compared to that of fully public sector banks i.e. 6.26 pc. The NPAs are a drag on the entire banking system in India and this is mainly due to the legacy of social control over the banks. There is no quick fix for this. The RBI and the Government of India have undertaken several measures to address the NPA problem, e.g. change in the legislative framework (like the recently introduced Securitization and Reconstruction of Financial Assets and Enforcement of Security Interest Act 2002 and the establishment of Assets Reconstruction Company), to provide inputs to the recovery efforts by the banks. However, it may take time before such measures yield significant results.

The C/D ratio, which shows the quality of the credit and deposits, is much better in post-privatized period than pre-privatized period. On an average, it was only 45.63 pc in the pre-privatized period and became 52.76 pc. It is also higher than the fully public sector banks (46.46 pc).

The Table also shows that new private sector banks don't have significant difference in ROA as compared to the partially privatized public sector banks. This seems to suggest that partially privatized public sector banks are fast catching up with the new private sector banks in terms of profitability. On the other hand, there is a difference in other financial performance ratios. But in terms of efficiency, new private sector banks show significant difference from the partially privatized public sector banks. P/E is 7.9 lakh in new private sector banks whereas it is only 1.76 lakh in partially privatized public sector banks. Similarly, D/E and C/E are excellently higher in the new private sector banks as compared to partially privatized public sector banks.

Challenges before Partially Privatized Public Sector Banks

- Strong opposition by the bank employee unions
- Poor HRD policies, especially VRS
- Heavy cost requirement for the adoption of latest technology
- Rationalization of branches
- Weak branches
- Risk management
- Severe competition with new private sector banks and foreign banks

- Difficulties in withdrawing facilities enjoyed by the banks when they were fully government owned banks
- Cultural transformation – work culture
- Structural issues
- Portfolio management
- Research and Development
- Business re-engineering i.e. CRM, social-banking, relationship marketing, universalization of business etc.
- Information technology
- Capital restructuring

Opportunities

As the new private sector banks and foreign banks have tremendous opportunities, the partially privatized public sector banks also have same opportunities but with some limitations.

- Introduction of innovative products/services
- New phase of VRS with effective HRM policies
- Transformation of work culture
- To explore the feasibility and viability of e-banking especially in the rural and semi-urban areas
- Strong CRM and relationship marketing
- Global competition with opening up branches in the foreign countries
- Improved efficiency to win the customers
- Proper and efficient risk management
- Separate research & development department in each bank.

Conclusion

This chapter analyzes the impact of privatization in the banks' performance and efficiency using the ratios given in the performance highlights of IBA. We calculated simple and combined mean, standard deviation and co-efficient of variations and compared the financial performance and efficiency of partially privatized public sector banks in the pre-privatized and post-privatized period, partially privatized public sector banks with fully public sector banks and than with the banks already in the private sector (new private sector banks).

Partially privatized public sector banks have performed better in the post-privatized period as compared to their performance in the pre-privatized period. Similarly, they performed better in terms of financial performance and efficiency than the fully public sector banks. The partially privatized public sector banks also seem to be catching up with the new private sector banks, although some efficiency ratios are better in the new private sector banks. Overall, going by the results of this study, partially privatized public sector banks continue to show improved financial performance and efficiency in the years after privatization. On the basis of this chapter, we suggest that Government of India should continue to dilute their stake in public sector banks, inspite of the fact that there an opposition by the bank employees and politicians.

Areas of Future Research

- Feasibility and viability of e-banking in the rural and semi-urban areas by partially privatized public sector banks.
- Perceptions and expectations of rural bank customer regarding banks.
- New Credit facilities in rural areas in the changing environment.
- Comparative cost analysis of rural, semi-urban, urban branches and metropolitan cities.
- To study and analyze the portfolio investment of partially privatized public sector banks.
- IT and transformation in the banks.

13

Recent Policies to Reform Indian Banking

With a view to enhance the efficiency of banking system and to align it with international practices, the Reserve Bank of India (RBI), in consultation with the Government of India, has taken a series of policy measures in recent years.

Transparency and Disclosures

The stability of a financial system stands enhanced when institutions and markets function on the basis of informed decisions. Adequate disclosure of information should act as a deterrent to excessive risk-taking and minimise adverse selection problems. Market discipline is believed to increase with interest from outside stakeholders such as depositors, creditors and investors. It is desirable to have greater transparency to ensure that the stakeholders have adequate information to be able to independently monitor the institutions. RBI has issued detailed guidelines, from time to time, to ensure banks' compliance with the accounting standards issued by the Institute of Chartered Accountants of India (ICAI).

The Joint Parliamentary Committee (JPC) on Stock Market Scam and Matters Relating Thereto in its report released in December 2002 had recommended that the comments made by the RBI in the inspection reports should be published in the annual reports of the banks along with the financial results to ensure greater transparency.

In November 2004, RBI decided that strictures or directions on the basis of inspection reports or other adverse findings be placed in the public domain. Also, disclosure of the details of the levy of penalty on a bank in public domain will be in the interests of the investors and depositors.

Best international practices require meaningful and appropriate disclosures of banks' exposures to risk and their strategy towards managing the risk. With a view to ensuring that the banks make meaningful disclosures of their derivative portfolios, a minimum framework for disclosures by banks on their risk exposures in derivatives was advised by the RBI to the commercial banks. The guidelines included both qualitative and quantitative aspects to provide a clear picture of the exposure to risks in derivatives, risk management systems, objectives and policies.

Board for Financial Supervision

The Board for Financial Supervision (BFS) was constituted by the RBI in November 1994 to exercise *undivided attention to supervision*. The BFS provides direction on a continuing basis on supervisory policies including governance issues and supervisory practices. It also provides direction on supervisory actions in specific cases. The BFS ensures an integrated approach to supervision of commercial banks, financial institutions, non-banking financial companies, urban co-operatives banks and primary dealers.

The BFS met reviews the monitoring with regard to frauds in banks and financial institutions (FIs) and house-keeping in public sector banks, including reconciliation of entries in inter-branch accounts, inter-bank accounts (also *Nostro* accounts) and balancing of the books of accounts. The Board also reviews the monitoring of all India financial institutions and non-banking financial companies. Besides, delineating the course of action to be pursued in respect of institution-specific supervisory concerns, the Board provides guidance on several regulatory and supervisory policy matters. The Board also reviews the financial performance of primary dealers (PDs) system as a whole and provided guidance. It also assesses the monitoring done with regard to the performance of urban co-operative banks and district central co-operative banks.

Monitoring of Frauds

With a view to reducing the incidence of frauds, the RBI advised banks in October 2002 to look into the existing mechanism for vigilance management in their institutions and remove the loopholes, if any, with regard to fixing of staff accountability and completion of staff side action in all fraud cases within the prescribed time limit, which would act as a deterrent. Banks were also urged to bring to the notice of the RBI large value frauds and the actions initiated in this regard.

A Technical Paper on Bank Frauds covering various aspects such as nature of frauds, present arrangement for follow-up of frauds, international legal framework relating to frauds, possible further measures with regard to legal and organisational perspectives was prepared by the RBI and placed in the Board for Financial Supervision (BFS) meeting held on April 8, 2004. The Technical Paper recommended the constitution of a separate Cell to monitor frauds not only in commercial banks but also in financial institutions, local area banks, urban co-operative banks and non-banking finance companies. As the proposal was accepted by the BFS, a separate Fraud Monitoring Cell (FrMC) was constituted on June 1, 2004 under the overall administrative control of the RBI's Department of Banking Supervision.

Ownership and Governance of Banks

Banks are special for several reasons. They accept and deploy large amount of uncollateralised public funds and leverage such funds through credit creation. Banks also administer the payment mechanism. Accordingly, ownership and governance of banks assume special significance. Legal prescriptions relating to ownership and governance laid down in the Banking Regulation Act, 1949 have, therefore, been supplemented by regulatory prescriptions issued by the RBI from time to time. The existing legal framework and significant current practices cover the following aspects.

* Composition of Boards of Directors.

- Guidelines on corporate governance.
- Guidelines for acknowledgement of transfer/allotment of shares in private sector banks issued as on February 3, 2004.
- Foreign investment in the banking sector.

The RBI, in consultation with the Government of India, laid down a comprehensive policy framework for ownership and governance in private sector banks on February 28, 2005. The broad principles underlying the framework ensure the following.

- Ultimate ownership and control is well diversified.
- Important shareholders are *fit and proper* (as per the guidelines of February 3, 2004 on acknowledgement for allotment and transfer of shares).
- Directors and CEO are 'fit and proper' and observe sound corporate governance principles.
- Private sector banks maintain minimum capital (initially Rs. 200 crore, with a commitment to increase to Rs. 300 crore within three years)/net worth (Rs. 300 crore at all times) for optimal operations and for systemic stability.
- Policy and processes are transparent and fair.

In order to attain a well-diversified ownership structure, it is to be ensured that no single entity or a group of related entities has shareholding or control, directly or indirectly, in excess of 10 per cent of the paid-up capital of a private sector bank. Where any existing shareholding by any individual entity/group of related entities is in excess of 10 per cent, the bank will be required to indicate a time table for reduction of holding to the permissible level. Any bank having shareholding in excess of 5 per cent in any other bank in India will be required to indicate a time bound plan for reduction of such holding to the permissible limit of 5 per cent. The parent of any foreign bank having presence in India having shareholding directly or indirectly through any other entity in the banking group in excess of 5 per cent in any other bank in India will be similarly required to indicate a time bound plan for reduction of such holding to 5 per cent. In the case of restructuring of problem/weak banks or in the interest of consolidation in the banking sector, the RBI could permit a higher level of shareholding, including by a bank.

Payment of Dividends

In an endeavour to further liberalise the norms of such payments, the RBI granted general permission to banks to declare dividends for the accounting year ended March 31, 2005 onwards, which comply with (a) CRAR of at least 9 per cent for preceding two completed years and the accounting year for which it proposes to declare dividend and (b) net NPA of less than 7 per cent.

In case any bank does not meet the above CRAR norm, but has a CRAR of at least 9 per cent for the accounting year for which it proposes to declare dividend, it would be eligible to declare dividend, provided its net NPA ratio is less than 5 per cent. The bank should comply with the provisions of Sections 15 and 17 of the Banking Regulation Act, 1949 and the prevailing regulations/guidelines issued by the RBI, including creating adequate provisions for impairment of assets and staff retirement benefits, transfer of profits to Statutory Reserves. The proposed dividend should be payable out of the current year's profit and the RBI should not have placed any explicit restrictions on the bank for declaration of dividends.

It has also been stipulated that the dividend payout ratio [percentage of 'dividend payable in a year' (excluding dividend tax) to 'net profit during the year'] shall not exceed 40 per cent. In case the profit for the relevant period includes any extraordinary profits/income, the payout ratio shall be computed after excluding such extraordinary items for reckoning compliance with the prudential payout ratio. The financial statements pertaining to the financial year for which the bank is declaring a dividend should be free of any qualifications by the statutory auditors, which have an adverse bearing on the profit during that year. In case of any qualification to that effect, the net profit should be suitably adjusted while computing the dividend payout ratio.

Managerial Autonomy for Public Sector Banks

Competition among the commercial banks has increased with the entry of private sector banks, permission to foreign banks to open up to 12 branches a year with effect from 1998-99 and relaxation of various restrictions on public sector banks which, *inter alia,* are now allowed to access the capital market to raise funds. This will dilute the shareholding of the Government.

In the changed scenario, public sector banks will have to improve their efficiency. The highly regulated and directed banking system is now transforming itself into one characterised by openness, competition and prudence. This development conforms to the liberalisation and globalisation needs of the Indian economy.

The Government of India issued a managerial autonomy package for the public sector banks on February 22, 2005 with a view to providing them a level playing field with the private sector banks in India. Under the new framework, the Boards of public sector banks would enjoy more freedom to carry out their functions efficiently without any impediment. The functions, however, have to be in sync with the extant statutory requirements, government policy prescription and regulatory guidelines issued by the RBI from time to time. The revised guidelines allow the following to public sector banks.

- Pursue new lines of business.
- Make suitable acquisitions of companies or businesses.
- Close/merge unviable branches.
- Open overseas offices.
- Set up subsidiaries.
- Exit a line of business.

Similarly, these banks have been allowed to decide human resource issues, including staffing pattern, recruitment, placement, transfer, training, promotions and pensions as well as visits to foreign countries to interact with investors, depositors and other stakeholders. Besides, the Boards of Directors of stronger banks would have additional autonomy for framing their own human resource (HR) policies. Prescription of standards for categorisation of branches, based on volume of business and other relevant factors, have been left to the banks to decide. Public sector banks have been permitted to lay down policy of accountability and responsibility of bank officials.

Mergers and Amalgamation of Banks

In pursuance of the recommendations of the Joint Parliamentary Committee (2002), the RBI had constituted a Working Group to evolve guidelines for voluntary mergers involving banking companies. Subsequently, guidelines for merger/amalgamation of private sector banks were issued on May 11, 2005 covering details of the process of merger proposal, determination of swap ratios, disclosures, and norms for buying/selling of shares by the promoters before and during the process of merger.

The guidelines on merger and amalgamation, *inter alia,* stipulate the following.

- The draft scheme of amalgamation be approved individually by two-thirds of the total strength of the total members of Board of Directors of each of the two banking companies.
- The members of the Boards of Directors who approve the draft scheme of amalgamation are required to be signatories of the Deed of Covenants as recommended by the Ganguly Working Group on Corporate Governance.
- The draft scheme of amalgamation be approved by shareholders of each banking company by a resolution passed by a majority in number representing two-thirds in value of shareholders, present in person or by proxy at a meeting called for the purpose.

- The swap ratio be determined by independent valuers having required competence and experience; the Board should indicate whether such swap ratio is fair and proper.
- The value to be paid by the respective banking company to the dissenting shareholders in respect of the shares held by them is to be determined by the RBI.
- The shareholding pattern and composition of the Board of the amalgamating banking company after the amalgamation are to be in conformity with the RBI's guidelines.
- Where an NBFC is proposed to be amalgamated into a banking company in terms of Sections 391 to 394 of the Companies Act, 1956, the banking company is required to obtain the approval of the RBI before the scheme of amalgamation is submitted to the High Court for approval.

While the guidelines deal with the merger proposals between two banking companies or between a banking company and a non-banking financial company, the principles underlying the guidelines would also be applicable as appropriate to public sector banks. Where an NBFC is proposed to be amalgamated with a banking company, the Board should also examine whether:

- the NBFC has violated/is likely to violate any of the RBI/Securities and Exchange Board of India (SEBI) norms and if so, ensure that these norms are complied with before the scheme of amalgamation is approved;
- the NBFC has complied with the Know Your Customer (KYC) norms for all the accounts, which will become accounts of the banking company after amalgamation; and
- the NBFC has availed of credit facilities from banks/FIs and if so, whether the loan agreements mandate the NBFC to seek consent of the bank/FI concerned for the proposed merger/amalgamation.

In the case of regional rural banks (RRBs), sponsor banks are being encouraged to amalgamate the RRBs sponsored by them at the State level. The Government of India (Ministry of

Finance), after consultation with NABARD, the concerned State Governments and the Sponsor banks, issued nine notifications on September 12, 2005 under Section 23-A of the Regional Rural Banks Act, 1976 providing for amalgamation of 28 RRBs into nine new RRBs sponsored by nine banks in six States, *viz.* Bihar, Gujarat, Karnataka, Maharashtra, Punjab and Uttar Pradesh. These amalgamations became effective from September 12, 2005.

Exposure Norms

The RBI has prescribed regulatory limits on banks' exposure to individual and group borrowers in India to avoid concentration of credit, and has advised banks to fix limits on their exposure to specific industries or sectors for ensuring better risk management. In addition, banks are also required to observe certain statutory and regulatory exposure limits in respect of advances against investments in shares, debentures and bonds. The exposure ceiling limits is fixed in relation to banks' capital funds. The applicable limit is 15 per cent of capital funds in the case of a single borrower and 40 per cent in the case of a group of borrowers. Credit exposure to borrowers belonging to a group may exceed the exposure norm of 40 per cent of the bank's capital funds by an additional 10 per cent (i.e. up to 50 per cent), provided the additional credit exposure is on account of extension of credit to infrastructure projects. Credit exposure to a single borrower may exceed the exposure norm of 15 per cent of bank's capital funds by an additional 5 per cent (i.e. up to 20 per cent) provided the additional credit exposure is on account of infrastructure. Banks, may in exceptional circumstances, with the approval of their Boards, consider enhancement of the exposure to a borrower up to a further 5 per cent of capital funds.

Investment of banks/FIs in equity shares and preference shares eligible for capital status, subordinated debt instruments, hybrid debt capital instruments and other instruments approved in the nature of capital, which are issued by other banks/FIs and are eligible for capital status for the investee bank/FI, should not exceed 10 per cent of the investing bank's capital funds. Banks/FIs should not acquire any fresh stake in a bank's equity shares, if by such acquisition, the investing bank's/FI's holding exceeds 5 per cent of the investee bank's equity capital.

In view of the growing need for putting in place proper risk management system for identification, assessment and containing risks involved in the banking business, and also with a view to sensitising the banks in this regard, the RBI has been issuing instructions/guidance notes on various risks for the benefit of banks. The position relating to risk management, reporting requirements and balance sheet disclosures in respect of real estate exposure of banks was reviewed and on June 29, 2005, the RBI issued a set of instructions for the guidance of banks. In terms of these guidelines, banks should have a Board mandated policy in respect of their real estate exposure. The policy may include exposure limits, collaterals to be considered, margins to be kept, sanctioning authority/level and sector to be financed, though the actual limits/margins may vary from bank to bank depending upon the individual bank's portfolio size, risk appetite and risk containing abilities. The policy should also include risk management system to be put in place for containing risks involved in this sector, including price risk and a monitoring mechanism to ensure that the policy stipulations are being followed by field level functionaries and that the exposure of banks to this sensitive sector is within the stipulated limits. Further, banks may disclose their gross exposure to the real estate sector as well as the details of the break-up as mentioned in direct and indirect exposure in real estate in their annual reports.

In order to encourage the flow of finance for venture capital, banks were advised that their investment in venture capital (including units of dedicated Venture Capital Funds meant for Information Technology) would be over and above the ceiling of 5 per cent of the banks' total outstanding advances (including Commercial Paper) as on March 31 of the previous year prescribed for the capital market.

The instruction that banks have to limit their commitment by way of unsecured guarantees was withdrawn to enable banks to formulate their own policies on unsecured exposures. With a view to ensuring uniformity in approach and implementation, 'unsecured exposure' was defined as an exposure where the realisable value of the security was not more than 10 per cent, *ab initio*, of the outstanding exposure.

New Capital Adequacy Framework (Basel II Norms)

Given the financial innovations and growing complexity of financial transactions, the Basel Committee on Banking Supervision released the New Capital Adequacy Framework (Basel II) on June 26, 2004 which is based on the following three pillars.

- Minimum capital requirements.
- Supervisory review.
- Market discipline.

The revised framework has been designed to provide options to banks and banking systems, for determining the capital requirements for credit risk, market risk and operational risk and enables banks/supervisors to select approaches that are most appropriate for their operations and financial markets. The revised framework is expected to promote adoption of stronger risk management practices in banks. Under Basel II, banks' capital requirements will be more closely aligned with the underlying risks in banks' balance sheets. One of the important features of the revised framework is the emphasis on operational risk

Operational risk is defined as the risk of loss resulting from inadequate or failed internal processes, people and systems or from external events. This definition includes legal risk, but excludes strategic and reputational risks. Operational risk differs from other banking risks in that it is typically not directly taken in return for an expected reward but is implicit in the ordinary course of corporate activity and has the potential to affect the risk management process. The Basel Committee identified the following seven types of operational risk events that have the potential to result in substantial losses.

- Internal fraud.
- External fraud.
- Employment practices and workplace safety.
- Clients, products and business practices.
- Damage to physical assets.
- Business disruption and system failures.
- Execution, delivery and process management.

The potential losses, in turn, vary according to the business line within the bank in which the event occurs.

Management of specific operational risks is not new. It has always been important for banks to try to prevent fraud, maintain the integrity of internal controls, reduce errors in transaction processing and so on. However, what is relatively new is the thrust on operational risk management as a comprehensive practice comparable to the management of credit risk and market risk. To manage operational risk, banks are gradually gearing to develop risk assessment techniques that are appropriate to the size and complexities of portfolios, their resources and data availability.

With a view to ensuring migration to Basel II in a non-disruptive manner given the complexities involved, a consultative approach is being followed. The RBI released draft guidelines for implementation of Basel II in India on February 15, 2005. In terms of the draft guidelines, banks are required to adopt standardised approach for credit risk and basic indicator approach for operational risk. The standardised duration method would continue to be applied to arrive at the capital charge for market risk. Banks would need the RBI's approval for migration to advanced approaches of risk measurement.

All scheduled commercial banks (except regional rural

banks), both at the solo level (global position) and the consolidated level, will be required to implement the revised capital adequacy framework with effect from March 31, 2007. With a view to ensuring smooth transition to the revised framework and providing opportunity to banks to streamline their systems and strategies, banks in India are required to commence a parallel run of the revised framework with effect from April 1, 2006.

Several measures have been undertaken by the RBI to prepare the banking system to make a smooth migration to Basle II. Following the amendment to the Banking Companies (Acquisition and Transfer of Undertakings) Act in 1994, several public sector banks (PSBs) have raised capital both in India and abroad through Global Depository Receipts (GDRs). Several PSBs have also raised subordinated debt through the private placement. There is a proposal to allow banks to raise subordinated debt from the capital market to augment their capital base by making suitable amendment to the Banking Regulation Act, 1949. Concurrently, a series of regulatory initiatives were taken by the RBI relevant for Basel II.

First, concerted efforts were made to ensure that the banks have suitable risk management framework oriented towards their requirements dictated by the size and complexity of business, risk philosophy, market perceptions and the expected level of capital.

Second, Risk Based Supervision (RBS) was introduced in 23 banks on a pilot basis.

Third, the RBI has been encouraging banks to formalise their Internal Capital Adequacy Assessment Programme (ICAAP) in alignment with their business plans and performance budgeting system.

Fourth, there has been a marked improvement in the area of disclosures, so as to have greater transparency in the financial position and risk profile of banks. Similarly, capacity building for ensuring the regulator's ability for identifying and permitting eligible banks to adopt Internal Ratings

Based/Advanced Measurement approaches was given due priority.

Investment Norms

With effect from September 2, 2004, banks were allowed to exceed the limit of 25 per cent of total investments limit under held to maturity (HTM) category provided that the excess comprises only SLR securities and the total SLR securities held in the HTM category are not more than 25 per cent of their demand and time liabilities (DTL). To facilitate this, banks were allowed to shift SLR securities to the HTM category once more during 2004-05 as a one-time measure. The non-SLR securities held as part of HTM would, however, remain in that category and no fresh non-SLR securities would be permitted to be included in the HTM category.

Banks are allowed to shift investments to/from HTM category with the approval of their Boards once a year. Similarly, banks could shift investments from *available for sale* category to *held for trading* category. Shifting of investments from *held for trading* category to *available for sale* category is allowed only under exceptional circumstances. Transfer of scrips from one category to another, under all circumstances, is to be done at the acquisition cost/book value/market value on the date of transfer, whichever is the least, and the depreciation, if any, on such transfers has to be fully provided for.

Securitisation of Standard Assets

With a view to ensuring healthy development of the securitisation market, the RBI issued draft guidelines on securitisation of standard assets on April 4, 2005 to banks, financial institutions and non-banking financial companies. The regulatory norms for capital adequacy, valuation, profit/loss on sale of assets, income recognition and provisioning for originators and service providers such as credit enhancers, liquidity support providers as also the accounting treatment for securitisation transactions and disclosure norms were laid down in the draft guidelines.

Under the proposed guidelines, for a transaction to be treated as securitisation, it must follow a two-stage process. In the first stage, there should be pooling and transferring of assets to a bankruptcy remote special purpose vehicle (SPV). In the second stage, repackaging and selling the security interests, representing claims on incoming cash flows from the pool of assets to the third party investors should be effected.

For enabling the transferred assets to be removed from the balance sheet of the seller in a securitisation structure, the isolation of assets or *true sale* from the seller or originator to the SPV would be an essential prerequisite. Therefore, an arm's length relationship between the originator/seller and the SPV has to be maintained. In case the transferred assets do not meet the true-sale criteria, the assets would be deemed to be an on-balance sheet asset of the seller who would be required to comply with all applicable accounting and prudential requirements in respect of those assets. The SPV would also be required to meet the criteria to enable originators to avail off-balance sheet treatment for the assets transferred by them to the SPV and also to enable the service providers and investors in the pass-through certificate (PTCs) to avail of the regulatory treatment for their respective exposures in a securitisation structure.

Further, in all cases of securitisation, the securities issued by the SPV should be independently rated by an external credit rating agency and such ratings are required to be updated at least semi-annually.

Management of NPAs by Banks

The enactment of the Securitisation, Reconstruction of Financial Assets and Enforcement of Security Interest (SARFAESI) Act, 2002 was an important landmark in the ongoing reforms in the financial sector. The Act enables the setting up of asset management companies, addressing the problem of non-performing assets (NPAs) of banks and financial institutions and enhancing creditor rights. The main provisions of the Act are as follows.

- A securitisation company or reconstruction company having own funds of not less than Rs. 2 crore or such other amount not exceeding 15 percent of total financial assets acquired or to be acquired as specified by the RBI can commence business after obtaining a certificate of registration, subject to fulfilling certain conditions and complying with the prudential norms set by the RBI.
- The securitisation or reconstruction company may acquire assets of any bank or financial institution by issuing a debenture or bond or any other security for consideration agreed upon between such company and the bank or the financial institution.
- Notice of acquisition of a financial asset may be sent by bank or financial institution to an obligor. The obligor on receipt of such notice will make payment to the securitisation company concerned.
- A securitisation company may raise funds from qualified institutional buyers by formulating schemes for acquiring financial assets.
- In the event of non-realisation of financial assets, qualified institutional buyers of a securitisation company holding not less than 75 per cent of the total value of securities issued by such company are entitled to call for a meeting of all institutional buyers and the resolution passed in such a meeting is binding on the company.
- A securitisation or a reconstruction company may provide for the proper management of the business of the borrower, sale or lease of a part or whole of the business of borrower, settlement of dues payable by the borrower and taking possession of secured assets within the framework of guidelines framed by the RBI.
- Other functions of the securitisation company include acting as an agent for any bank or financial institution for

the purpose of recovery of their dues.

- Secured creditor is entitled to enforce any security interest created in its favour without the intervention of the court or tribunal.
- In case of non-performing debts, the secured creditor is entitled to serve a notice to the borrower to discharge his liabilities within 60 days.
- In case of failure to discharge the liabilities in the stipulated period, the secured creditor is entitled to take possession of secured assets, take over the management of secured assets and to appoint any person to manage the same.
- Borrowers are entitled to prefer an appeal with the Debts Recovery Tribunal after depositing 75 percent of the amount claimed by the secured creditor. Borrowers aggrieved by the order of the Debts Recovery Tribunal may prefer an appeal to an Appellate Tribunal within 30 days from the date of receipt of the order of Debts Recovery Tribunal.

The RBI and the Central Government have initiated several institutional measures to contain the levels of NPAs, including the following: (a) Corporate Debt Restructuring (CDR), (b) Debt Recovery Tribunals (DRTs) and (c) *Lok Adalats* (people's courts).

Settlement Advisory Committees have also been formed at regional and head office levels of commercial banks. Furthermore, banks can also issue notices under the Securitisation and Reconstruction of Financial Assets and Enforcement of Security Interest (SARFAESI) Act, 2002 for enforcement of security interest without intervention of courts. Thus, banks have a menu of options to resolve their problem of NPAs.

With a view to providing an additional option and developing a healthy secondary market for NPAs, guidelines on sale/purchase of non-performing assets were issued in July 2005 where securitisation companies and reconstruction companies are not involved. The draft guidelines cover the following broad areas: (a) procedure for purchase/sale of non-performing financial assets by banks, including valuation and pricing aspects and (b) prudential norms relating to asset classification, provisioning, accounting of recoveries, capital adequacy and exposure norms and disclosure requirements.

The guidelines include several specific provisions, including the following.

- A non-performing asset in the books of a bank shall be eligible for sale to other banks only if it has remained a non-performing asset for at least two years in the books of the selling bank and such selling should be only on a cash basis.

- A non-performing financial asset should be held by the purchasing bank in its books at least for a period of 15 months before it is sold to other banks.

- A bank may purchase/sell non-performing financial assets from/to other banks only on a 'without recourse' basis.

- Banks should ensure that subsequent to sale of the non-performing financial assets to other banks, they do not have any involvement with reference to assets sold and do not assume operational, legal or any other type of risks relating to the financial assets sold.

- A non-performing financial asset may be classified as 'standard' in the books of the purchasing bank for a period of 90 days from the date of purchase. Thereafter, the asset classification status of the account shall be determined by the record of recovery in the books of the purchasing bank with reference to cash flows estimated while purchasing the asset. The asset shall attract provisioning requirement appropriate to its asset classification status in the books of the purchasing bank.

- Any recovery in respect of a non-performing asset purchased from other banks should first be adjusted against its acquisition cost. Recoveries in excess of the acquisition cost can be recognised as profit.

- The asset classification status of an existing exposure to the same obligor in the books of the purchasing bank will continue to be governed by the record of recovery of that exposure and hence may be different.
- For the purpose of capital adequacy, banks should assign 100 per cent risk weights to the non-performing financial assets purchased from other banks.
- In the case the non-performing asset purchased is an investment, then it would attract capital charge for market risks also.
- Purchasing bank should ensure compliance with the prudential credit exposure ceilings (both single and group) after reckoning the exposures to the obligors arising on account of the purchase.

Corporate Debt Restructuring: A Special Group (Chairperson: Smt. S. Gopinath) was appointed by RBI to undertake a further review of the corporate debt restructuring (CDR) mechanism and suggest certain changes/improvements in the existing scheme for enhancing its scope and to make it more efficient. In pursuance of the recommendations made by the Special Group, major modifications were proposed in the draft guidelines issued on May 6, 2005 in the existing CDR scheme which included the following.

- Extension of scheme to corporate entities where banks and institutions have an outstanding exposure of Rs.10 crore or more from the earlier exposure of Rs. 20 crore and above.
- Requirement of support of 60 per cent of creditors by number in addition to the support of 75 per cent of creditors by value with a view to making the decision-making process more equitable.
- Linking the restoration of asset classification prevailing on the date of reference to CDR Cell for implementation of package within three months from the date of approval of the package.
- Restricting the regulatory concession in asset classification and provisioning requirement to the first restructuring

where the package also has to meet certain norms relating to turnaround period and minimum sacrifice and funds infusion by promoters.

- Convergence in the methodology for computation of economic sacrifice among banks and FIs.
- Regulatory treatment of non-SLR instruments acquired while funding interest or in *lieu* of outstanding principal and valuation of such instruments.
- Limiting the RBI's role to providing broad guidelines for the CDR system.
- Enhancing balance sheet disclosures.
- Pro-rata sharing of additional finance requirement.
- Including one-time settlement (OTS) as part of the CDR scheme to make the exit option more flexible.
- Discretion to the core group in dealing with wilful defaulters in certain cases.

Debt Recovery Tribunals: Debt Recovery Tribunals (DRTs) were set up under the Recovery of Debts Due to Banks and Financial Institutions Act, 1993 for expeditious adjudication and recovery of debts due to banks and financial institutions. On the recommendation of the RBI, the Government of India set up a Working Group in July 2004 to improve the functioning of DRTs. The Working Group is to examine issues and recommend appropriate measures regarding (a) the need to extend the provisions of the Recovery of Debts Due to Banks And Financial Institutions Act to cases for less than Rs. 10 lakh (b) redistribution of the jurisdiction of the various DRTs (c) modification in the existing strength of the DRTs/Debt Recovery Appellate Tribunals (DRATs) and (d) legal and institutional provisions.

Lok Adalats: The RBI issued guidelines to commercial banks and financial institutions to enable them to make increasing use of the forum of *Lok Adalats*. In terms of the guidelines, banks could settle banking disputes involving an amount up to Rs. 5 lakh through the forum of *Lok Adalats*. Further, banks were advised to participate in the *Lok Adalats* convened by various DRTs/DRATs for resolving cases involving Rs. 10 lakh and above to reduce the stock of NPAs. The Central Government, in consultation with the RBI, decided to increase the monetary ceiling of cases to be referred to the *Lok Adalats* organised by Civil Courts. Accordingly, on August 3, 2004, the RBI enhanced the monetary ceiling of cases to be referred to *Lok Adalats* organised by Civil Courts to Rs. 20 lakh as against the earlier ceiling of Rs. 5 lakh.

Anti-Money Laundering Guidelines

In recent years, prevention of money laundering has assumed importance in international financial relationships. In this context, in November 2004, the RBI revised the guidelines on 'know your customer' (KYC) principles in line with the recommendations made by the Financial Action Task Force (FATF) on anti-money laundering (AML) standards and combating financing of terrorism (CFT). Banks were advised to frame their KYC policies with the approval of their Boards and ensure they are compliant with its provisions by December 31, 2005. The salient features of the policy relate to the procedure prescribed with regard to (a) customer acceptance, (b) customer identification, (c) risk management and (d) monitoring as required under Prevention of Money Laundering Act (PMLA), 2002.

The revised guidelines make the verification of the identity of the customer and address through independent source documents mandatory. Banks are also required to classify the accounts according to the risk perceived by the bank. However, in order to ensure that the inability of persons belonging to low income groups to produce documents to establish their identity and address does not lead to their financial exclusion and denial of banking services further, simplified procedure has been provided for opening of accounts for those persons who do not intend to keep balances above Rs. 50,000 and whose total credit in one year is not expected to exceed Rs. 1,00,000. In addition, the RBI issued instructions emphasising the obligation on banks to follow the provisions of the Foreign Contribution (Regulation) Act, 1976 in respect of acceptance of foreign donations on behalf of associations/organisations maintaining accounts with them.

Off-site Monitoring and Surveillance

The RBI instituted a state-of-the-art Off-site Monitoring and Surveillance (OSMOS) system for banks in 1995 as part of crisis management framework for Early Warning System (EWS) and as a trigger for on-site inspections of vulnerable institutions. The scope and coverage of off-site surveillance has since been widened to capture various facets of efficiency and risk management of banks. They were also advised to increase the level of utilisation of the INFINET for regulatory-cum-supervisory reporting.

While taking up on-site inspection of banks, data from the OSMOS system are used by the inspecting officers for assessing the performance of banks. On-line connectivity has been provided to all the Regional Offices having head offices of banks under their jurisdictions to enable them to access the data directly and generate standard reports. The system was revised to collect certain additional data on derivatives, interest rate risk in investment portfolio, capital charge for market risk and risk weights on housing loans and consumer credit. To identify areas requiring urgent supervisory action and initiate timely action, the time limit for submission of monthly returns was reduced to 15 days and for quarterly returns to 21 days, across all categories of banks from June 2005. To improve the data quality, several measures were initiated. These included (a) modification of the 'guidance note on off-site returns' in the light of the latest revision of the system, relevant regulatory changes and common reporting mistakes observed in various returns and (b) meetings with individual identified banks to highlight the mistakes committed in the returns, removing conceptual ambiguities and sensitising them to the importance of off-site returns.

Supervision of Financial Conglomerates

The financial sector in India is becoming increasingly complex due to the entry of some of the large banks into non-traditional financial activities such as merchant banking, insurance and mutual funds. A few non-banking financial intermediaries have also become large enough to cause systemic impact. The number of cross-border financial conglomerates operating in and out of India is also growing. From a regulatory perspective, the above developments have led to an appreciation of the limitations of the segmented approach to supervision in addressing the potential risks arising out of operations of financial conglomerates. The Working Group on Financial Conglomerates (Convenor: Smt. Shyamala Gopinath) in its Report submitted in May 2004, *inter alia,* suggested criteria for identifying financial conglomerates, a monitoring system for capturing intra-group transactions and exposures and a mechanism for inter-regulatory exchange of information in respect of financial conglomerates.

The Working Group identified 22 financial conglomerates. As part of operationalisation of the monitoring mechanism, a pilot process envisaging submission of data/ information in the prescribed format by the designated entities (DEs) to their principal regulators [Reserve Bank of India (RBI), Securities and Exchange Board of India (SEBI) and Insurance Regulatory and Development Authority (IRDA)] followed by a dialogue between the DEs and the regulators on issues of concern has been set in motion. The reporting format was revised with effect from quarter ended December 31, 2004 to make the reporting system user-friendly. A system of half-yearly discussion with the CEO of financial conglomerates in association with other principal regulators has been introduced to address outstanding issues/supervisory concerns.

Credit Information Bureau of India Ltd. (CIBIL)

The compilation and dissemination of credit information

covering data on defaults to the financial system has been undertaken by the Credit Information Bureau of India Ltd. (CIBIL) set up in 2001. Banks/FIs were advised to take immediate steps to ensure submission of periodical data to CIBIL and progress reports to the RBI. Boards of banks/FIs were also advised to oversee furnishing of requisite information of all borrowers to CIBIL and report compliance of the same to the RBI. The role of CIBIL in dissemination of credit information was clarified. CIBIL should move towards a sufficiently diversified ownership structure with no single entity owning more than 10 per cent of its paid-up capital.

With a view to strengthening the legal mechanism and facilitating credit information bureaus to collect, process and share credit information on borrowers of banks/FIs, a draft Credit Information Companies (Regulation) Bill was introduced in the Parliament. The Bill was passed by the Rajya Sabha and the Lok Sabha in May 2005 and received the assent of the President in June 2005. The new legislation empowers CIBIL to collect information relating to all borrowers and confers upon the RBI the power to determine policy in relation to functioning of credit information companies and also giving directions to credit information companies.

Customer Service

Several steps have been taken by the RBI in recent years to improve customer service of commercial banks.

Customer Service Committee of the Board: The RBI constituted a Standing Committee on Procedures and Performance Audit on Public Services (CPPAPS) [Chairman: S. S. Tarapore] in December 2003.

Keeping in view the recommendations of the CPPAPS, all the public sector/private sector banks and select foreign banks were advised to constitute a Customer Service Committee of the Board with a view to strengthening the corporate governance structure in the banking system and also to bringing about ongoing improvements in the quality of customer service provided by bank. Furthermore, based on the recommendations of the Committee, banks were advised in April 2005 to take necessary action to convert the existing *Ad hoc* Committees into Standing Committees on Customer Service. It was felt that the *Ad hoc* Committee when converted as a permanent Standing Committee cutting across various departments could serve as a micro level executive committee driving the implementation process and providing relevant feedback, while the Customer Service Committee of the Board would oversee and review/modify the initiatives. Thus, the two committees would be mutually reinforcing.

Banking Ombudsman: With a view to enhancing the effectiveness of the Banking Ombudsman Scheme, banks were advised in April 2005 that Customer Service Committee of the Board should play a more active role with regard to complaints/grievances received by the Banking Ombudsmen of the various States. Furthermore, to ensure that the awards of the Banking Ombudsmen are implemented immediately and with active involvement of top Management, banks were also advised to (a) place all the awards before the Customer Service Committee to enable it to address issues of systemic deficiencies existing in banks, if any, brought out by the awards and (b) place all the awards remaining unimplemented for more than three months with the reasons therefore before the Customer Service Committee to enable it to report to the Board such delays in implementation without valid reasons and for initiating necessary remedial action.

Credit Card Facilities: In order to ensure orderly growth of the card segment of consumer credit and protect the interests of banks/NBFCs and their customers, the RBI constituted a Working Group on Regulatory Mechanism for Cards (Chairman: R. Gandhi). Based of the recommendations of the Working Group, draft guidelines on credit cards were framed by the RBI in June 2005 for all commercial banks/non-banking financial companies (NBFCs) with regard to their credit card operations.

The draft guidelines delineated the broad parameters that banks/NBFCs should, at the minimum, take into account with regard to the following.

- Issue of cards with respect to clear mentioning of Most Important Terms and Conditions (MITCs).
- Interest rates and other charges on customers.
- Corrective mechanism on account of wrongful billing.
- Use of Direct Sale Agents and other agents for outsourcing various credit card operations.
- Protection of customer rights especially in respect of right to privacy, customer confidentiality and fair practices in debt collection.
- Redressal avenues of customer grievances.
- Internal control and monitoring systems of the banks/NBFCs for such card operations.

The draft guidelines further stipulate that each bank/NBFC must have a well documented policy and a 'Fair Practices Code' for credit card operations. The 'Fair Practices Code' for credit card operations released by the IBA in March 2005 could also be used by banks/NBFCs. The bank/ NBFCs code should, at the minimum, however, incorporate the relevant guidelines contained in the draft guidelines released by the RBI.

Collection and Processing of Cheques: The RBI has been advising banks from time to time on issues relating to (a) immediate credit of local/outstation cheques, (b) time frame for collection of local/outstation cheques and (c) interest payment for delayed collection.

On a comprehensive review of the technological progress in payment and settlement systems and the qualitative changes in operational systems and processes undertaken by a number of banks, the RBI felt that prescription of a single set of rules may not be appropriate. Banks were, therefore, advised in November 2004 to formulate a comprehensive and transparent policy covering all the above three aspects, taking into account their technological capabilities, systems and processes adopted for clearing arrangements and other internal arrangements for collection through correspondents. Banks were also advised that adequate care be taken to ensure that the interests of small depositors are fully protected.

Grievances Redressal Mechanism: The Central Vigilance Commission (CVC) had expressed concerns regarding lack of redressal machinery in private sector banks. The issue was examined in detail and the RBI instructed the IBA to advise all the members to ensure, *inter alia*, that a suitable mechanism exists for receiving and addressing complaints from their customers/constituents and that the time frame is fixed for resolving the complaints received at different levels.

Settlement of Claims of Deceased Depositors: The RBI's Committee on Procedures and Performance Audit on Public Services (Chairman: S.S. Tarapore), 2003 had observed that the tortuous procedures, particularly those applicable to settlement of claim of a deceased depositor, caused considerable distress to family members. Accordingly, the RBI advised banks in June 2005 that while making payment to the survivor(s)/nominee(s) of the deceased depositor, they should desist from insisting on production of a succession certificate, letter of administration or probate or obtain any bond of indemnity or surety from the survivor(s)/nominee(s), irrespective of the amount standing to the credit of the deceased account holder.

Furthermore, in those cases where the deceased depositor had not made any nomination or for the accounts other than those styled as "either or survivor" (such as single or jointly operated accounts), banks were advised to adopt a simplified procedure for repayment to legal heir(s). In the case of term deposits, banks have been advised to incorporate a clause in the account opening form itself to the effect that in the event of the death of the depositor, premature termination of term deposits would be allowed.

Still further, banks have been advised to obtain appropriate agreement/authorisation from the survivor(s)/nominee(s) with regard to treatment of pipeline flows. Banks were also advised to settle the claims in respect of deceased depositors and release payments to survivor(s)/nominee(s) within a period not exceeding 15 days from the date of receipt of the claim, subject to the production of proof of death of the depositor and suitable identification of the claim(s) to the bank's satisfaction.

Door-step Banking: In May 1983, banks were advised by the RBI not to extend any banking facilities at the premises of their customers without obtaining its prior permission. Several requests, however, were received from Government departments such as Railways requesting to make available banking services including collection of cash at their premises. Keeping this and representations from certain banks in view, it was decided in April 2005 that a scheme for providing services at the premises of a customer within the framework of Section 23 of the Banking Regulation Act, 1949 may be formulated by banks with the approval of their Boards and submitted to the RBI for approval. In order to ensure that Central and State Government departments are not inconvenienced, agency banks in the interregnum may continue to lift cash and collect credit instruments from their premises.

Banking Codes and Standards Board of India: The RBI's Committee on Procedures and Performance Audit of Public Services (Chairman: S.S. Tarapore), 2003 had recommended that Banking Codes and Standards Board of India (BCSBI) be set up as an independent organisation but strongly supported and fully funded by the RBI. Accordingly, in the Annual Policy Statement of the RBI for 2005-06, it was proposed to set up an independent Banking Codes and Standards Board of India on the lines of the Banking Code of the British Bankers' Association of the UK in order to ensure that comprehensive code of conduct for fair treatment of customers is evolved and adhered to.

Remittance Facility to NRIs/PIOs: On May 13, 2005, the remittance facility to a non-resident Indian (NRI)/person of

Indian origin (PIO) out of balances in the NRO account was further extended by allowing remittances up to US$ 1 million, per calendar year, under legacy/ inheritance acquired out of settlement. However, the existing guidelines regarding remittance of sale proceeds of immovable property to a citizen of Pakistan, Bangladesh, Sri Lanka, China, Afghanistan, Iran, Nepal and Bhutan would continue. In view of the recommendations of the RBI's Committee on Procedures and Performance Audit on Public Services (Chairman: S.S. Tarapore), 2003 it was decided that with effect from March 15, 2005, in addition to the earlier facility, a resident power of attorney holder would be permitted to remit, through normal banking channels, funds out of the balances in NRE/FCNR(B) account to the nonresident account holder provided specific powers for the purpose have been given.

Appendices

Appendix 1

Highlights of the Annual Policy Statement of the Reserve Bank of India for the Year 2008-09

(announced on April 29, 2008)

Highlights

- The overall moderation in real sector activity was reflected in the evolution of monetary and banking developments in 2007-08. Non-food credit extended by the scheduled commercial banks (SCBs) increased by 22.3 per cent (Rs.4,19,425 crore) as compared with 28.5 per cent (Rs.4,18,282 crore) in the previous year. The incremental non-food credit-deposit ratio for the banking system declined to 72.3 per cent during 2007-08 from 83.2 per cent in 2006-07, 109.3 per cent in 2005-06 and 130.0 per cent in 2004-05. Food credit of SCBs declined by Rs.2,121 crore in 2007-08 as against an increase of Rs.5,830 crore in the previous year.

- Provisional information on the sectoral deployment of bank credit available up to February 2008 indicates, as anticipated, a gradual deceleration over the year. On a year-on-year basis, credit to services sector recorded the highest growth (28.4 per cent), followed by industry (25.9 per cent) and agriculture sector (16.4 per cent). On the other hand, growth in personal loans decelerated to 13.2 per cent (30.6 per cent). Growth in housing and real estate loans decelerated to 12.0 per cent (25.8 per cent) and 26.7 per cent (79.0 per cent), respectively. Within the industrial sector, there was a sizeable credit pick-up in respect of infrastructure (42.1 per cent as against 28.2 per cent a year ago), food processing (32.0 per cent as against 27.6 per cent) and engineering (26.2 per cent as against 18.1 per cent). There was moderation in credit growth to basic metals and metal products (19.0 per cent as against 33.3 per cent), textiles (23.0 per cent as against 35.5 per cent), petroleum (23.3 per cent as against 64.4 per cent) and chemicals (13.9 per cent as against 19.2 per cent). Credit to industry constituted 45.2 per cent of the total expansion in non-food bank credit up to February 2008, followed by services (29.8 per cent), personal loans (15.8 per cent) and agriculture (9.2 per cent). The share of infrastructure in total credit to industry increased from 20.5 per cent to 23.1 per cent. On the contrary, the share of credit to metals, textiles, chemicals and petroleum declined from 12.4 per cent, 11.3 per cent, 8.3 per cent and 4.9 per cent, respectively, to 11.7 per cent, 11.1 per cent, 7.5 per cent and 4.8 per cent. Priority sector advances grew by 16.9 per cent with a moderation in their share in outstanding gross bank credit to 33.3 per cent in February 2008 from 34.7 per cent a year ago.

- Commercial banks' investment in Government and other approved securities increased by 22.9 per cent (Rs.1,81,222 crore) during 2007-08 significantly higher than 10.3 per cent (Rs.74,062 crore) in 2006-07. Accordingly, their stock of statutory liquidity ratio (SLR) eligible securities marginally increased to 27.4 per cent of the banking system's net demand and time liabilities (NDTL) in March 2008 from 27.3 per cent in March 2007. Bank's holdings of SLR securities in excess of the prescribed ratio of 25 per cent amounted to Rs.1,02,422 crore although several banks are operating their SLR portfolios close to the prescribed level. Adjusted for collateral securities under the liquidity adjustment facility (LAF) and issuances under the market stabilisation scheme (MSS), banks' investment in SLR-eligible securities would amount to 23.7 per cent of NDTL.

- During the year, the financial markets experienced alternating shifts in liquidity conditions. Tightness in liquidity on account of year-end adjustments in March 2007 persisted up to April-May, necessitating net repo injections under the LAF. There was substantial drawdown in the Centre's cash balances during May-July 2007 and a dip in MSS outstanding in June-

July 2007 due to redemptions. The total overhang of liquidity as reflected in the balances under the LAF, the MSS and surplus cash balances of the Central Government taken together declined from an average of Rs.97,412 crore in March 2007 to Rs.63,994 crore in July 2007. The resumption of net issuances under the MSS, accretions to Centre's cash balances and the increase in CRR by 100 basis points during August-November 2007 led to a reduction in the liquidity in the banking system and intermittent net liquidity injections of Rs.2,742 crore and Rs.10,804 crore on a daily average basis in November and December 2007, respectively. Auctions of dated securities under MSS were discontinued between November 2, 2007-January 16, 2008 to ease the stringency in liquidity. The liquidity overhang ruled steady in the range of Rs.2,13,847 crore-Rs.2,18,224 crore during October-December 2007.

- Movements in interest rates in the domestic financial markets reflected the factors driving changes in liquidity with the banking system during 2007-08. The weighted average call market rates declined from 8.33 per cent in April 2007 to 0.73 per cent in July 2007 coincident with a ceiling of Rs.3,000 crore placed on daily reverse repo from March 5, 2007. The rates moved up in August following the removal of the ceiling but generally stayed within the informal LAF rate corridor up to December 2007. As liquidity conditions tightened, call money rates strayed, *albeit* marginally, above the repo rate during the last fortnight of February and in March 2008. The daily weighted average call rate during March 2008 was much lower at 7.37 per cent as compared with 14.10 per cent in March 2007. In April 2008, call rates declined further and the weighted average call rate stood at 5.93 per cent as on April 25, 2008. Interest rates in the CBLO and market repo segments moved in sympathy with call rates and declined from December 2007 peaks to 6.37 per cent and 6.72 per cent, respectively, in March 2008 and further to 4.93 per cent and 5.45 per cent in April 2008 (up to April 25, 2008). The daily average volume (one leg) in the call money market declined from Rs.14,845 crore in April 2007 to Rs.11,182 crore in March 2008 and further to Rs.9,374 crore in April 2008 (up to April 25, 2008). The corresponding volumes in the market repo (outside the LAF) were Rs.7,173 crore, Rs.14,800 crore and Rs.11,911 crore respectively, whereas in the CBLO segment, the volumes were Rs.18,086 crore, Rs.37,413 crore and Rs.31,297 crore, respectively.

- During March 2007-March 2008, public sector banks (PSBs) readjusted their deposit rates downwards by 25-50 basis points, while those offering lower deposit rates for similar maturity earlier increased their deposit rates by 50-100 basis points. Similarly, PSBs paying higher interest rates earlier on shorter term deposits of up to one year maturity also revised their deposit rates downwards by 25 basis points. In particular, the interest rates offered by the PSBs on deposits of above one year maturity moved from the range of 7.25-9.50 per cent in March 2007 to 8.00-9.25 per cent in March 2008, while deposit rates for shorter term deposits of up to one year maturity decreased from the range of 2.75-8.75 per cent to 2.75-8.50 per cent during the same period. On the other hand, private sector banks increased their interest rates for long term deposits of above one year maturity from a range of 6.75-9.75 per cent to 7.25-9.75 per cent during the same period. Foreign banks set deposit rates lower for maturities of less than one year while they have marginally raised their rates for deposits of longer maturities.

Developments in the Global Economy

- Since the beginning of the turbulence in August 2007, central banks of advanced economies have responded with both conventional and unconventional measures to ease liquidity stress in financial markets and solvency issues among large financial institutions. There has, however, been several aspects that differentiate the approaches of the central banks. Some central banks, notably the ECB, the Reserve Bank of

Australia and the Swiss National Bank have responded by providing liquidity to inter-bank markets, implicitly viewing the financial turmoil as essentially a problem of liquidity tightness. These central banks have provided liquidity through fine-tuning operations aimed at assuring orderly conditions in their respective money markets. On the other hand, some central banks like the US Fed, the Bank of England and the Bank of Canada have responded in a more diverse fashion, regarding the market stress as reflecting both liquidity seizure as well as broader threats to financial stability, coupled with dangers of the slowdown in economic activity becoming protracted. Accordingly, they have moved to inject liquidity into money markets through normal and special facilities. They have also relaxed the class of eligible securities for liquidity availment from the central bank. Furthermore, they have also cut policy rates substantially amid fears that the subprime crisis could turn into a major credit crunch with adverse implications for the real sector. The US Fed has also been involved in resolution of problems arising in non-bank entities like investment banks and insurance companies. The Bank of England has provided generalised and institution-specific emergency liquidity and facilities for swapping securities.

- Some central banks have cut policy rates since the third quarter of 2007 when the financial market turmoil surfaced. During September 18, 2007 to March 18, 2008 the US Federal Reserve cut its policy rate by 300 basis points to 2.25 per cent after seventeen increases to 5.25 per cent between June 2004 and June 2006. The Bank of England reduced its repo rate to 5.0 per cent by 25 basis points each in February and April 2008. The Bank of Canada reduced its rate to 3.0 per cent by 25 basis points reductions each in December 2007 and January 2008 and 50 basis points each in March and April 2008. Central banks of several countries, including the euro area, New Zealand, Japan, Korea, Malaysia, Thailand and Mexico have not changed their rates since the last quarter of

2007. Some central banks that have tightened their policy rates in recent months include the Reserve Bank of Australia (Cash Rate raised by 25 basis points in February-March 2008 to 7.25 per cent); the People's Bank of China (lending rate raised to 7.47 per cent in December 2007 from 7.29 per cent in September 2007); the Banco Central de Chile (benchmark lending rate raised to 6.25 per cent in January 2008 from 5.75 per cent in October 2007), and Banco Central do Brasil (overnight Selic rate raised by 50 basis points to 11.75 per cent in April 2008).

• There are several issues emerging out of recent financial developments that are interacting with global macroeconomic changes and carry implications for the conduct of monetary policy globally. First, financial markets are currently at the heart of the turmoil and are regarded as sources of higher potential instability going forward. Despite sizeable central bank action over a wide spectrum, market interest rates and policy rates continue to be widely divergent. Second, there are renewed concerns about the gaps in the financial architecture and its limited capability for withstanding shocks or for preventing spillovers. Third, the effectiveness of financial regulations and supervision has come under scrutiny, especially in the context of appropriately assessing capital adequacy in large financial institutions, complex financial products and vehicles and risk management practices. In this context, it is important to note that even the Basel II and related processes are being reviewed in their granularities. Fourth, the role of credit rating agencies is being subjected to critical reassessment, particularly in view of their envisaged role under Basel II. There is active discussion on the need for credit rating agencies to clearly differentiate the ratings for structured products, improve their disclosure of rating methodologies, and assess the quality of information provided by originators, arrangers, and issuers of structured products. Fifth, current practices relating to transparency and disclosure are being subject to careful appraisal in view of their inadequacy in the context of structured financial products and special purpose vehicles. Sixth, the role of investment banks and their adequacy of capital needs to be reviewed, along with stipulation of separate yet complementary sets of best practices for hedge fund investors and asset managers to increase accountability for participants in this industry.

Stance of Monetary Policy for 2008-09

- The Reserve Bank will continue with its policy of active demand management of liquidity through appropriate use of the CRR stipulations and open market operations (OMO) including the MSS and the LAF, using all the policy instruments at its disposal flexibly, as and when the situation warrants.
- In sum, barring the emergence of any adverse and unexpected developments in various sectors of the economy, assuming that capital flows are effectively managed, and keeping in view the current assessment of the economy including the outlook for growth and inflation, the overall stance of monetary policy in 2008-09 will broadly be:
  - To ensure a monetary and interest rate environment that accords high priority to price stability, well-anchored inflation expectations and orderly conditions in financial markets while being conducive to continuation of the growth momentum.
  - To respond swiftly on a continuing basis to the evolving constellation of adverse international developments and to the domestic situation impinging on inflation expectations, financial stability and growth momentum, with both conventional and unconventional measures, as appropriate.
  - To emphasise credit quality as well as credit delivery, in particular, for employment-intensive sectors, while pursuing financial inclusion.

Monetary Measures

Bank Rate: The Bank Rate has been kept unchanged at 6.0 per cent.

Repo Rate/Reverse Repo Rate: The repo rate under the LAF is kept unchanged at 7.75 per cent. The reverse repo rate under the LAF is kept unchanged at 6.0 per cent. The Reserve Bank has the flexibility to conduct repo/reverse repo auctions at a fixed rate or at variable rates as circumstances warrant. The Reserve Bank retains the option to conduct overnight or longer term repo/reverse repo under the LAF depending on market conditions and other relevant factors. The Reserve Bank will continue to use this flexibility including the right to accept or reject tender(s) under the LAF, wholly or partially, if deemed fit, so as to make efficient use of the LAF in daily liquidity management.

Cash Reserve Ratio: Scheduled banks are required to maintain cash reserve ratio (CRR) of 7.75 per cent with effect from the fortnight beginning April 26, 2008 and 8.0 per cent with effect from the fortnight beginning May 10, 2008 as announced on April 17, 2008. On a review of the evolving liquidity situation, it is considered desirable to increase the CRR by 25 basis points to 8.25 per cent with effect from the fortnight beginning May 24, 2008.

Developmental and Regulatory Policies for the Year 2008-09

- The setting of developmental and regulatory policies for 2008-09 will continue to focus on developing a sound, efficient and vibrant financial system that ensures the efficient provision of financial services to the widest sections of society. In the context of recent financial developments internationally, the securing and maintenance of financial stability will continue to receive priority from a policy perspective. Credible communication, adequate and timely availability of information and a broad-based, participative and consultative approach in the conduct of its developmental and regulatory policies with involvement of all stakeholders would shape the Reserve Bank's responses to the emerging challenges.

- According to the Institute of International Finance (IIF), banks should commit themselves to follow best practices in a number of areas where the financial crisis has revealed weaknesses. 'Best practice' should not imply legal obligations but high standards for entities to develop their own tailor-made solutions. The proposals made by the Financial Stability Forum (FSF) [a forum of select senior representatives of national financial authorities - including central banks, supervisory authorities and treasury departments _ international financial institutions, international regulatory and supervisory groupings and committees of central bank experts] and ratified in early April 2008 by the G-7 to be implemented over the next 100 days are comprehensive and cover full and prompt disclosure of risk exposures, write downs and fair value estimates for complex and illiquid instruments; urgent action by setters of accounting standards and other relevant standard setters to improve accounting and disclosure standards for off-balance sheet or entities and to enhance guidance on fair value accounting, particularly on valuing financial instruments in periods of stress; strengthening of risk management practices, supported by supervisors' oversight, including rigorous stress testing; and strengthening of capital positions as needed. In addition, proposals made by the FSF for implementation by end-2008 include: strengthening prudential oversight of capital, liquidity, and risk management under Basel II, especially for complex structured credit instruments and off-balance sheet vehicles; enhancing transparency and valuation for off-balance sheet entities, securitisation exposures, and liquidity commitments under the Basel Committee's guidance; enhancing due diligence in the use of ratings; adherence by credit rating agencies to the revised code of conduct of the International Organisation of Securities Commissions (IOSCO); strengthening the authorities' responsiveness to risk through cooperation and exchange of information so as to act swiftly to investigate and penalise fraud, market abuse, and manipulation; implementing robust arrangements for dealing with stress in the financial system such as liquidity support from the central banks; and, strengthening arrangements for dealing with weak and failing banks, domestically and cross border.

Credit Delivery Mechanisms and Other Banking Services

- With a view to augmenting RRBs' funds/resource base, commercial banks/sponsor banks have been allowed to classify loans granted to RRBs for on-lending to agriculture and allied activities as indirect finance to agriculture in their books.

- In terms of the revised guidelines on lending to priority sector effective from April 30, 2007 domestic SCBs are required to lend 40 per cent of adjusted net bank credit (net bank credit plus investments made by banks in non-SLR bonds held in the held to maturity category) or credit equivalent of off-balance sheet exposures, whichever is higher, to the priority sector. These SCBs are also required to lend at least 18 per cent to the agriculture sector and 10 per cent to weaker sections covering small and marginal farmers with land holding of five acres and less; landless labourers, tenant farmers and share croppers; artisans, village and cottage industries where individual credit limits do not exceed Rs. 50,000; beneficiaries of Swarnjayanti Gram Swarozgar Yojana (SGSY), Swarna Jayanti Shahari Rozgar Yojana (SJSRY), the Scheme for Liberation and Rehabilitation of Scavengers (SLRS) and the Differential Rate of Interest (DRI) scheme; scheduled castes and scheduled tribes; self-help groups (SHGs); and distressed poor who have to prepay their debt to the informal sector against appropriate collateral or group security. It has been observed that banks have not been achieving the sub-target of 10 per cent for lending to weaker sections. At present, domestic SCBs having shortfall in the priority sector lending target and/or the agriculture sub-target are allocated amounts for contribution to the Rural Infrastructure Development Fund (RIDF) maintained with the National Bank for Agriculture and Rural Development (NABARD).

- In terms of the revised guidelines on lending to the priority sector, SCBs can undertake outright purchase of any loan asset eligible to be categorised under the priority sector from other banks and financial institutions and classify the same under the respective categories of priority sector lending (direct or indirect), provided the loans purchased are held at least for a period of six months. To enable greater flow of credit to the priority sectors, it is proposed to allow RRBs to sell loan assets held by them under priority sector categories in excess of the prescribed priority sector lending target of 60 per cent.

- In collaboration with the Indian Banks' Association (IBA), the Banking Codes and Standards Board of India (BSCBI) is evolving a banking code for small and micro enterprises which will go a long way in empowering the sector.

- The Lead Bank Scheme, introduced in 1969, aimed at coordinating the activities/efforts of banks, State Governments and other developmental agencies for promoting overall development of the rural sector. Although the Scheme was reviewed in 1989 when the service area approach was adopted, there have been significant changes in the financial system in the post-reform period. More recently, there is increased focus on financial inclusion. At the same time, planning has become more decentralised with greater devolution of expenditure to the grassroots levels. In the revised context and in order to improve the effectiveness of the Scheme as announced in the Mid-Term Review of October 2007, a High Level Committee (Chairperson: Smt. Usha Thorat) with members drawn from various financial institutions, banks and State Governments was constituted to review the Lead Bank Scheme. The Committee has so far held seven meetings and has interacted with most of the State Governments and banks. Interactions are also proposed with academics and Non-Governmental Organisations (NGOs). The Committee is expected to submit its report by July 2008.

- In the last few years, the Reserve Bank has been focusing on safeguarding the interest of common persons in their interface with banks while improving the ease and efficiency of conducting banking transactions. The measures taken by the Reserve Bank include setting up of the Banking Codes and Standards Board of India, revamping the Banking Ombudsman scheme, constitution of board-level customer service committees in banks, dissemination of customer-centric information in local languages and promoting fair and transparent policies and practices, especially in the matter of bank charges, interest rates, customer acquisition and debt collection. Banks have also responded positively, including adoption of the Code of Commitment to their customers. Nevertheless, analyses of the types, frequency and trends of complaints reaching the Reserve Bank and the offices of the Banking Ombudsmen suggest that the essence of the Code still needs to percolate down to the level of the customer service delivery interface in banks. Banks, therefore, need to pay closer attention to these aspects, particularly, sensitivity of the staff to meeting the legitimate expectations of customers. They also need to ensure that they have in place effective internal arrangements for customer grievance redressal.

- In 2007, on account of concerns about high bank charges and excessive interest rates in personal segment, the Reserve Bank laid down principles for ensuring reasonableness of bank charges and communicating them in respect of identified basic banking services. Banks were also cautioned against excessive interest rates, which are not sustainable and may be seen as usurious and broad guidelines in this regard were laid down. For greater transparency in setting interest rates banks were advised that they must use external or market-based rupee benchmark interest rates for pricing their floating rate loan products. The Reserve Bank has, thus, attempted to involve banks' boards in implementation of various guidelines to ensure fairness, reasonableness and transparency in bank charges for various services and setting interest rates and use of external transparent benchmark for this purpose while giving them flexibility on consideration of commercial judgement. It is expected that banks' boards will take necessary care that these objectives are met and need for more prescriptive regulation is avoided.

- The Reserve Bank has adopted a three-track approach to capital adequacy regulation in India with the norms stipulated at varying degrees of stringency for different categories of banks given the variations in size, nature and complexity of operations and relevance of different types of banks to the Indian financial sector, the need to achieve greater financial inclusion and to provide an efficient credit delivery mechanism. Accordingly, commercial banks, which account for a major share in the total assets of the banking system and are Basel II standards compliant, would be on Track I, banks which are Basel I compliant would be on Track II and banks which are in the nature of local community banks would be on Track III.

- In view of the rapid expansion of overseas operations, introduction of new products and processes, increasing off-balance sheet exposures including derivative products, a need has arisen for a review of the reporting system. Accordingly, an inter-departmental Group has been constituted to review the existing regulatory and supervisory framework for overseas operations of Indian banks and recommend appropriate changes, including off-site reporting systems.

Institutional Developments
- The Payment and Settlement Systems Bill was passed by the Parliament and became an Act known as 'Payment and Settlement Systems Act, 2007' after receiving the assent of

the President on the December 20, 2007. The Act empowers the Reserve Bank to regulate and supervise the payment and settlement systems in the country; gives it authority to permit the setting up/continuance of such systems and to call for information/data and issue directions from/to payment system providers. The Act defines a payment system and gives legal recognition to multilateral netting and settlement finality. Accordingly, the Reserve Bank has placed the draft regulations under the Payment and Settlement Systems Act, 2007 on its website inviting public comments to be received latest by May 15, 2008. The regulations will be finalised in consultation with the Government

- Information Technology (IT) has enhanced the scope of financial inclusion with low cost technology by reaching out to hitherto unexplored sectors of the economy. The usage of card-based products for multiple applications is cost-effective and holds potential for large-scale deployment. With a wide range of IT-based products such as smart cards, hand held devices and secured message transfers, there is an imperative need to ensure that these instruments blend seamlessly with the existing operative systems at the bank level. Accordingly, banks are urged to ensure that security of banking transactions is adequately addressed while using such products.

- The RTGS system implemented by the Reserve Bank has been in operation for nearly four years. The system has also stabilised over the years and has been witnessing increased coverage in terms of bank branches and transaction volume. The Bank for International Settlements (BIS) has published a set of Core Principles in 2001 which are in the nature of standards to measure the efficiency of the systemically important payment systems and the Reserve Bank has been assessing the compliance of the Indian RTGS system with these principles on annual basis. As per the latest review, the system is fully compliant with six core principles, broadly compliant with three, and one principle is not applicable for the Indian RTGS system. Out of the four responsibilities of the central bank under the core principles, full compliance has been achieved in respect of two core principles, broad compliance with one and one responsibility is not applicable in the Indian context.

- The reach of mobile phones has been increasing at a rapid pace in India. There were about 231 million mobile phone connections in the country at the end of December 2007. The rapid expansion of this mode of communication has thrown up a new payment delivery channel for banks. Many countries in the world have adopted this mode of delivery to successfully spread the reach of the banking facility to the remote parts of their respective countries. This channel facilitates small value payments to merchants, utility service providers and the like and money transfers at a low cost.

- The Reserve Bank has been continuously taking initiatives to migrate from paper-based payment to electronic payment systems by creating the appropriate technological infrastructure. In this context, an Internal Group was constituted to examine various issues connected with the use of electronic payment systems. Based on the Group's report, an approach paper was placed on the Reserve Bank's website inviting comments/suggestions from the public. On the basis of the feedback, effective from April 1, 2008 all payment transactions of Rs. one crore and above in the money, Government securities and foreign exchange markets and the regulated entities (banks, PDs and NBFCs) have been made mandatory to be routed through the electronic payment mechanism.

Appendix 2

Main Recommendations of the Narasimham Committee on Banking Sector Reforms

Strengthening Banking System

- Capital adequacy requirements should take into account market risks in addition to the credit risks.
- In the next three years the entire portfolio of government securities should be marked to market and the schedule for the same announced at the earliest (since announced in the monetary and credit policy for the first half of 1998-99); government and other approved securities which are now subject to a zero risk weight, should have a 5 per cent weight for market risk.
- Risk weight on a government guaranteed advance should be the same as for other advances. This should be made prospective from the time the new prescription is put in place.
- Foreign exchange open credit limit risks should be integrated into the calculation of risk weighted assets and should carry a 100 per cent risk weight.
- Minimum capital to risk assets ratio (CRAR) be increased from the existing 8 per cent to 10 per cent; and intermediate minimum target of 9 per cent be achieved by 2000 and the ratio of 10 per cent by 2002; RBI to be empowered to raise this further for individual banks if the risk profile warrants such an increase. Individual banks' shortfalls in the CRAR be treated on the same line as adopted for reserve requirements, viz. uniformity across weak and strong banks. There should be penal provisions for banks that do not maintain CRAR.
- Public Sector Banks in a position to access the capital market at home or abroad be encouraged, as subscription to bank

capital funds cannot be regarded as a priority claim on budgetary resources.

Asset Quality

- An asset be classified as doubtful if it is in the substandard category for 18 months in the first instance and eventually for 12 months and loss if it has been identified but not written off. These norms should be regarded as the minimum and brought into force in a phased manner.

- For evaluating the quality of assets portfolio, advances covered by Government guarantees, which have turned sticky, be treated as NPAs. Exclusion of such advances should be separately shown to facilitate fuller disclosure and greater transparency of operations.

- For banks with a high NPA portfolio, two alternative approaches could be adopted. One approach can be that all loan assets in the doubtful and loss categories, should be identified and their realisable value determined. These assets could be transferred to an Assets Reconstruction Company (ARC) which would issue NPA Swap Bonds.

- An alternative approach could be to enable the banks in difficulty to issue bonds which could form part of Tier II capital, backed by government guarantee to make these instruments eligible for SLR investment by banks and approved instruments by LIC, GIC and Provident Funds.

- The interest subsidy element in credit for the priority sector should be totally eliminated and interest rate on loans under Rs. 2 lakh should be deregulated for scheduled commercial banks as has been done in the case of Regional Rural Banks and cooperative credit institutions.

Prudential Norms and Disclosure Requirements

- In India, income stops accruing when interest or instalment of principal is not paid within 180 days, which should be reduced to 90 days in a phased manner by 2002.

- Introduction of a general provision of 1 per cent on standard assets in a phased manner be considered by RBI.
- As an incentive to make specific provisions, they may be made tax deductible.

Structural Issues

- With the conversion of activities between banks and DFIs, the DFIs should, over a period of time convert themselves to bank. A DFI which converts to bank be given time to face in reserve equipment in respect of its liability to bring it on par with requirement relating to commercial bank.
- Mergers of Public Sector Banks should emanate from the management of the banks with the Government as the common shareholder playing a supportive role. Merger should not be seen as a means of bailing out weak banks. Mergers between strong banks/FIs would make for greater economic and commercial sense.
- 'Weak Banks' may be nurtured into healthy units by slowing down on expansion, eschewing high cost funds/borrowings etc.
- The minimum share of holding by Government/Reserve Bank in the equity of the nationalised banks and the State Bank should be brought down to 33 per cent. The RBI regulator of the monetary system should not be also the owner of a bank in view of the potential for possible conflict of interest.
- There is a need for reform of the deposit insurance scheme based on CAMELs ratings awarded by RBI to banks.
- Inter-bank call and notice money market and inter-bank term money market should be strictly restricted to banks; only exception to be made is primary dealers.
- Non-bank parties be provided free access to bill rediscounts, CPs, CDs, Treasury Bills, MMMF.
- RBI should totally withdraw from the primary market in 91 days Treasury Bills.

Appendix 3

Main Recommendations of the Working Group for Harmonising the Role and Operations of Development Finance Institutions and Banks

Role, Structure and Operations

- To enable Indian financial institutions and commercial banks to compete in a deregulated and increasingly global market place, a progressive move towards universal banking, supported by an enabling regulatory framework, is necessary.
- Pending a full banking licence, DFIs be permitted to have a banking subsidiary (with holdings up to 100 per cent); DFIs themselves to continue to play their existing role.
- The appropriate corporate structure for the universal bank should be an internal management/shareholder decision. The structure can be a single company or a holding company with individually capitalised but wholly owned subsidiaries, a group of entities with cross holdings or a flagship company with subsidiaries which may or may not have independent shareholders.
- Keeping in view the importance of size, expertise and reach for sustained viability and future survival in the financial sector, management and shareholders of banks and DFIs should be permitted to explore and enter into gainful mergers. Such mergers can be between banks or between banks and DFIs. However, restructuring/ consolidation should be brought about in a market-oriented fashion and led solely by considerations of viability and profitability.
- DFIs in India have started moving in the direction of universal banking and increasingly operate on commercial as opposed

to developmental considerations. Developmental obligations would require financial support from RBI/Government.

Regulatory and Legal Framework

- Establish a 'super regulator' to supervise and coordinate the activities of multiple regulators.
- Undertake legal reforms with focus on debt recovery area of Banks and FIs thorough revamp of the 1993 Act on Recovery of Debts from Banks and DFIs.

Supervisory practices

- Supervisory framework be risk-based with focus on macro-management.
- Consolidated supervision for financial subsidiaries and conglomerates and global consolidated supervision by banking supervisor.

Statutory obligations

- CRR should be confined to cash and cash-like instruments; it should be brought down progressively within a time-bound frame to international levels.
- Given the stringent asset classification and provisioning norms and Government borrowing at market determined rates, the need for SLR has declined; SLR may therefore be phased out in line with international practice.
- There is a need to develop an alternative mechanism for financing specific sectors which require concessional funds which can be provided by specifically targeted subsidies rather than via statutory obligation on the entire banking system.
- Definition of priority sector should be modified to reflect the growing importance of infrastructure finance. However, infrastructure lending may not be included in the definition of "net bank credit" used in computing priority sector obligations.

- To facilitate sound credit planning and efficient disbursal of loans, priority sector obligation should be linked to the net bank credit at the end of the previous financial year.

State Level Institutions (SLIs)

- Eventual merger of SFCs, SIDCs and SSIDCs in each state into a single entity.
- Strong SFCs to go public with state government holdings gradually brought down to below 50 per cent.
- Transfer of present share holdings of IDBI in SLIs to SIDBI
- Ownership of SIDBI to be transferred to RBI/Govt. on the same lines as NABARD.

Harmonising the Role, Operations and Regulatory Framework

In view of the large amount of funding required, both DFIs and Banks have a role in working capital finance and long-term funding with different levels of emphasis on each segment. Since the basic functional differences will continue (at least for the present), removal of the following restrictions/stipulations be considered:-

- Prior approval for bond issues by DFIs with either maturity of less than 5 years or maturity or maturity of 5 years and above but with interest rate exceeding 200 basis points over the GOI securities of equal residual maturity.
- Overall ceiling for DFIs' mobilisation of resources by way of term money bonds, CDs, term deposits and inter-corporate deposits at 100 per cent of net owned funds of DFIs.
- Maturity ceiling of five years on deposits from the public and capping of interest rate on deposits of DFIs at interest rate offered by SBI for similar maturities.
- Minimum size of deposits to be accepted by DFIs.

Appendix 4

Main Recommendations of the Committee on Capital Account Convertibility

- The Committee recommended that the implementation of CAC be spread over 1997-98 to 1999-2000, and sequenced along with progress towards attainment of the pre-conditions/signposts stipulated for the relevant year, and depending on the assessment of authorities, the implementation of measures could be accelerated or decelerated.

- Fiscal consolidation, a mandated inflation target and strengthening of the financial system should be regarded as crucial pre-conditions/signposts for CAC in India. In addition, a few important macro economic indicators, viz. exchange rate policy, the balance of payments and the adequacy of foreign exchange reserves should be assessed on an on-going basis.

Measures Recommended to be Progressively Phased Over Three Years

- For resident corporate/business: liberalisation of measures in respect of issue of foreign currency denominated bonds (rupee settlements), financial capital transfer abroad, loans from non residents, opening offices abroad, direct investments abroad, repatriation of dividends, and use of foreign exchange by the exporters and the foreign exchange earners. Long term ECB be kept outside ceiling. Queuing for the implementation of ceiling to avoid crowding out of the small borrowers by the big ones. Recommendations for the FCCB/FRNs same as that of ECB.

- For the resident banks: liberalisation in matters of Bank's borrowing from overseas market, use of funds and repayments, accepting deposits and extending loans in foreign currencies, investing in overseas market, use of funds and repayments, accepting deposits and extending loans in foreign currencies, investing in overseas market, fund based/non fund based facilities to Indian joint ventures, buyers' credit/acceptance for financing importers buying from India and forfeiting.

- For the non resident banks, allowing forward cover in Rupee Accounts, cancelling/re-booking, enhanced overdraft limit and limited investment.

- Overseas investments by SEBI registered Indian investors (including Mutual Funds), and short-term borrowing by the All India Financial Institutions within limits.

- Maturity restrictions on FII investments in debt instruments be removed, and investment in rupee debt securities be subjected to a separate ceiling and not ECB ceiling.

- For resident individuals: allowing foreign currency denominated deposits, foreign capital transfer, and liberalisation of repatriation norms.

- For non residents: capital transfers from non-repatriable assets held in India be allowed subject to ceilings.

- To allow forward market, derivatives, and futures.

- Participation in international commodity market.

- Deregulation of deposit rates with removal of minimum period restrictions. Level playing field for all banks, FIs, and NBFCs regarding reserve requirements and prudential norms.

- Development of Treasury bill market and access to FIIs in it.

- Prominent roles of the Primary Dealers and the Satellite Dealers.

- Setting up Office of the Public Debt to handle part of issue of dated securities and Treasury bills.

- Development of gold market with participation of banks and financial institutions, gold denominated deposits and loans, and gold derivatives.

- Replacement of the requirement of prior approval of the RBI with subsequent reporting, and dispensing with such requirements in case of disinvestment in a number of cases concerning investments by both residents and non residents.

Banking Statistics at a Glance

Table 1: Scheduled Commercial Banks in India: Major Indicators, 1950-51 to 2006-2007

(Rs. crore)

Year	Demand Deposits (1)	Time Deposits (2)	Aggregate Deposits (1+ 2)
1950-51	593	290	882
1960-61	710	1,026	1,736
1970-71	2,626	3,280	5,906
1980-81	7,798	30,190	37,988
1990-91	33,192	1,59,349	1,92,541
1991-92	45,088	1,85,670	2,30,758
1994-95	76,903	3,09,956	3,86,859
1998-99	1,17,423	5,96,602	7,14,025
1999-00	1,27,366	6,85,978	8,13,345
2000-01	1,42,552	8,20,066	9,62,618
2001-02	1,53,048	9,50,312	11,03,360
2002-03	1,70,289	11,10,564	12,80,853
2003-04	2,25,022	12,79,394	15,04,416
2004-05	2,48,028	14,52,171	17,00,198
2005-06	3,64,640	17,44,409	21,09,049
2006-07	4,29,137	21,79,172	26,08,309

Contd…

Year	Investments	Bank Credit	Cash in Hand	Assets
1950-51	N.A	547	35	N.A.
1960-61	N.A.	1,336	46	N.A.
1970-71	1,772	4,684	167	147
1980-81	13,186	25,371	766	1,028
1990-91	75,065	1,16,301	1,804	5,582
1991-92	90,196	1,25,592	2,008	7,927
1994-95	1,49,253	2,11,560	2,972	14,277
1998-99	2,54,595	3,68,837	4,362	34,787
1999-00	3,08,944	4,35,958	5,330	43,448
2000-01	3,70,159	5,11,434	5,658	62,355
2001-02	4,38,269	5,89,723	6,245	52,864
2002-03	5,47,546	7,29,215	7,567	59,019
2003-04	6,77,588	8,40,785	7,898	48,179
2004-05	7,39,154	11,00,428	8,472	51,297
2005-06	7,17,454	1,50,7077	13,046	54,392
2006-07	7,90,431	1,92,8913	16,108	77,060

Source: Reserve Bank of India, *Handbook of Monetary Statistics of India, 2006; Handbook of Statistics on the Indian Economy, 2006-07* and other Issues.

Table 2: Savings Deposits with Indian and Foreign Banks, 1951-52 to 2006-2007

(Rs. crore)

Year	Indian Banks	Foreign Banks	Total
1951-52	125	10	136
1960-61	256	26	282
1970-71	1,408	117	1,524
1980-81	10,664	270	10,934
1990-91	49,542	959	50,501
1991-92	55,554	1,348	56,902
1994-95	89,019	2,305	91,324
1998-99	1,60,947	3,836	1,64,783
1999-00	1,87,173	4,727	1,91,900
2000-01	2,17,452	5,531	2,22,982
2001-02	2,72,119	6,988	2,79,107
2002-03	3,02,816	8,748	3,11,565
2003-04	3,73,137	12,232	3,85,369
2004-05	4,43,573	15,045	4,58,618
2005-06	5,56,303	18,827	5,75,130
2006-07	6,49,586	21,839	6,71,425

Source: Reserve Bank of India, *Handbook of Monetary Statistics of India, 2006* and *Handbook of Statistics on the Indian Economy, 2006-07.*

Table 3: Growth of Various Components of Money Stock in Indian Economy, 1950-51 to 2006-2007

(Rs. crore)

Year	Currency in Circulation	Cash with Banks	Currency with Public	Other Deposits with RBI
1950-51	N.A.	N.A.	1,405	24
1960-61	2,154	56	2,098	13
1970-71	4,557	186	4,371	60
1980-81	14,307	881	13,426	411
1990-91	55,282	2,234	53,048	674
1991-92	63,738	2,640	61,098	885
1998-99	1,75,846	6,902	1,68,944	3,736
1999-00	1,97,061	7,979	1,89,082	3,034
2000-01	2,18,205	8,654	2,09,950	3,630
2001-02	2,50,974	10,179	2,40,794	2,850
2002-03	2,82,473	10,892	2,71,581	3,242
2003-04	3,27,028	12,057	3,14,971	5,119
2004-05	3,68,661	12,893	3,55,863	6,478
2005-06	4,30,676	17,557	4,13,119	6,869
2006-07	5,04,225	20,754	4,83,477	7,496

Contd...

Year	Bankers' Deposits with RBI	Reserve Money (M_0)	Narrow Money (M_1)	Broad Money (M_3)
1950-51	59	1,494	2,021	2,352
1960-61	71	2,239	2,869	3,964
1970-71	˙205	4,822	7,374	11,020
1980-81	4,734	19,452	23,424	55,774
1990-91	31,823	87,779	92,892	2,65,828
1991-92	34,882	99,505	1,14,406	3,17,049
1998-99	79,703	2,59,286	3,09,068	9,80,960
1999-00	80,460	2,80,555	3,41,796	11,24,174
2000-01	81,477	3,03,311	3,79,450	13,13,220
2001-02	84,147	3,37,970	4,22,843	14,98,355
2002-03	83,346	3,69,061	4,73,581	17,17,960
2003-04	1,04,365	4,36,512	5,78,716	20,05,676
2004-05	1,13,996	4,89,135	6,46,263	22,53,938
2005-06	1,35,511	5,73,055	8,26,375	27,29,545
2006-07	1,97,295	7,09,016	9,65,195	33,10,278

Note: Figures for the Years 2003-04, 2004-05, 2005-06 and 2006-07 are provisional.

Source: Reserve Bank of India, *Handbook of Monetary Statistics of India, 2006* and *Handbook of Statistics on the Indian Economy, 2006-07.*

Table 4: Growth of Regional Rural Banks (RRBs) in India, 1979-80 to 2004-2005

(Rs. crore)

Year	Demand Deposits	Time Deposits	Bank Credit.
1979-80	72	72	173
1980-81	74	157	285
1984-85	258	715	1,134
1990-91	941	3,619	3,497
1991-92	1,044	4,227	3,951
1994-95	2,115	8,733	6,201
1998-99	4,688	20,740	11,016
1999-00	5,105	24,946	12,663
2000-01	6,098	29,897	15,211
2001-02	7,305	35,189	18,033
2002-03	8,513	39,131	21,359
2003-04	10,727	42,663	25,057
2004-05	12,757	45,529	31,651

Contd...

Year	Investments in Govt. Securities	Investments in other Securities	Cash in Hand
1979-80	0	0	5
1980-81	0	0	8
1984-85	0	0	24
1990-91	9	6	56
1991-92	8	17	64
1994-95	459	375	216
1998-99	1,191	3,816	300
1999-00	1,224	4,786	343
2000-01	1,642	5,847	357
2001-02	1,970	4,901	400
2002-03	7,673	4,335	471
2003-04	13,324	4,208	547
2004-05	16,970	3,242	598

Source: Reserve Bank of India, *Handbook of Monetary Statistics of India, 2006.*

Bibliography

Bibliography

Aggarwal, P.C. (1987), 'Frauds in Banks – An Analytical Study', The Chartered Accountant, Vol. XXIX, No. 6, December.

Aggarwal, B.P. (1981), Commercial Banking in India: New Delhi; Classical Publishing Company.

Aggarwal, H.N. (1979), A Portrait of Nationalized Banks - A Study With Reference to Their Social Obligations, New Delhi: Inter-India Publishers.

Aggeler, H & Feldman, R (1998), 'Record Bank Profitability: How, Who and What Mean?' *Federal Reserve Bank of Minneapolis*, Fedgazette, April, Vol. 10, No. 2.

Ahluwalia, M.S. (2001), 'Second Generation Reforms in the Banks; Major Issues', paper presented at the Bank Economists' Conference (January), New Delhi.

Allen, F. (1988), 'The Determinants of Bank Interest Rate Margins', Journal of Financial and Quantitative Analysis, Vol. XXIX, No. 6 (Dec.).

Altunbus, Y, Evans, L & Molyneux, P (2000), "Bank Ownership and Efficiency", *Journal of Money, Credit and Banking,* Vol. 33, No. 4, pp. 926-954.

Angadi and Devaraj, 'Productivity & Profitability of Banks in India', (1983), Economic and Political Weekly Vol. 18, (Nov. 26).

Angadi, V.B. (1987), 'Integrated Approach to Study Bank's 'Profitability', Prajnan, (Oct.- Dec.).

Arora, U. & Verma, R. (2005), "Banking Sector Reforms and Performance Evaluation of Public Sector Banks in India", *Punjab Journal of Business Studies*, Vol. 1, No. 1 (April – Sept.), pp. 11-25

Avasthi, G.P.M. (2000-01), 'Information Technology in Banking: Challenges for Regulators', Prajnan, Vol. XXIX, No. 4.

B, Jaski. (2002), 'Unleashing Employee Productivity: Need for a Paradigm Shift', IBA Bulletin Vol. XXIV, No. 3 (March).
Bajaj, K.K. (2000), 'E-Commerce Issues in the Emerging Hi - Tech. Banking Environment' The Journal of The Indian Institute of Bankers. (Jan- March).

Bajaj, M.K. (2000), 'Customer Relations Management' IBA Bulletin, (Sept.).

Bajwa, K.S. (1983), 'Productivity in Banks', Indian Banking Today and Tomorrow, (April).

Bakshi, S. (2001), 'Banks Foray into Insurance - Prospects and Problems', Bank Quest, The Journal of The Indian Institute of Bankers. Vol.72. No.4 (Oct – Dec.).

Ballabh, J (2001), 'The Indian Banking Industry: Challenges Ahead', *IBA Bulletin,* Vol. XXIII, No. 4 & 5, April, pp.8-10.

Basu, D. (1989), 'Diversification of Financial Markets and Challenges Confronting Banks' SBI Monthly Review , (Feb.).

Bedi, S. (1984), 'Universal Banking System', Prajnan, NIBM (July-Sept.).

Berg, S.A., Forsund, F. and Jansen, E. (1991), "Technical efficiency of Norwegian Banks: A Nonparametric Approach to Efficiency Measurement", *Journal of Productivity Analysis*, 2, pp. 127-42.

Bhasin, T.M. (2001), 'E-Commerce in Indian Banking', IBA Bulletin, Vol. XXIII, Nos. 4 & 5 (April – May).

Bhatt, P.R. (1999), 'Profitability of Commercial Banks in India', Indian Journal of Economics (March).

Bhattacharya, S.K.(1988), 'The Need for Optimizing the Banking Industry Structure,' The Journal of The Indian Institute of Bankers (Janu.- March).

Bossone, B. (2001), 'Should Banks Be Narrowed?', IMF Working Paper No. 159. Washington, IMF.

Chander, S. (1987), 'Productivity in Banking Industry', The Chartered Accountant (Sept.).

Chopra, K. (1987), Managing Profitability and Productivity in Public Sector Banking (Jalandhar: ABS Publications).

Das, A. (2002), 'Risk and Productivity Change of Public Sector Banks', Economic and Political Weekly, Vol. XXXVII, No. 5 (Feb. 2).

De Kock, M. 1974. Central Banking. St. Martin's Press. New York.

De Young R. & Rice T. (2003), 'Non-Interest Income and Financial Performance at US Commercial Banks', Policy Studies, Federal Reserve Bank of Chicago.

Desai, V. (1980), Indian Banking – Nature and Problems (Bombay: Himalaya Publishing House).

Eapen, P.G. (2000), 'Automated Teller Machines- Security Issues', IBA Bulletin , Vol. XXII, No. 9 (Sept.).

Ganesh, K. (1979), 'Monitoring Profitability in Banks', The Commerce (July).

Ganesh, S. (2001), 'Frauds in a Computerized Environment', IBA Bulletin, Vol. XXIII No. 12 (Dec.).

Garg, S.C. (1982), Indian Banking Cost & Profitability (New Delhi: Anmol Publ.).

Ghosh, D. N. (1988), 'Commercial Banking: Lessons From Indian Experience', SBI Monthly Review, (Nov.).

Goiporia, M. N. (1987), 'Emerging Banking Challenges', The Journal of The Indian Institute of Bankers (July-Sep).

Government of India. 1972. Banking Committee Report.

Grossk, S. (1993), Efficiency and Productivity in The Measurement of Productive Efficiency, Techniques and Applications (UK: Oxford University Press).
Gupta, R P. (2001), 'Banking In The New Millennium: Strategic Management Issues', IBA Bulletin, Vol. XXIII, No. 3 (March).

Heggade, O.D. (2000), Banker – Customer Relationship in India (New Delhi: Mohit Publ.).

Honohan, P (2001), 'Recapitalising Banking Systems: Implications for Incentives and Fiscal and Monetary Policy', Policy Research Working Paper No. 2540

IMF.1998. "Currency Crises: The Role of Monetary Policy." Finance and Development. 46-48. March.

Jalan, B. (2000), 'Finance and Development: Which Way Now?,' RBI Bulletin , (Janu.).

Johri & Jauhari, (1994), Role of Computers in Banking Operation Systems (New Delhi: Himalaya Publishing House).

Joshi, N.C. (1978), Indian Banking (New Delhi: Ashish Publ. House).

Kaveri, V. S. (2001), 'Loan Default and Profitability of Banks', IBA Bulletin (Janu.).

Kohli, S.S. (2001), 'Indian Banking Industry: Emerging Challenge', IBA Bulletin, Vol. XXIII, No. 3 (March).

Kshirsagar, S.S.(1979), 'Decentralization in Banks', Prajnan, NIBM (April-June).

Kulkarni, R. V. (2000), 'Changing Face of Banking from Brick and Mortar Banking to E- Banking', IBA Bulletin (Janu.).

Malhotra, R.N. 1990. The Evolution of Financial System, The Nineteenth Frank Moraes Memorial Lecture.
Mathur, O.P. (1978), Public Sector Banks in India – A Case Study of State Bank (New Delhi: Sterling Publishers Private Ltd.).

Mehta, V. P. 1985. "FERA: Exchange Control in India." Asia Publishing House: Bombay.

Metzer, S.R. (2000), 'Strategic Planning for Future Bank Growth', The Banker's Magazine (July- Aug.).

Mittal, S.R. A. (2000), 'Payment Systems in High – Tech. Banking', The Journal of The Indian Institute of Bankers, Vol.71 No. 3 (July- Aug.).

Mohan, Rakesh. 2003. "Transforming Indian Banking: In Search of a Better Tomorrow." *RBI Bulletin*,

———2004. "Agricultural Credit in India: Status, Issues and Future Agenda." *RBI Bulletin.*

———2004, "Indian Banking and e-Security." *RBI Bulletin,* November.

———2004, "Ownership and Governance in Private Sector Banks in India." *RBI Bulletin,*

Murthy, C.S. (1999), Fundamentals of Information Technology (New Delhi: Himalaya Publishing House).

N. Vittal. (2001), 'The Emerging Challenges: strategies and solutions for Indian Banking', IBA Bulletin, Vol. XXIII, No. 3 (March).

Nachane, D.M. (1999), 'Capital Adequacy Ratios: An Agnostic Viewpoint', Economic and Political Weekly, Special Nos. 3 & 4.

Naha, P.K. (1990), 'Two Year Action Plans in Banks – A Review', PNB Monthly Review, (Nov.).

Nagam, B.M.L. (1987),   Banking and Economic Growth. (Bombay: Vora & Co.).

Nair, S.N. (2000), 'E-Commerce and the Emergence of E-Banking', IBA Bulletin , Vol. XXII, No. 10 (Oct.).

Narayanan, V. (2000), 'NPA Reduction – The New   Mantra of Slippage Management', IBA Bulletin, Vol. XXII, No. 10 (Oct.).

Nayan, K. (1982), Performance Evaluation of Commercial Banks: Development of an Evaluation Model Ph.D. Thesis, H.P. Uni., Shimla.

Ojha, J. (1997), 'Productivity and Profitability of Public Sector Banks in India: An International Comparison', SBI Monthly Review (July).

Padmini, E.V.K. (1989),'Profitability Analysis of Commercial Banks: A Case Study Indian Banking', Today & Tomorrow, (Dec.).

Pai, D.T. (2001), 'Indian Banking – Changing Scenario', IBA Bulletin, Vol. XXIII, No. 3 (March).

Panandikar, S.G. (1975), Banking in India (Bombay: Orient Longman).

Pathrose, P.P. (2001), 'Hi-Tech. Banking Prospects and Problems', IBA Bulletin , Vol. XXIII, No. 7. (July).

Ram, T.T . (2002), 'Deregulation and Performance of Public Sector Banks', EPW, Vol. XXXVII, No. 5.

Ramachandaran, C (2005), 'Boosting of Fee-Based Income of Banks- Ways and Means', *IBA Bulletin,* Vol. XXVII, No. 12, (December), pp. 18-20.

Ramaswamy, M. (1977), 'Bank Deposits and Interest Rate Reduction', The Journal of The Indian Institute of Bankers (July-Sept)

Rangarajan, C. (2000), 'Banking in The Hi -Tech. Environment', The Journal of The Indian Institute of Bankers. (Jan-March).

Rao, N.V. (2000), 'Changing Indian Banking Scenario: a Paradigm shift' IBA Bulletin , Vol. XXIV No. 1.

Rao, P. (1978), 'Profits in a Bind', Business India (Nov.).

Rao, P.K. (1999), 'IT in Financial Services Industry: Innovations and Implications', Chartered Secretary , (Sept.).

Reserve Bank of India, Annual Report, Various Issues.
——1970, The History of the Reserve Bank of India: 1935-5.
——1985, Reserve Bank of India: Fifty Years (1935-85).
——1997, Report of the Committee on Capital Account Convertibility (Chairman: Shri S.S. Tarapore)."
——1998, Committee on Banking Sector Reforms (Chairman: M. Narasimham)
——1998, Payment Systems in India.
——2000, Report of the Advisory Group on Transparency in Monetary and Financial Policies.
——2001, Report on Internet Banking.
——2002, Report of the Working Group on Electronic Money.
——2003, Risk-Based Supervision Manual.
——2004, Financial Sector Reforms in India: Policies and Performance Analysis." RBI Bulletin, October.
——2005, Report on Trend and Progress of Banking in India.
——2006, Report on Trend and Progress of Banking in India.
——2007, Report on Trend and Progress of Banking in India.

Sabnani, P. (2000), 'Universal Banking', IBA Bulletin, Vol. XXII No.7 (July).

Sachdeva, U.S. (1987), Frauds and Bankers: Prevention and Detection Techniques (New Delhi: UDH Publishing House).

Sachdeva, U.S.(1985), 'Limitation Period and Registration of Charges :A Bankers' Concern', Prajnan, (Oct.-Dec.), pp.361-72

Satya, (1984), 'Banks: Improving Productivity and Profitability' The Journal of India Institute of Bankers, (Sept.).
Satyamurty, B. (1994), 'A Study on Interests Spread Management in Commercial Banks in India', NIBM, Working Paper.

Saxena, K.K (1985), 'Evolution of Bank Marketing in India', SBI Monthly Review, (Janu.).

Saxena, M(2001), 'Banker's Choice: Tech it or Leave it', Strategic Marketing (Feb.).

Sayers, R. 1961, The Role of Central Bank in a Developing Economy.

Senapati, M. (1999), 'Financial Services in the Internet Era', ICFAI Reader, (Nov.).

Shah, S.G (1979), 'Bank Profitability: The Real Issues', The Journal of India Institute of Bankers, (July- Sept.).

Shah, V. D. (1986), 'Empirical Relationship between Size & Cost at Branch Level', Prajnan Vol. XV, No. 318, (Janu.- March).

Sham, L. (1978), 'Performance of Commercial Banks Since Nationalization of Major Banks: Promise and Reality', EPW, (Aug.).

Shanti, S. (1984), Customer Services in Banks. (Bombay: Him. Publ. House).

Shapiro, C (2000), 'Will E-Commerce Erode Liberty', Harvard Business Review (May- June).

Shastri, R.V (2001), 'Technology for Banks in India- Challenges', IBA Bulletin , Vol. XXIII, No. 3 (March).

Shrives, Dhal (1992), 'The Relationship between Risk and Capital in Commercial Banks'. Journal of Banking and Finance.

Shurethy, S. (1999), E-Business with Net. Commerce. (Singapore: Addison Wesley Longman).

Shyam, R. (1988), Workshop on Profit Planning (Bombay: Bankers Training College, RBI).

Singh, R.P. (1999), Working of the Nationalized Banks (New Delhi: Radha Publications).

Singh, S. (1989), 'Profitability in Commercial Banks in India', PNB Monthly Review (Oct.).

Singla, A. & Arora, R.S. (2005), "Financial Performance of Public Sector Banks: A Comparative Study of Canara Bank and Indian Bank", Punjab Journal of Business Studies, Vol. 1, No. 1 (April-September), pp. 87-93

Subal, K. and Sarkar, S. (2004), "Deregulation, Ownership and Efficiency Change in Indian Banking", Dept. of Economics, State University of New York.

Subrahmanyam, G. 'Some Conceptual Issues in Productivity 1984), Measurement', Prajnan (April-June).

Sushila, S. (1987), Banks and Customers: A Behavioural Analysis. (New Delhi: Shri Ram Center for Industrial Relations and Human Resources).

Swamy, B.N.A. (2001), 'New Competition, Deregulation and Emerging Changes in Indian Banking: An Analysis of the Comparative Performance of Different Bank- Groups', Bank Quest, The Journal of India Institute of Bankers, Vol. 72 No.3 (July- Sept.).

Talwar, S P (2001), "Competition, Consolidation and Systemic Stability in the Indian Banking Industry", in BIS Papers, No. 4 – The Banking Industry in the Emerging Market Economies: Competition, Consolidation and Systemic Stability, Bank for International Settlement, Basel available at http://www.bis.org/publ/bispap04.htm

The Central Banking Enquiry Committee, 1931 (Chairman: Sir Bhupendra Nath Mitra).

Vageesh, N.S (2000), 'New Private Banks; New Kids on the Block', Business Line, (March).

Varde, 1988), 'Effectiveness, Efficiency and Customer Services in Banks', RBI Bulletin , (April).

Varde, S. (1983), Profitability of Commercial Bank (Bombay: NIBM)

Vaswani, T.A. (1968), Indian Banking System (Bombay: Lalvani Publ. Hou.).

Verghese, S.K (1983), 'Profits and Profitability of Indian Commercial Banks in the Seventies', EPW, (Nov.).

Verghese, S.K. (1983), Profits and Profitability of Indian Commercial Banks in the Seventies (Bombay: NIBM).

Verma, D. (2000), 'Banking on Change', ICFAI Reader, (May).

Index